WITHDRAWN

THE DECLINE
AND FALL OF THE
SUPREME COURT

THE DECLINE
AND FALL OF THE
SUPREME COURT

Living Out the Nightmares of the Federalists

Christopher C. Faille

Foreword by William C. Olson

Westport, Connecticut
London

Library of Congress Cataloging-in-Publication Data

Faille, Christopher C.
    The decline and fall of the Supreme Court : living out the
nightmares of the Federalists / Christopher C. Faille; foreword by
William C. Olson.
        p.   cm.
    Includes bibliographical references and index.
    ISBN 0–275–94826–9 (alk. paper)
    1. United States. Supreme Court—Officials and employees—
Selection and appointment—History.   2. Judges—Selection and
appointment—United States—History.   3. Judicial review—United
States—History.   4. United States—Constitutional history.
I. Title.
KF8748.F28   1995
347.73′2634—dc20
[347.3073534]   94–13733

British Library Cataloguing in Publication Data is available.

Library of Congress Catalog Card Number: 94–13733
ISBN: 0–275–94826–9

First published in 1995

Praeger Publishers, 88 Post Road West, Westport, CT 06881
An imprint of Greenwood Publishing Group, Inc.

Printed in the United States of America

The paper used in this book complies with the
Permanent Paper Standard issued by the National
Information Standards Organization (Z39.48–1984).

10 9 8 7 6 5 4 3 2

Copyright Acknowledgment

From *The Federalist* by Hamilton, Jay and Madison, intro. by Edward Mead Earle, Copyright ©
1941 by Random House, Inc. Reprinted by permission of Random House, Inc.

For Jacques Barzun

E quant' io l'abbia in grado, mentre io vivo
convien che nella mia lingua si scerna.

Dante, <u>Comm.</u>, <u>Inf</u>. xv, 86–87

Contents

Foreword

John Marshall is one of my heroes. His jurisprudential steadfastness and political adroitness combined to make the Federal judiciary in general and the Supreme Court in particular coequal with the Congress and the Executive branch. From <u>Marbury</u> through <u>Barron</u> the Chief Justice defined the very meaning of Federalism, and, in consequence, created the most independent, powerful judiciary in the world. This is John Marshall's legacy, and so, too, is legal formalism.

As an undergraduate in my course in American Constitutional Law, Christopher Faille probably tired of the emphasis that I place on Marshall as the key to unlocking the vast power which the Federal judiciary enjoys, a power negatively evidenced only once in the nineteenth century in the infamous Dred Scott case in 1857. Associate justices were appointed by presidents and confirmed by the Senate rather routinely: the American Bar Association was not asked to inquire about the credentials of nominees to the Federal judiciary. Indeed, the Federal judiciary generally mirrored American life. Probably the one most important exception was the dissent of Associate Justice John Marshall Harlan in <u>Plessy</u>. But during the Roosevelt administration, things changed.

The Supreme Court in particular began to become politicized. What one thought about Constitutional issues would perhaps become votes on the Supreme Court for those very same issues. Thus began legal realism, a concept which Faille describes as a judicial response to the failure of legislative/executive action, and more. The Federal judiciary becomes, in effect, a law-making and executing body, doing what the other two branches are fearful or unwilling to do. Correctly, Faille observes in Chapter 9 that, "The Court ought to walk with small steps through a field of broken glass." To do more at this point in time would further diminish the authenticating function of the Court.

Faille focuses, and properly so, on the Burger Court as a turning point. The "litmus tests" that began to apply not only eroded the careful system of checks and balances that, under Marshall, had led to the increased power of the Court; they also winnowed away the independence of the judiciary, what Faille calls "legal realism." I happen to think that Faille is right about this trend, and worry that a continued erosion of the authority of the Federal courts will have a fundamental impact on American government.

Ultimately, a key to Constitutional interpretation rests on the Fourteenth Amendment. Faille has done a fine job of presenting in each chapter the potential impact of realism on the Fourteenth. Readers should pay particular attention to his evidence in this regard.

Faille has written a book that raises seminal questions about the future of the Supreme Court. If he is right, and the Supreme Court loses its moral authority, then as a nation we have lost a key ingredient in our political fabric. This book is a valuable resource for all who wish to understand the direction of American jurisprudence.

I do not agree with every point that Faille makes, and I am absolutely certain that he would shudder if I did. But his fundamental premise that the authority of the Supreme Court is eroding should command a wide audience of undergraduates, law students and professors. It is about the very essence of the transformation of the Federal judiciary and of the Supreme Court of the United States.

William C. Olson

Acknowledgments

I would like to acknowledge, first, my mother and father, for having embedded in my consciousness a wholesome set of prejudices, one of which operates powerfully in favor of perseverance.

Second, Dwight Murphey, author of *Understanding the Modern Predicament*, a four-volume series on ideologies since the Enlightenment, has proven to be a friend of astonishing generosity as well as a scholar of astounding range.

Third, I wish to thank the staff of all the libraries of north central Connecticut and western Massachusetts. Collectively, their services amounted to a poor person's research grant.

Fourth, Rosalie Schultz, is acknowledged for her intellectual comradeship and stimulation.

Fifth, Stanley S. Jaspan of the law firm of Foley & Lardner, Milwaukee, Wisconsin, gave freely of his time to explain to me the fetal protection policy of Johnson Controls, Inc.

Finally, thanks are due to Theresa, for going to Holyoke and for pronouncing her name in a way that sounds like "Lisa."

Introduction: The Triumph of Realism

In this book, I describe the consequences of the triumph of a set of ideas, a triumph consummated both in legal academe and (though to a lesser extent) on the bench and at the bar. These domains have fallen to a conqueror that goes by the name "legal realism." In one paragraph, the story I want to tell is as follows:

Over the course of fifty-four years, from 1937 until the time of the Clarence Thomas hearings in 1991, the Supreme Court of the United States suffered a grievous loss of institutional stature and of its once-clear function within a constitutional system of government. A Court that was meant to be free of faction is now perceived by all the pertinent publics, by politicians in office and out, as a mere collection of nine power seekers and power keepers. The nine are now politicians in a city that swarms with politicians; they are indistinguishable from the rest. The Court has lost its sanctity. Because of this loss, members of the Court are now subject to the same power machinations as are presidential candidates and activist movie stars. If the Court is not special, not unique, then there is no reason the selection of its members should be an elevated or even a particularly deliberative act. The decline and fall of the Supreme Court—through its disastrous acceptance of the jurisprudence of realism—came first. The decline and fall of senatorial "advice and consent" are a consequence.

In the first two chapters, I provide some essential historical background. In Chapter 1, I glean what I can from the *Federalist Papers* on the meaning and intended operation of the "advice and consent" clause as it applies to judicial nominees. In Chapter 2, I describe a critical constitutional turning point, the shift in the Court's view of its own responsibilities in 1937, a shift justified then and since by the language of "restraint." In the rest of the book, I treat a variety of constitutional, statutory, and partisan developments in the years since the ascension of Earl Warren to the post of chief justice. My narrative continues until and through the Supreme Court's 1991 term, because some of the final decisions of that term, Justice Thomas's freshman year, give clarity and meaning to the phrase "the Rehnquist Court."

To some, the events with which my tale concludes may already seem antique. Immediate impressions have faded into memories, the newspapers that generated those impressions have faded into yellow, industrious librarians have reduced their pages to microfiche. A new president is in the White House now, and at least two new justices are on the Court. But I trust that my efforts will prove to be of more than archival interest through the years of the Clinton administration and whatever administrations shall follow. Judicial confirmation fights—bitterly contested, confusing the public's understanding of the constitutional system, and pumping poison into the bloodstream of the body politic—are not, we can be sure, things of the past. The present administration's spokespeople may speak in disparaging tones of "the gridlock of the last twelve years," in the spirit of old-fashioned partisan fun. But nothing with which this book is concerned had its start in January 1981. The narrative to come makes that clear. Likewise, nothing can be supposed to have come to an end in January 1993. A moment's meditation should make that clear.

There are at least two sorts of issues in the politics of the United States today: those addressed to the brain and those addressed to the gut. When a politician considers the merits of a rewrite of the tax code or a modification of foreign trade policy, the questions at issue concern who gets what, from whom, and with the application of how much muscle, by what means applied. These are issues for the calculating brain. On the other hand, when a politician stands up after some deadly disaster and announces, using a still-powerful phrase almost fifty years old, "The buck stops here," while her anxious cabinet colleagues await the results of the overnight polls, the questions at issue concern who is what kind of person, seeking the favor of what kind of electorate.

There is a large reservoir of support for a gut-issue political platform one might well describe as the presumptive endorsement of the actions of duly constituted authority. There is, however, also a considerable (and much publicized) store of support for a gut-issue politics one might better describe as reflexive opposition to officialdom. The most powerful and the most polarizing of our political struggles pit one of these sentiments against the other.

I might best generalize two labels from the era of the Vietnam War and call the politics of authority "hawkish" and the politics of reflexive opposition, or of insurgency, "dovish."

The characteristic stance of the Clinton administration, like that of the Johnson administration of thirty years ago, is that of a *hawkish social democracy.* Bill Clinton addressed issues of the gut when, during his campaign, he made a point of criticizing a black rapper, Sister Souljah, at a forum where words to that effect were likely to, and where they did, embarrass the Reverend Jesse Jackson. Clinton, as president, withdrew the nomination of Lani Guinier for an important Justice Department position, declaring as he did so that her support of race-conscious reapportionment of voting districts is outside the pale of political respectability. "This has nothing to do with the political center," he said of this decision, "it's about _my_ center."[1] He praised his attorney general for authorizing an armored assault on a commune of religious dissidents. On each of these matters and on others, President Clinton has taken the side of traditional authority at the expense of insurgencies. In only one such case did the side-taking come to the point of deadly force. But in each case it was "hawkish" in the sense I have tried to describe.

Yet none of these matters stand at the heart of Clinton's agenda. The antirevolutionary side of his program chiefly serves to grant legitimacy to the extreme social-democratic economic platform that this administration regards as its mandate. The president has offered a sweeping proposal to nationalize health care and health insurance. He has adopted as his own the traditional Keynesian fiscal policies, in which redistribution is justified as a countercyclical stimulus. He has exerted a constant pressure upon the Federal Reserve to inflate the currency. Finally, he has increased the level of federal intervention in the processes of collective bargaining, always at the expense of the employer.

This configuration, this hawkish social democracy, may be, if _anything_ is, the meaning of the phrase "new Democrat." But why is it a matter germane to a study of the decline and fall of the Supreme Court? For at least this one reason: judicial appointments are today often regarded as issues of the gut, as issues of precisely the sort on which a Clinton Democrat must prove himself to be a hawk. In this sense, it should have come as no surprise when, in May 1994, President Clinton nominated to the Supreme Court Judge Stephen Breyer, the most prominent craftsman and advocate of a tough and inflexible set of sentencing guidelines binding upon federal district court judges.[2]

I return to the political considerations behind Clinton's judicial appointments in the epilogue. I simply assert my conclusions here.

President Clinton's conception of the future of the party he heads requires that he place himself periodically in opposition to those whom he calls the "Old Democrats" or "bean counters"; those whom I have been calling "doves." There will be opportunities for an alignment of Republicans with Clinton loyalists among the Democrats. Indeed, the analogy I introduced between this administration and that of Lyndon Johnson is apt. On a variety of foreign policy and defense issues Democrats loyal to Johnson aligned themselves with Republicans in opposition to the doves within their own party. Clinton has already had to rely upon the same coalition for some crucial initiatives, and he will no doubt call upon it again in the future. What follows is that the people who worked so hard to "bork" the nominees of Presidents Reagan and Bush may well find themselves attempting to "bork" some of the nominees of President Clinton, as well.

Whether they succeed depends very much upon whether the public understands how the sport of "borking" came to be and of what a decayed state of our constitutional system it is a symptom.[3]

NOTES

1. Hitchens, "Minority Report," The Nation, July 5, 1993, p. 6.

2. Noble, "With uniform sentencing: same crime, same time," New York Times, April 19, 1987, E5.

3. Indeed, the borkers do seem to have considered Breyer as a potential target for vilification, though in the end they backed away, determined to fight another day.

See Lewis, "In a sea of praise, discouraging words," New York Times, May 16, 1994, A10, and especially the quote there attributed to Ralph Nader. Nader said that Breyer has no concern "for the pain of the ordinary worker, the unequal distribution of death, injuries and contamination suffered by the ordinary worker."

1

What the Founders Wanted

The Constitution provides for a federal judiciary, which consists of "one supreme Court, and such inferior Courts as the Congress may from time to time ordain and establish." The judges of this judiciary are appointed by the president, with the "advice and consent" of the Senate. In the late twentieth century, the Senate's discharge of this responsibility, especially with regard to confirmation of the justices of the Supreme Court, has become caught within, and contributes to, the embitterment and polarization of American politics.

James Madison, Alexander Hamilton, and John Jay, under the collective pseudonym "Publius," wrote eighty-five essays in defense of the Constitution, essays that they published serially in New York newspapers and later reissued as a book, The Federalist Papers. (I speak throughout of Publius in the singular, as the only author of one coherent production, but there are, in fact, disputes as to which contributor wrote which of these essays. Hamilton wrote papers 1, 6–9, 11–13, 15–17, 21–36, 59–61, and 65–85. Madison wrote 7–10, 14, and 37–48. Jay wrote 2–5 and 64. In dispute are papers 18–20, 49–58, and 62–63. External evidence for authorship of most of these papers seems to favor Madison. Internal, or stylistic, evidence is unhelpful as the style of Publius is uniform throughout.)

Much that Publius had to say touches, directly or indirectly, upon the "advice and consent" clause.[1] Since it was pursuant to the Senate's discharge of its responsibilities under this clause that recent confirmation battles have about, I must begin here. Publius argued that the Constitution is the founding document of a republic, in that the Constitution conforms to the "true principles of republican government."[2] After all, the Publius of antiquity was the statesman who overthrew the king of Rome in the late sixth century B.C. and who founded the republic in that city that was to last for half a millennium.[3] In the spirit of his ancient namesake, then, our American Publius spent half of one essay establishing that a republic is a government "which derives all its powers directly or indirectly from the great body of the people" and that the Constitution in dispute is a plan for just such a government.[4] In America, nothing else is possible.

But Publius was not eager to argue the fine points of that or any alternative definition of a republic or to reason by deduction from definition. Publius took the republican character of American institutions as a datum, a given, and concerned himself quite consistently with showing how the Constitution solves the problems distinctive to that character.

The single greatest of these problems, from which the others flow, is what Publius calls the "spirit of faction." This is the spirit that puts party or sect above nation, some private interest or temporary passion above the public good. Factionalism does not cease to be an evil, a "vice," when the faction in question or a coalition of factions commands a majority of the voting population, for a combination of any size may seek measures injurious to "the rights of other citizens, or to the permanent and aggregate interests of the community."[5]

Indeed, factionalism is dangerous, in part because its tendency is to elevate majority rule, making of that the only principle in politics. Publius warned in his first essay that "of those men who have overturned the liberties of republics, the greatest number have begun their career by paying an obsequious court to the people; commencing demagogues, and ending tyrants." One constant theme of these papers is, How shall America avoid that fate?

The examples in paper 10 strike closer to home, speaking to the condition of America in the late twentieth century. Here Publius warns that faction is behind "a rage for paper money, for the abolition of debts, for an equal division of property, or for any other improper or wicked project." It is a reasonable inference, then, that the soundness of the currency, the reliability of instruments of debt, private or public, and the protection of property rights all come within Publius's notion of the public good, the permanent and aggregate interests of the community.[6]

Upon what institutions must the community rely for the protection of this public good, for vigilance against this dangerous spirit of faction and its improper or wicked effects?

THE FEDERAL JUDICIARY

The judiciary is certainly among these institutions of vigilance. The intentions of the framers in creating a federal judicial system and the arguments of Publius in their defense are best understood as a reaction to the ad hoc character of the federal courts under the Articles of Confederation. Those articles authorized Congress to "appoint courts" for the hearing of criminal cases in which no individual state could exercise jurisdiction, especially piracy on the high seas. Also, these articles gave

Congress the "last resort on appeal" in litigation between states, as over boundaries. But, for the most part, there were to be no separate body of federal law and no federal court system to hear litigation not arising under those nonexisting statutes.[7]

This lacuna contributed to the vulnerability and chaos that brought so many distinguished statesmen together in Philadelphia in May 1787. The Confederation had to beg the constituent states for money, because it had no power to raise revenue on its own. Likewise, the Confederation had no authority to institute uniform conditions of commerce or to bargain for trade terms with other nations. These circumstances left our potential prosperity "fettered, interrupted, and narrowed by a multiplicity of causes."[8] The remedy required a federal system of laws, and if there must be federal laws, then there must be federal courts, on the sensible ground that "laws are a dead letter without courts to expound and define their true meaning and operation."[9] For such reasons, Publius referred to the absence of a permanent judicial power within the United States as "a circumstance which crowns the defects of the Confederation."

Must this federal system include trial courts? The Constitution allows that it might, authorizing Congress to establish such "inferior courts" as it shall find necessary.[10] Opponents of this provision argued that all questions of fact ought to be left in the hands of the state courts. A federal system, if it must exist, need take only appeals on issues of federal law once those issues have arisen in the course of a state proceeding. To that argument Publius answered:

> The most discerning cannot foresee how far the prevalency of a local spirit may be found to disqualify the local tribunals for the jurisdiction of national causes; whilst every man may discover, that courts constituted like those of some of the States would be improper channels for the judicial authority of the Union. State judges, holding their offices during pleasure, or from year to year, will be too little independent to be relied upon for an inflexible execution of the national laws.[11]

One sees the ghost of a "faction" again, this time relabeled as a local spirit. Some state courts, Publius says, are clearly possessed by this spirit, whereas any of the others might yet fall under its power. The United States, then, needs a full judicial system, not just a truncated portion of one, to satisfy one of the goals set forth in the Constitution's preamble, to "establish justice."

Even granting all the steps of the argument thus far, there was an alternative to the creation of a "supreme court" of the United States. It is not enough to say, although Publius did say it, that "all nations have found it necessary to establish one court paramount to the rest, possessing a general superintendence," because, in the case of this nation, there was a much-discussed alternative.

The framers might have given the Senate a judicial role analogous to that performed by the House of Lords in the United Kingdom. The Senate itself (or the Congress, said the advocates of unicamerality) could serve as the highest court, vitiating any need for a distinct appointive body. This prospect Publius rejected as a violation of the principle of separation of powers. Indeed, he has some fun at the expense of the antiratification forces here, for, in some respects, they complained that the proposed Constitution did not separate powers sufficiently, yet to avoid the necessity of a Supreme Court, they called for a blatant merging of the judicial and legislative roles.

One good reason for separating powers (for creating a Supreme Court, in particular) is the expectation that such a Court will serve to protect the Constitution against legislative encroachments. The power presumed by such expectations is known, in shorthand, as judicial review. Its foundations are furiously debated by historians and political scientists alike, but Publius appears to have had no doubt that it would exist:

> The interpretation of the laws is the proper and peculiar province of the courts. A constitution is, in fact, and must be regarded by the judges, as a fundamental law. It therefore belongs to them to ascertain its meaning, as well as the meaning of any particular act proceeding from any legislative body. If there should happen to be an irreconcilable variance between the two, that which has the superior obligation and validity ought, of course, to be preferred; or, in other words, the Constitution ought to be preferred to the statute.[12]

This is precisely the reasoning that Justice John Marshall was to employ in Marbury v. Madison when he exercised this power of judicial review for the first time in our nation's history.[13]

As Professor Herbert Wechsler has memorably argued, a court possesses not merely the power, which term implies discretion, but the duty to choose the Constitution over a statute as the governing authority when it determines that the former is in conflict with the latter.[14]

Here, as throughout the Federalist Papers, Publius argues that the wisdom of the Constitution lies in the barriers it erects against the mischief of faction. On one hand, factionalism, even if it should overtake the judiciary, would be less dangerous there than elsewhere. With or without this power of review, the judiciary is the least dangerous branch, possessed as it is of neither purse nor sword, confined as it must be by the legislature with the former and the executive with the latter. On the other hand, factionalism is less likely to overcome the deliberations of the judiciary than it is those of the legislature.[15]

So certain is Publius that the federal courts shall have the authority to void statutes, that he builds his argument for the lifetime tenure of judges upon this premise. Only with secure tenure can judges maintain their "independent spirit," the spirit most conducive to the "faithful performance of so arduous a duty." In other words, lifetime tenure gives a judge the wherewithal to resist the temptations of factionalism. It is "one of the most valuable of the modern improvements in the practice of government. In a monarchy it is an excellent barrier to the despotism of the prince; in a republic it is a no less excellent barrier to the encroachments and oppressions of the representative body. And it is the best expedient which can be devised in any government, to secure a steady, upright, and impartial administration of the laws."[16] This passage implies a point that deserves explicit statement. In the United States, a republic, Congress is the <u>most</u> dangerous branch. It is the legislative body whose "encroachments and oppressions" are especially to be feared as a threat to the impartial administration of the laws. An independent judiciary, then, is to be praised as a security for the laws and as a barrier against the partiality of legislators, who in the previous passage are presumed to be creatures of faction.

If one has found Publius's reasoning persuasive, then one has seen why the United States requires a federal judicial system, a final non-legislative court of appeal within this system, and lifetime tenure for the judges ("justices") of that Supreme Court. Even if one has not found Publius's reasoning persuasive, one has seen why certain astute and well-placed gentlemen of that time believed that such institutions are necessary. How are positions on this Supreme Court filled?

A PRESIDENTIAL PREROGATIVE

Publius tells us that an energetic executive is "a leading character in the definition of good government."[17] It is consistent with this general principle that the framers have given the chief executive, the president of the United States, the exclusive authority to nominate a justice of the Supreme Court. This undivided duty, performed with an eye to the president's own reputation, creates the greatest of incentives to "investigate with care the qualities requisite to the stations to be filled, and to prefer with impartiality the persons who may have the fairest pretensions to them."[18]

In defense of this presidential prerogative, Publius explains that the selection of judges by a <u>body</u> of men will not work. Publius finds it abhorrent to consider that such appointments might become a bone of contention among political factions, and his desire to allow for nonpartisan judiciousness is precisely his desire to avoid collective selection. Again one sees the fear of faction that pervades all the key decisions of the framers:

> The choice [of an assembly] . . . will of course be the result either of a victory gained by one party over the other, or of a compromise between the parties. In either case, the intrinsic merit of the candidate will be too often out of sight. In the first, the qualifications best adapted to uniting the suffrages of the party, will be more considered than those which fit the person for that

station. In the last, the coalition will commonly turn upon some interested equivalent, Give us the man we wish for this office, and you will have the one you wish for that. This will be the usual condition of the bargain. And it will rarely happen that the advancement of the public service will be the primary object either of party victories or of party negotiations.[19]

One cannot read that passage without understanding that the very result Publius hoped to avoid and expected that the sole presidential prerogative of nomination would avoid has, in fact, come about. There are three explanations for the resemblance of warning to fact. First, Publius and the framers may have failed at a task that is, in principle, impossible—the removal of partisan politics from intrinsically political questions. Second, the resemblance of the parade of horribles I have just quoted to what does take place in the contemporary Senate may be a consequence of the fact that we no longer have precisely the system Publius expounded. Some changes by tradition, some by formal amendment (notably the direct election of senators) have rendered it otherwise.[20] Third and of greatest significance, the social and economic context for both nomination and confirmation is vastly different from anything Publius could have expected. He imagined that the federal government would play a comparatively small role in the life of the nation, in contrast to the ubiquity of federal interventions in our own era of social democracy.

Although Publius did consider that the dangers of plural appointment may attach to confirmation by the Senate, he thought that risk slight. After all, he reasoned, senatorial rejection of one nominee could lead only to a second nomination by the same chief executive and then, as necessary, a third or fourth. In the case of such a conflict, the Senate can never assure itself that subsequent nominations will prove any more to its liking than those just rejected. Accordingly, Publius concluded, consent will be refused only when there are "strong and special reasons for the refusal." The appointment method provided in this Constitution loses none of the benefits of one-man selection.

Indeed, although senatorial advice and consent are conceived as a check upon presidential power, it is a check thought most effective and least harmful if it remains only a threat. The need to submit a name to the Senate has a "powerful, though in general a *silent* operation . . . the *possibility* of rejection would be a strong motive to care in proposing" (emphasis added).

The important essay that expounds the advice and consent clause[21] ends with a backhanded compliment to the House of Commons. Although this body has, Publius reminds us, a reputation for corruption that is wellfounded "to a considerable extent," it nonetheless serves as a valuable check "to control the inclinations of the monarch, both with regard to men and to measures." The House of Commons had then, and indeed as a formal matter has now, no such role as the "advice and consent" clause gives the U.S. Senate. Its only "check" on the "men" appointed by King George III was impeachment. The allusion, then, was most likely to the ongoing Warren Hastings impeachment trial.[22] Although the reference is rather mysteriously employed, it seems that Publius intended that his audience should take Hastings as a warning: it is better to let an assembly stop an occasional Hastings before he takes office than to require a protracted impeachment proceeding later.

The Senate is more closely patterned after the House of Lords than after the House of Commons. It is clear that Publius considered the Senate a "select" body, charged with duties requiring "greater extent of information and stability of character" than those assigned to the lower house.[23] This select character was not thought to depend upon the indirect method of election, although, of course, the latter was meant to reflect the former. Publius made only cursory mention of the means of election of senators, and that one mention states only that it was more "congenial to public opinion" than any alternative. The truly distinguishing features of the upper body are, rather, the lesser number of members and the long terms for which they are elected. In the first Congress there were sixty-five members of the House of Representatives,[24] but only twenty-six senators. Here, as in every other clause examined, we can see the operation of the fear of faction in the designs of the framers. The larger body shall be more subject than the smaller to what Publius calls "the impulse of sudden and violent passions," while greater length of service shall give senators greater "acquaintance with the objects and principles of legislation" than their colleagues in the other assembly will acquire. It is largely because America under the Articles of Confederation has lacked such an institution as a Senate, opines Publius, that "she is held in no respect by her friends . . . the derision of her enemies . . . a prey to every nation which has an interest in speculating on her fluctuating councils and embarrassed affairs."[25]

This argument in favor of an upper house hardly completes the case for the advice and consent clause. Federal judges might be elected rather than appointed. Some of those whom Publius called "the more respectable adversaries" of ratification argued that only separately elected judges would have independence from the other two branches and that the principle of separation of powers requires that no branch can appoint the members of any other. To this, Publius replied with a survey of the constitutions of the various states within the confederation system, which showed that the separation of powers is not absolute in any of them.[26]

More particularly, Publius saw two objections to an elective federal judiciary. First, "peculiar qualifications being essential in its members," the method by which judges are chosen must secure those qualifications.[27] Election, in other words, would undermine merit selection in the one branch in which merit can, otherwise, be objectively determined and secured. Second, elections are unnecessary to give judges independence. The permanence of their tenure (i.e., "on good behavior") has the same effect, for such security soon destroys "all sense of dependence on the authority" from whom it came.

From much of the foregoing it ought to be clear that the framers—or at least the three very important framers combined as Publius—did not believe that senatorial debates over the confirmation of judicial nominees would become a partisan and ideological struggle, a competition between what that composite author could only have called competing factions. Yet it is clear to anyone who has followed such debates in recent years that this is exactly what they have become. Among the changes in our constitutional and political system that have helped to produce this unexpected result, one stands out. The functions of the federal judiciary (and of the Supreme Court especially) are now much more extensive, its impact on the daily lives even of politically inconspicuous citizens much more pervasive than its inventors could have imagined.

There are five broad reasons for this change: the enactment of a Bill of Rights; the application of that bill as a limit on the authority of the several states; the laying of rails, the opening of canals, and the pervasively interstate character of commerce that followed from such progress; the unraveling of America's racial problems, a colonial inheritance; and, finally, the assumption by the United States of an unlimited role as ensurer of last resort for the other levels of government, so that those other levels, so ensured, may seek to protect their residents against virtually all the travails of everyday life. I now discuss each of these five developments.

A DIFFERENT AMERICA

In all but the last of his papers, Publius addressed an objection to the Constitution founded not upon what it did but upon what it left undone. It contained no Bill of Rights. He gives several replies to this objection, most of which but nibble about the edge of his problem. This is what he says when finally he gets to the heart of the matter:

> Bills of rights are, in their origin, stipulations between kings and their subjects, abridgements of prerogative in favor of privilege, reservations of rights not surrendered to the prince . . . . It is evident, therefore, that according to their primitive signification they have no application to constitutions, professedly founded upon the power of the people, and executed by their immediate representatives and servants. Here, in strictness, the people surrender nothing; and, as they retain everything they have no need of particular reservations.[28]

This argument resembles the lawyerly equivocation that gives the professional bar a bad name. As a historical generalization, it is irrelevant. Why should not the same sort of document that, in its "primitive signification," abridged the prerogatives of a king be employed now for a somewhat different end and as an integral part of a constitution? As a bit of conceptual analysis, the passage just quoted is still less impressive. It is entirely possible that "the people" may be oppressed, as a public or as individuals, by those persons whom they had, mistakenly or viciously, trusted as their "immediate servants and representatives." It is that possibility that a Bill of Rights, combined especially with the institution of judicial review, can thwart and, in fact, has helped to thwart.

Publius had a better answer available. He might have written: "Yes, a Bill of Rights would be good. The ratification of this Constitution will also ratify the amendment machinery and clear the way for the introduction of such a bill. Its advocates ought to be on our side or, at least, need not be against us." Unfortunately, the polemical instinct, the desire to show every argument of one's opponents to be worthless, seems to have gotten the better of our author's judgment here.

It was not until after the Civil War that the first eight amendments came to be applied to actions, not just of the federal government but of the state governments as well. The Fourteenth Amendment prohibits any state from "making or enforcing any law which shall abridge the privileges or immunities of citizens of the United States." This is not an elegant but is a precise way of saying that what the feds cannot do to you, the states cannot, either.

Challenges to federal or state actions on constitutional grounds are not the only or even the chief sources for the swelling prominence of the federal courts in our lives. One must give those challenges a billing no higher than our departure from the horse-and-buggy age of commerce in which Publius wrote, an age in which it was natural to expect that most transactions of commerce would be intrastate and that most regulation of contracts, sales, and securities would remain the province of the thirteen state legislatures. We have departed from that age via railroads, internal combustion, airplanes, and fax transmissions. The continent-sized United States unquestionably is a single entity for purposes of virtually all meaningful commercial regulation or for purposes of the deliberate political decision not to regulate or to deregulate a field previously encumbered. Antitrust, securities law, labor relations, and occupational, consumer, health, and safety regulation—all are fields now thoroughly federalized, and the federalization of each has had the effect of raising the stakes of every Supreme Court appointment, making the dispassionate examination of qualifications that Publius expected of both the president and the Senate ever more moot, ever more remote as an ideal.

Still other developments have had this stakes-raising effect. Publius was certainly aware that the country was bound to experience continued agitation over the institution of slavery. The end of the slave trade and the count, for representational purposes, of slaves as part-persons were two of the issues requiring delicate compromise in Philadelphia and defense before diverse publics throughout the ratification debates.[29] It is even possible that, if he had been asked, Publius could have suggested that the days of this institution were numbered and that continued racial difficulties would follow its collapse.[30] But it is hardly possible that Publius would have gone much further, or would have predicted anything akin to the complicated system of congressional statutes, court orders, and constitutional doctrines that now goes under the name of "civil rights"—a body of federal law that constitutes another enormous addition to the tasks of the Supreme Court as the final arbiter of issues of federal law.

They say, in late night television commercials for multi-faceted kitchen utensils, "but wait! there's more!" The most important of all these accretions to the supremacy of the Supreme Court awaited the first half of the twentieth century, a time of transformation for the United States from a system of limited government to one that Americans now describe as "the welfare state", but that Europeans would call "social democracy."

This system operates at all levels, from town hall to state capital to Washington, D.C. But the central government is the Rome to which all roads lead. The essential feature of social democracy (I use that more descriptive imported label throughout this volume) is its systematic effort to eliminate risk. First, risk is to be banished from economic decisions. In time, it is expected to disappear from all of life. Under such slogans as "security from cradle to grave," a system of consensus politics has developed, incorporating first one constituency, then another as beneficiaries of the socialization of risk, then banishing to the margins of public discourse those whom it could not incorporate.

In this new America, Supreme Court justices became brokers of risk. This is what has made of a confirmation hearing an event charged with passions and dominated by a spirit of faction that would have made old Publius blush.

Imagine that the westward crew and the eastward crew working on the transcontinental railroad missed one another, one set of tracks passing through Promontory, Utah, and the other through Provo, one hundred miles to the south. The golden stake would never have been struck, and the only sound that would have resounded in the air instead of that famous metallic clang would perhaps have been the whine of mutual recrimination. Likewise, we can see an eighteenth-century political system tracking well to the north of our late twentieth-century political expectations, and the golden stake, the calm, nonfactious use of the Senate's power of advice and consent, is never struck.

Among those who have noticed this missed rendezvous, some have concluded that the United States needs a new Constitution or such a sweeping set of constitutional amendments as to amount to a new document altogether.[31] But one might more plausibly conclude that the strain consists of expectations that violate the nature of things. An insistence upon eliminating risk could not be satisfied with any imaginable Constitution. Perhaps the United States ought to show more respect for its Enlightenment founding by limiting its public ends to those that can be accomplished by Enlightenment means.

The great debate between activist government and limited government rests on the competition between those two inferences. The premise that they share is sound. The Constitution, with its advice and consent clause, was not intended for a world in which the Supreme Court is called upon to do all that social democracy requires.

NOTES

1. U.S. Constitution, Article II, §2, ¶2: the president "shall nominate, and by and with the advice and consent of the Senate, shall appoint, other public ministers and counsels, judges of the Supreme Court, and all other officers of the United States, whose appointments are not herein otherwise provided for."

2. E. M. Earle, ed., The Federalist: A Commentary on the Constitution of the United States (New York, 1937), No. 9. The Earle edition is cited throughout this chapter, hereafter as Publius, followed by the number.

3. M. Hecht, Odd Destiny (New York, 1982), 137.

4. Publius, No. 39.

5. Publius, No. 10.

6. Alexander Hamilton would guide the nation's early finances on this principle, as in the report on public credit that he presented to the House of Representatives on January 14, 1790.

7. Article IX, ¶¶ 1 & 2.

8. Publius, No. 11.

9. Publius, No. 22.

10. U.S. Constitution, Article III, §1.

11. Publius, No. 81.

12. Publius, No. 78.

13. Marbury v. Madison, 1 Cranch 137 (1803).

14. Wechsler, "Toward Neutral Principles of Constitutional Law," 73 Harv. L. Rev. 1 (1959) at 5–6.

15. "The benefits of the integrity and moderation of the judiciary have already been felt in more states than one; and . . . they must have commanded the esteem and applause of all the virtuous and disinterested" (Publius, No. 78).

16. Id.

17. Publius, No. 70.

18. Publius, No. 76.

19. Id.

20. U.S. Constitution, Amendment XVII (1916).

21. Publius, No. 76.

22. In 1773, King George III appointed Warren Hastings governor-general of the East India Company. In that capacity Hastings helped organize the opium trade into a rich source of revenue for the Crown, and he made his company the paramount source of power throughout the subcontinent. In 1784 he resigned his office and returned to England to face an impeachment inquiry in the House of Commons. Impeachment carried. Hastings faced trial in the House of Lords. That latter ordeal began in February 1788 and dragged on to eventual acquittal, in April 1795. There are many fine accounts of this controversy, most recently that which appears in Conor Cruise O'Brien's biography of Edmund Burke, The Great Melody (Chicago, 1992).

23. Publius, No. 62.

24. U.S. Constitution, Article I, §2, ¶3.

25. Publius, No. 62.

26. Publius, No. 47. The authoritative compendium of antifederalist thought, sometimes answered by, and sometimes answering, Publius, is the edition prepared by H. J. Storing, The Complete Anti-Federalist (Chicago, 1981).

27. Publius, No. 51.

28. Publius, No. 84.

29. U.S. Constitution, Article I, §2, ¶3; §9, ¶1. For a discussion of the role of slavery in the creation of the Constitution, see Wiecek, "The Witch at the Christening," L. Levy & D. Mahoney, eds., The Framing and Ratification of the Constitution 167–184 (New York, 1987).

30. In the course of the Lincoln-Douglas debates, Abraham Lincoln argued that the Founders, even the slaveholders among them, expected the gradual dissolution of the institution of slavery, as evidenced by the free-soil provision of the Northwest Ordinance. He inferred that the efforts of the Slave Power to save and spread that institution constituted a violation of the original compact. For the classic study of Lincoln's reasoning, see H. Jaffa, Crisis of the House Divided (New York, 1959) esp. 277–293.

31. The Constitution and the structures it created cannot, argued one prominent New Dealer, "serve to modernize a government that must make itself master of the environment, acting for citizens caught up in the multifarious changes brought about by scientific discoveries and the following technology" (R. Tugwell, Off Course [New York, 1971] at 109). In The Emerging Constitution (New York, 1974) Tugwell offered his alternative draft.

2

What the New Deal Required

The fifth amendment to the Constitution directs that the United States shall deprive no person of life, liberty, or property without due process of law. The Fourteenth Amendment offers the same direction to the several states. But by the time of the Thomas hearing of 1991 it was a matter of common observation that the Supreme Court never employs its power of judicial review to protect commercial liberty or otherwise to strike laws that violate property rights. This chapter narrates the onset of the abnegation of judicial responsibility behind that common observation.

In 1918 Congress passed a Minimum Wage Act providing for the creation in the District of Columbia of a Minimum Wage Board.[1] This Board was authorized, first, to ascertain the actual wages of women and minors (the two groups for whose particular protection the act was drafted), then, to establish a standard wage for members of those groups. Employers within the District were forbidden to offer any wage to a woman or child below the established standard.

The plaintiff in the first minimum wage case, a woman named Willie A. Lyons, and her employer, Children's Hospital of the District of Columbia, brought suit against the members of the Minimum Wage Board. Jessie C. Adkins was the first named of those members. The District Court dismissed the suit. The Court of Appeals reversed that dismissal.[2] This is a remarkable spectacle. A worker brought suit because a statute passed at the insistence of the supposedly progressive, pro-labor, political faction of her day, threatened to deprive her of her wage. Yet such a spectacle reminds us of the real, if not always the obvious, effect of all minimum wage laws that have any market "bite" at all.

In 1923 the U.S. Supreme Court, in a five to three decision by Justice George Sutherland, reminded the government that the Fifth Amendment protects "liberty" and that the framers of that clause did not add, "except, of course, for liberty of contract, which may be abridged at will." They wrote "liberty," and presumably they meant liberty. Of course, as Sutherland acknowledged, liberty of contract cannot be an absolute. Under common law there is quite a panoply of restrictions on this liberty, such as the prohibition of fraud and protection of the mentally ill. But the justice reminded Congress that in the United States, liberty is the rule, and its limits are the exceptions. This law deprived both employers and employees of liberty in a very sweeping manner without so much as a pretense of due process, and, so Sutherland concluded for the majority, it was of no effect as in violation of the supreme law of the land.[3]

A little simple logic will persuade anyone who needs to be persuaded that Sutherland's opinion was not among the causes of the Great Depression that followed it by several years and that its reversal was not a candidate for cure. Delusions of desperate times aside, no one gets a job because the government sets a wage or loses a job because an attempt at wagesetting fails. The most likely effect of "setting a floor below wages" is to squeeze people like Lyons out of the room. A more benevolent possibility is that a minimum wage set low enough to do no harm will have no effect at all, on recovery or anything else.

THE HUNDRED DAYS AND AFTER

The period of frenetic activity that put in place the new president's economic program, the New Deal, lasted from March 4, 1933, the day of Franklin Roosevelt's inauguration, until June 26, 1933, when Congress passed the National Industrial Recovery Act (NIRA). This period lasted 114 days, but historians with more regard for the Napoleonic precedent than for calendrical literalness have tagged it "the Hundred Days."

The year 1933 also saw parallel flurries of legislation in the states, for the legislatures and their governors had to respond to the general outcry that all authorities "do something" about the grave economic crisis. State assertions of control over local industries, analogous to the federal assertion of control over interstate industry, were, in the climate of that time, regarded as one of a piece with the New Deal—both defended and assailed in the same breath. In this sense it was important to the new administration that, for example, both New York and Washington state enact minimum wage laws at this time. Both laws were challenged.

Early in 1936 the New York case came before the Supreme Court. Counsel for that state, defending the constitutionality of the law, insisted that he was arguing not for an overturn of <u>Adkins</u>, only for a distinction. On one hand, counsel argued from the fact that the Fifth Amendment, invoked in <u>Adkins</u>, limits only the acts of the federal government, not those of the states. That is true but proved irrelevant. The Fourteenth Amendment repeats the pertinent language of the Fifth verbatim and applies it to the states. On the other hand, counsel argued that New York had done its homework more carefully than had the District of Columbia and ought to be rewarded with a higher grade. Specifically, if the holding of the Court in Adkins can be read to mean only that the Wage Board mistook the labor market in the nation's capital, then the same Court could, without inconsistency, find in 1936 that the lawmakers of New York possessed a correct understanding of the labor pool there.

Such an argument was patently untenable, analogous to the contention that the Constitution is different in New York because the air is colder there. In conference, the justices soon discovered that there was no one among the nine who believed that there was any distinction to be drawn between Adkins and the case at hand, Morehead. Four justices intended to overturn Adkins and find the New York statute unconstitutional. The other four intended to affirm Adkins and strike the statute. The decision was in the hands of Justice Owen J. Roberts.

Roberts chose the narrowest of rulings. He voted to uphold Adkins, on the ground that New York had failed to make the argument that it should be overturned. He, and with him the five-man majority his vote created, would indicate willingness to listen to an argument to overturn on the merits in another case. In the meantime, as the result of the timidity of New York's argument, its law failed.

Justice Roberts did not write an opinion stating the reason for his decisive vote. Chief Justice Charles Evans Hughes assigned the honor of drafting the majority opinion to Pierce Butler, who, in an act of judicial gamesmanship, wrote a very broad decision that sought to forestall any continued challenges to Adkins, repeating the arguments from that decision of 1923.[4] Roberts later admitted that he erred by remaining silent. The publication of a "concurring opinion," a common event now, was a rare one in 1936, and since Roberts wrote none, Butler's reasoning alone spoke for the majority.[5]

That summer President Roosevelt informed the platform committee of the Democratic National Convention, meeting in Philadelphia, that there would be "no short cuts of any kind" in the treatment of constitutional issues.[6] That platform accordingly declared that if constitutional reform should prove a means necessary to the ends of the New Deal, that reform would come about through the established procedures of constitutional amendment. This pledge was to the credit of the president and his party.* Keeping it, would have been more so.

---

* The talk of constitutional reform in 1936 was instigated not only by Morehead. In 1935 a unanimous Court struck the NIRA. In 1936 the Court, by a six to three vote, struck the Agricultural Adjustment Act (AAA), which sought to employ the taxing power to control agricultural output. These were the twin mandates for sweeping executive regulation to come out of the hundred days.

In October 1936 the Supreme Court agreed to hear an appeal from still another minimum wage case, West Coast Hotel v. Parrish.[7] Due to the illness of Justice Harlan F. Stone, the Court could not vote on Parrish at its December 19 conference and deferred the matter for two months. Yet Roberts made his view known to his colleagues at this conference, and it was clear to each of the eight that when the ninth had recovered his health, there would be a five-man majority in favor of sustaining minimum wage legislation, for the first time in U.S. constitutional history.

Such judges' conferences are of necessity secret. No one, then, knew of these developments on February 5, 1937, when the president sent to Congress a plan for a revolutionary reorganization of the judiciary. The plan was couched in terms of an effort to improve the efficiency of the federal courts, but behind the scenes the president was perfectly willing to admit,[8] and everyone else in the country recognized at once,[9] that the real purpose was a leveling of Supreme Court resistance to Roosevelt's programs. The president sought the power to increase the membership of the Court by one member for every sitting justice over the age of seventy who did not agree to retire within six months. This would give Roosevelt the immediate authority to appoint six new justices, breaking at one fell swoop any pestily persistent independence on the part of that body, the sort of persistent posture Publius had presumed it would always preserve.

Parrish came up for discussion in the justices' conference of February 7, and the Court soon announced a five to four vote upholding minimum wage statutes. The key passage in that decision follows:

The Constitution does not speak of freedom of contract. It speaks of liberty and prohibits the deprivation of liberty without due process of law. In prohibiting that deprivation, the Constitution does not recognize an absolute, an uncontrollable liberty . . . the liberty safeguarded is liberty in a social organization which requires the protection of law against the evils which menace the health, safety, morals and welfare of the people.[10]

That passage, which is as cogent an explanation as the whole opinion contains, gets us nowhere. First, it seems to assume a distinction between the meaning of the words *liberty* and *freedom*. But the right to enter into a contract can be described, in the idiom of either the eighteenth century or the twentieth, under either word indifferently. The framers of the Constitution used *liberty* in connection with due process for reasons dating to the Lockean origin of the triad "life, liberty, and property."

Second, Chief Justice Hughes carefully explains that liberty cannot be absolute. Each of the two decisions examined, Adkins and Morehead, had conceded as much, while reaching a contrary result on indistinguishable facts. My liberty in waving my fist in the air, as is often said, comes to an end at the tip of your nose. The Parrish decision does nothing to establish whose nose is punched by means of a contract for employment at a politically disfavored wage.

Third, the reader is offered a laundry list of reasons for regulation: "health, safety, morals and welfare." All of these are rather too broad for comfort. They amount to the bare claim that the state will regulate contracts because it knows what is good for the contracting parties better than they know for themselves. One is hard put to it to find any justification in this opinion for the particular limit on freedom it represents, for treating wages at a politically disfavored level of compensation as contracts outside the protected scope of liberty.

The minimum wage controversy, more than controversies over crop quotas or the delegation of legislative authority, stimulated the legend of a one-justice "switch" in 1937, a switch that is said to have "saved nine" from the court-packing bill. This is only a legend. The five to four vote in <u>Parrish</u> was evident in December 1936, a month and a half before Roosevelt fired the opening shot of his court-packing campaign, and nobody's vote changed following that first shot.

The real switch came in April 1937, when the Supreme Court ruled in favor of the constitutionality of the National Labor Relations Act (NLRA), in effect abandoning the straightforward view of the interstate commerce clause that it had employed in the "sick chicken" case of just two years before.[11]

In its NLRA decision the Court announced, again through the chief justice, that: "although activities may be intrastate in character when separately considered, if they have such a close and substantial relationship to interstate commerce that their control is essential and appropriate to protect that commerce from burdens and obstructions, Congress cannot be denied the power to exercise that control."[12]

In subsequent cases the Court diluted this "close and substantial relation" test until it became clear that everything that happens anywhere can be deemed to be in interstate commerce,[13] so the specific enumeration of the powers of Congress no longer functions as a barrier to the size or pervasive influence of the federal government. The most important phrase in the last-quoted passage is the last, "Congress cannot be denied the power." By April 1937 the Supreme Court no longer believed itself legitimate in denying Congress any power that Congress judged it had to have.

But the NLRA decision broke the unity of the Democrats in the Congress of that year.[14] Roosevelt was selling his court-packing plan on the hypothesis that there was no alternative, no other means to enact the New Deal. Now an alternative presented itself, simply to let an ongoing jurisprudential process take its course in the expectation that the constitutional obstacles to the New Deal would clear by themselves. Although Roosevelt persisted for another three months before final defeat in July, from April it was clear that his party was not behind him and that he would have to back off as soon as a facesaving opportunity presented itself.

ROOSEVELT PARTISANS

At the end of February, in the earliest stages of the controversy over the president's plan for the Court, Congressman James P. Buchanan of the Tenth District, Texas, died of a heart attack. The Texas director of the National Youth Administration (NYA), Lyndon Johnson, saw the headlines of Buchanan's death and thought at once, "This is my chance."[15] Seven other Tenth District residents came to the same conclusion regarding their own respective "chances." Johnson had six weeks in which to prove his superiority to the alternatives in the eyes of the electorate. He ran as Roosevelt's man, of course. But, then, so did several of his opponents. How could Johnson prove that he was the most fervently pro-Rooseveltian of the lot? One method suggested itself. Johnson became the first of the eight to declare himself in favor of the court-packing plan: "The paramount issue of this campaign," he said when he announced that he was running one, "is whether the President shall be sustained in his program for readjustment of the judicial system. . . . I have always been a supporter of President Roosevelt and I am wholeheartedly in favor of his present plan."[16]

Of course, there were many people in the country and in Texas especially who were supporters of Roosevelt, very often heatedly so, yet who had reservations about that particular plan. But Johnson would brook no such subtleties. Any doubt about the destruction of the independence of the Supreme Court was a doubt about the leadership of the president, an enormously popular president in the district at issue. Any such doubt was plainly anti-Roosevelt. Thus, Johnson won election as the only 100 percent pure Rooseveltian available. Still, he was elected with the smallest total of votes of any of the nation's congressmen at that time. In part this was due to the large number of candidates and in part to the low voter turnout characteristic of a special election in an odd-numbered year.

The future president's election to Congress came on a slow news day and made headlines throughout the country. The Washington Post, for example, displayed these words prominently: "TEXAS SUPPORTER OF COURT CHANGE APPEARS ELECTED."[17] Before the congressman-elect had a chance to go to Washington, his hero came to Texas. The presidential yacht Potomac was cruising in the Gulf of Mexico, and it stopped in Galveston on May 11. Johnson made the best of what was not yet known as a "photo op," and the picture of his handshake with Roosevelt, he made sure, received wide distribution throughout the state in years to come, so long as the Roosevelt name retained its political magic.[18]

In the decades from that time to this, Roosevelt has had no dearth of supporters, partisans, or admirers among professional historians. Few of those fail to qualify their admiration at least in this respect, withholding their approval from his attack upon the Court. Samuel Morison, in a history of the United States widely used as a text a generation ago, called it that president's "first big mistake."[19]

The bill was a mistake in a predictive sense. Roosevelt seems to have believed that it would pass, and in that belief he was wrong. But it was not a mistake in a tactical sense. The introduction of the bill and the campaign for its passage accomplished the end the New Deal required: it changed the direction of Supreme Court decisions. In the following year, Congress would even reenact, with some changes, the old AAA, and the new version survived the judicial review its predecessor had flunked.[20] In the strategic sense, the court-packing bill may have proven to be a mistake after all. The fight helped create the Dixiecrat-Republican alliance in Congress that would bedevil Democratic presidents for a generation to come, and it stripped from FDR himself the aura of legislative invincibility he had worn since the hurried victories of the hundred days.[21]

Legislative victory or no, the simple and dependable transience of human flesh was about to give Roosevelt all the vacancies he could desire. There was going to be a Rooseveltian revolution in jurisprudence, simply by virtue of the longevity of that administration. In the period 1933–37, the members of the Supreme Court were (listed now by seniority): Willis Van Devanter, James McReynolds, Louis D. Brandeis, George Sutherland, Pierce Butler, Harlan F. Stone, Chief Justice Charles Evans Hughes, Owen J. Roberts, and Benjamin Cardozo. By the end of 1941, the members were as follows: Harlan F. Stone (now chief justice), Owen J. Roberts, Hugo Black, Stanley Reed, Felix Frankfurter, William O. Douglas, Frank Murphy, James F. Byrnes, and Robert H. Jackson. This new lineup was dedicated to the new jurisprudence, a conception of the law that did not merely allow but embodied the evermore complete system of social controls that has enwrapped the economic and social realities of the United States from that day to this, a conception of the role of the Court that made it not an opponent but an administrator of that system. The best one-word label for the form this new jurisprudence took, circa 1941, is "restraintism."

From one point of view, every time the Supreme Court exercises its power of judicial review and in the course of that exercise strikes an unconstitutional statute, regulation, or order, it is exerting power, an unelected power, at the expense of some decision of the elected branches of government, the branches closer to the great body of the people. A Court within a generally republican system should, therefore, exert its power very sparingly; it should "restrain" itself from such actions whenever there is so much as a colorable constitutional justification for the challenged law. On this same view, every time a Court does not exercise this power, although asked to do so by one of the litigants, every time it upholds a law, it is engaging in the true virtue of a republic, deferring to the voice of the people. That is the view of restraintism, which won its way in the years 1937–41.

But there is a paradox hidden in such language. For the Supreme Court does much more than allow or strike bills on constitutional grounds. The Supreme Court is the forum of last resort in controversies over the interpretation and construction of such law as may survive its review. Accordingly, the more lenient the Court becomes as to constitutional tests, the broader the body of law in operation at either the federal or the state levels, and the more necessary, the more intrusive into everyday life, become the Court's deliberations as the interpreter of those expanded bodies of law. The Supreme Court gains (interpretive) power by abandoning responsible exercise of its (review) power.

This paradox of restraint may be hidden from some eyes, as the result of the automatic Left/Right polarization of American politics. Some otherwise obvious points are lost to the sight of otherwise insightful people, people with minds as acute as Felix Frankfurter's, in the mist generated by the fog machine of this polarity.

Neither Left nor Right nor those moderates whose political imagination is dominated by the Left-to-Right spectrum have any interest in observing the paradox that a Court restrained in the face of legislative action on school prayer and workplace safety alike will end by deciding questions on everything, from matters of faith to matters of finance, its power increasing along with its gestures of humility. Perhaps a more truly restrained court will one day use its power of judicial review to keep all of government, inclusive of itself in its interpretive role, out of all such fields—using power in order to abdicate it, rather than the reverse.

In the meantime, the only consideration that could justify the great falling away from the Publian system that the New Deal and its judicial revolution imply, is the force of sheer necessity. It is in order, then, to consider whether the Great Depression constituted the necessity that, in turn, justified the developments I have briefly chronicled.

It is in order to do so but difficult to do so well. I cannot answer the questions that would have to be asked in any full inquiry, much less respond to the most likely objections to whatever answers I would propose, simply because this is not a work of economic history. But if I try to ignore the realities of business, everything I might want to suggest about American law or politics will make no sense to some, will give needless offense to others.

My solution, then, is to state my own view quite dogmatically: no explanation, no defense. (I offer the authorities in the notes at the end of the chapter.)

Cause. The depression was a monetary phenomenon, brought about by persistent adherence to a gold standard and by related or analogous monetary constraints throughout the Herbert Hoover and the early Roosevelt years.[22]

Timing. There were two distinct recoveries. The first had begun by the end of 1933 and continued through 1936. But the economy slid backward through 1937, and the word *recession* came into the language.[23] The second recovery began in 1938 and continued through the war years.

Policy. The trends in productivity and employment of the 1930s correlate quite well with monetary policy and not at all well with anything else that was going on at the time. A growing economy needs money. In some of its least-heralded actions, the Roosevelt administration, to its deserved credit, gave the economy that. But to this recovery, virtually the whole of the program that went then and that goes now under the name New Deal was at best a harmless sideshow, at worst a positive hindrance.[24] If the defense of necessity fails, then no other plausible defense remains, and the New Deal must be judged a bad thing, from the points of view of the citizen, the economist, and the student of law alike, and a departure from the limited government and its concomitantly limited judiciary, free of the spirit of faction, described by, and familiar to, Publius. Whether it is a departure that one can expect to reverse is a matter for consideration only at the end of the journey toward and through the Clarence Thomas hearings.

HUGO BLACK AND A CONFIRMATION

On May 18, 1937, only a week after Johnson met Roosevelt at Galveston, Justice Van Devanter, a man whose opposition to all New Deal legislation and to every act redolent of such legislation to come to his attention was almost mythic in its consistency, retired from the bench. In August the president nominated Senator Hugo Black to fill the post Van Devanter left vacant.

Black was an attorney from Birmingham, Alabama, and in the course of his practice he had found it expedient to join the Ku Klux Klan. In an interview near the end of his life, published posthumously, Black would explain: "I was trying a lot of cases against corporations, jury cases, and I found out that all the corporation lawyers were in the Klan. A lot of jurors were, too, so I figured I'd better be evenup."[25]

Black withdrew from the practice of law in 1926, the year of his election to the Senate. One of his last acts as a senator, in 1937, was sponsorship of a wages and hours bill which took advantage of the Supreme Court's recent retreat from Adkins and Morehead to federalize this field.[26] That fact might have helped set the stage for a very ideological, very polarized confirmation fight, the sort of fight we have come to expect from Court appointments in recent years. Principled supporters of economic due process might have been expected to raise the issue of minimum wage legislation and its relation to the Fifth or Fourteenth amendments as among the reasons for their opposition to Black.

There was a confirmation fight, but it was fought over Black's personal history and qualifications, over rumors of his former Klan membership, over the manner in which he had conducted his investigations as a committee chairman and whether that conduct displayed an insufficient regard for the rights of critics of administration policy, and finally over whether Senator

Black's career as a whole had displayed the "wide culture and juristic detachment" to be required of a justice of the Supreme Court.[27]

The Judiciary Committee did not, at this time, make a habit of calling judicial nominees to attend public hearings and give testimony on everything from their finances to their constitutional philosophy. After a favorable subcommittee vote Walter White, executive secretary of the National Association for the Advancement of Colored People (NAACP), aware of the Klan rumors, telegrammed Congress to ask that the full committee hold such a hearing. But nothing of that sort was done. The entire confirmation controversy, insofar as it took place in the public eye, consisted of a six-hour debate on the Senate floor. That debate ended with senatorial consent to the appointment by a vote of sixty-three to sixteen.[28]

Proof on the Klan issue surfaced at a constitutionally awkward moment—after the confirmation vote but before the new justice was to take his oath. For two weeks, from the press accounts of mid-September to October, Black kept reporters at bay, saying, "When I have a statement to make . . . I will make it in such a way that I cannot be misquoted and that the nation can hear."[29] On October 1, Black addressed America in a radio broadcast.

He confessed that he had been a member of the Klan, asserted that he had had "nothing to do" with that organization since before his election to the Senate, left the exact date of the disconnection unclear, and offered nothing by way of explanation. This policy of minimal admission was coupled with an assault on those who had raised the point in a "planned and concerted attack . . . calculated to create racial and religious hatred."[30]

Black's speech gained the largest radio audience assembled since the abdication address of King Edward VIII nearly a year before. But only one man's opinion counted. That man, Roosevelt, described Black's talk as "a grand job" that "did the trick."[31]

Three days later, after the new justice had taken his oath in a private ceremony, a lawyer from New Haven, Connecticut, brought an action asking that the Supreme Court bar Black from taking his seat. This action was grounded in the Constitution, Article I, §6, par. 2: "No Senator or representative shall, during the time for which he was elected, be appointed to any civil office under the authority of the United States, which shall have been created, or the emoluments where of shall have been increased, during such time." During Black's term of office as senator the Congress had increased pension rights for retired federal judges. The petitioner wanted the Court to decide whether such a bill is an increase of the emoluments of the former senator's new civil office.

The Court promptly dismissed this petition on the ground that the petitioner had no standing in the matter.[32] That was the first, and it remains the only, time in our history that the Supreme Court has had to determine the validity of an appointment to the Supreme Court. It was a fittingly controverted beginning for the service of the first justice in what was soon, through other such retirements and replacements, to become a thoroughly Rooseveltian Court.

In later years, Black became inextricably intertwined in the public mind with his distinctive view of the First Amendment, known as the "literalist" or the "absolutist" reading. Black decided that it is wrong, and an abdication of responsibility for the Supreme Court or any court to engage in any "balancing" of the interest or considerations at controversy that is not already contained within the language of the document before the tribunal. Specifically, when the First Amendment of the U.S. Constitution tells us that "Congress shall make no law . . . abridging the freedom of speech," it does not leave to the Court any discretion to balance free speech against other values—against, say, national security or public morals or the protection of private reputations. The framers have already done that balancing, and the way that the scales came down in their eyes, or rather in their words, is the way those scales must remain poised for so long as we have a constitutional republic at all. In its concise form, this position reads, "No law means no law."[33]

Black's view of the First Amendment and of the active role the courts must play in the enforcement of that absolute command was bound to clash with the language of judicial restraint, so successful in paving the way for economic regulation at the expense of freedom of contract. The clash that was bound to come, came.

NOTES

1. U.S. Constitution, Article I, §8, ¶17.
2. Children's Hospital v. Adkins, 284 F. 613 (D.C. Cir. 1922).
3. Adkins v. Children's Hospital, 261 U.S. 525 (1923).
4. M. Freedman, ed., Roosevelt and Frankfurter: Their Correspondence, 1928–1945 (Boston, 1969), 392–395 (hereafter Correspondence).
5. Morehead v. New York, 298 U.S. 587 (1936).
6. Correspondence, at 379 (editor's note).
7. West Coast Hotel v. Parrish, 300 U.S. 379 (1937).
8. Correspondence at 377 (a letter from Roosevelt to Frankfurter, January 15, 1937).
9. TRB, The New Republic (February 24, 1937) at 72.
10. 300 U.S. 379 at 391.
11. Schechter Corp. v. United States, 295 U.S. 495 (1935).
12. National Labor Relations Board v. Jones and Laughlin Steel Corp., 301 U.S. 1 (1937).
13. Wickard v. Filburn, 317 U.S. 111 (1942).
14. L. Baker, Felix Frankfurter (New York, 1969), 188–191.

15. D. Kearns, Lyndon Johnson and the American Dream (New York, 1976),
85–86.

16. R. Caro, The Years of Lyndon Johnson: Vol. I, The Path to Power (New
York, 1982), 404–405.

17. Washington Post (early edition) April 11, 1937, p. 1.

18. Caro, supra, photo following p. 358.

19. S. Morison, The Oxford History of the American People (New York, 1965),
970.

20. Mulford v. Smith, 307 U.S. 38 (1939); Wickard v. Filburn, 317 U.S. 111
(1942).

21. G. T. Dunne, Hugo Black and the Judicial Revolution (New York, 1977),
168.

22. M. Friedman & A. Schwartz, Monetary History of the United States,
1867–1960 (Princeton, NJ, 1963) is the definitive account. President Roosevelt
acknowledged a monetary dimension to the crisis of 1933 when, during his inaugural
address, he promised a "sound but adequate currency." Friedman, in "Too Tight for
a Strong Recovery," Wall Street Journal (October 23, 1992), A12, argues that in the
very different circumstances of the 1990s it is still the case that where "money moves,
factories follow."

Also, see D. Murphey, Liberalism in Contemporary America (McLean, VA, 1992),
45–60, where the depression is placed into the context of the ideological crosscurrents
of the time.

23. E. A. Goldenweiser, American Monetary Policy (New York, 1951), 174–182.
Goldenweiser stays within the postwar Keynesian orthodoxy and so cannot credit the
correspondence between money supply and business activity that his work suggests.
See p. 179: "It is difficult to accept the view of some critics that this action of the
Board [an increase in bank reserve requirements] was a serious factor in the
downturn of business which occurred in 1937." Nonetheless, his facts support the
inference that his theory does not allow.

24. Those historians who have learned their Keynesian economic lessons will
object: "Didn't the New Deal introduce deficit spending and the multiplier effect?
Didn't this policy prime the pump of private investment? Isn't that a countercyclical
benefit distinct from any monetary effects?" P. Samuelson, Economics (New York,
1976) sets out the orthodoxy, as at 368.

But if deficit spending had the consequences this theory predicts, then the United
States around 1995 should be an economic utopia. See D. L. May, From New Deal
to the New Economics (New York, 1981).

It is tempting to associate the 1937–38 recession with the oftenvoiced expression
"the second New Deal" and to suppose that just as the first New Deal met the Great
Depression, the second phase arose in reaction to the economic aftershock. But that
is not how Arthur Schlesinger, Jr., used the distinction in the canonical work The Age
of Roosevelt: The Politics of Upheaval (Boston, 1960). Schlesinger contrasted the
improvisational policies of 1933–34 with the systematic Keynesian of 1935–36. On
that account, both of the two New Deals preceded the recession of Roosevelt's
second term. See Murphey, Liberalism, 54–56, and notes.

25. Dunne at 111.

26. Dunne, 169–172.

27. Correspondence, 407–408 (a letter from Frankfurter to Roosevelt,
September 1, 1937).

28. Dunne, 56–59.

29.   "Justice Black," Newsweek (October 11, 1937) at 12.

30.   C. Williams, Hugo Black (Baltimore, 1950) reprints this address, 27–30.

31.   Dunne at 75.

32.   Ex Parte Albert Levitt, 302 U.S. 633 (1937).

33.   Jacobellis v. Ohio, 378 U.S. 184, 197 (1964). Black, "The Bill of Rights," 35 N.Y. University L. Rev. 865 (1960).

3

The Making and the Meaning
of the Warren Court

In 1948, Justice Hugo Black heard a petition that arose out of an accusation of ballot stuffing in a Texas senatorial primary. That case is worth notice not merely because on it turned the ambitions of a future president but because it illustrates the distinction between two philosophies of law, "realism" and "formalism." The appointment of a new chief justice in 1953 brought into being what became known as the "Warren Court," and the jurisprudence of that Court over the next fifteen years was predominantly realist.

Half a century ago a conception of law came under attack, in both the popular and the academic arena, under the invidious label "formalism." Its adversaries called their alternative "legal realism." The debates in Senate hearing rooms in the late 1980s and early 1990s over the suitability of nominees for the Supreme Court often echo these old debates over the meaning and nature of law.[1]

The term *formalism* stands, roughly, for four propositions:

1. The duty of a judge can be understood and must be exercised independently of all party affiliations or political ideology. As the Founders might have put it, judges must be above the spirit of faction.
2. There are a right and a wrong in the nature of things, which existed as such before they were declared by any authority.
3. The legal minds of earlier generations have already formulated this rightness for us, in easily understood and quite general terms.
4. The duty of a judge today is to apply those general terms to the particulars of the cases that come before him, so that the conclusion, the necessary judgment, will appear of itself, as does the conclusion of a well-formed syllogism upon presentation of both the major and the minor premise. In a case of some complexity, an inferential chain of several links may be necessary, but an educated guess or the calculation of mere probabilities need play no part.

Realists attacked this structure at every point. They believed that all law, inclusive of (indeed, especially) judge-made law, is the response of a decision maker to sociological facts and political pressures, and thus that there is no distinction of principle between law on one hand and policy on the other. Two famous phrases associated with Justice Oliver Wendell Holmes epitomize the opposition between formalism and realism. Holmes defined law as "a prediction of what the judge will do in fact," and in so saying he contradicted the first two of the four propositions just listed. On the other hand, Holmes said that "the life of the law is not logic, but experience," and in so saying he contradicted the last two of the four propositions.[2]

As the paradox of judicial restraint unraveled after 1937 and through the war years, as the judicial role expanded, such realism allowed judges to face their new responsibilities unafraid. The robe-wearing realists reasoned that, since there is no distinction between law and policy, there were nothing qualitatively new in their expanded caseload and no unique level of complexity in the facts through which they now had to sift.

The language of restraint and the theory of realism are distinct phenomena, but they combine to make modern government, at all branches and levels, the behemoth that it is. The language of restraint implies that elected officials are of unlimited competence. The theory of realism presumes that the judges themselves brandish an equally unlimited competence.

In order to illustrate the meaning and effects of realism, I turn to an incident in the career of Lyndon Johnson. In 1948 he ran for the Senate. He won the August 28 Democratic primary, tantamount to victory in the election, by a mere eighty-seven votes out of nine hundred thousand cast. His opponent, Coke Stevenson, immediately charged Johnson's campaign with ballot stuffing. In the normal course of events, that accusation would not have been cause of alarm. But Stevenson found a judge who agreed with him.

Johnson called Abe Fortas, who was in Dallas at the time, taking depositions on an antitrust case. This was Fortas of Arnold, Fortas & Porter, one of the nation's best-connected law partnerships, which brought together three of the legal stars of the New Deal. Fortas knew that Johnson had been a fervently pro-Roosevelt congressman from the Tenth District in Texas, and he was eager to lend a hand.

Unfortunately, every other lawyer in, or passing through, Texas also seemed eager to lend Johnson a hand. When Fortas arrived at the hotel suite in Fort Worth, where the crisis meeting was under way, the meeting itself was the crisis, with "acres of lawyers" reveling in their arguments, getting nothing done. Fortas's great service to Johnson was simply to take charge.

Stevenson first brought his accusation of vote fraud to the attention of a federal judge. Why was that? Simply put, the district court judge who took over the case was an old ally of Stevenson's. He proved it, too. Judge T. Whitfield Davidson signed an order temporarily invalidating the primary results and set September 21 as the date for a full hearing. On the twenty-second, the invalidation became permanent.

Johnson's team had a good legal argument available that the matter belonged in the state courts, that the conduct of a primary is a question of state law. Neither the court of appeals itself nor the full Supreme Court was available to judge the merits of that argument. Each would remain in recess until after the state deadline for the printing of general election ballots. Johnson's team decided that it would have to direct its points to the attention of the one Supreme Court justice whose special duty it was to preside over the Fifth Circuit. That justice was Hugo Black.

Fortas, in taking charge of the acres of lawyers, directed their collective attention to the task at hand, that of persuading Justice Black that Judge Davidson had no authority to invalidate the results of a state-run primary and so persuading him to dissolve Davidson's order to that effect.

There seems to be some confusion or conflict over the room in which Justice Black heard oral argument. Was it in the relative informality of his office or in open court? In such a matter it would not be at all unusual for a justice to invite the lawyers from both sides and a stenographer into his office, and that is how Fortas's biographer re-creates the scene.[3] Tucked away in the notes of Bruce Murphy's biography, though, is a reference to Paul Porter's recollection (in the oral history collection of the Lyndon Baines Johnson Library) of a four-hour argument in open court.[4] This conflict of recollections matters only in that it symbolizes one of the great ironies of the proceeding. The firm of Arnold, Fortas & Porter, itself prospering mightily from the climate of legal realism, stood now in opposition to the classically realist arguments of the lawyers for Coke Stevenson.

Those lawyers spent those four hours trying to persuade Black that an injustice had been done. Let us get beyond the formalities, they urged. Ballot boxes have been stuffed, a squeaker of a victory manufactured. How can the question of the differing jurisdictions of state and federal court systems stand in the way of any judge's duty to prevent the success of electoral fraud? To Black was addressed the appeal one addresses to a policymaker: Right this wrong!

The quintessential realists on Johnson's side argued for formalism. After a morning of argument and a break for lunch, Black announced his decision:

> It would be a drastic break with the past to permit Federal courts to go into elections. Believing, therefore, that I have jurisdiction, that it is a matter of supreme importance not only to Texas but beyond the borders of Texas, and that there is no statutory provision for a federal court to enjoin a step in an

election, until the full court shall have time to consider the matter the restraining order heretofore issued by Judge Davidson is no longer in effect.[5]

Black's commitment to formalism in legal philosophy was important in many contexts over the next twenty years. But I cannot expound that importance without first offering a glossary of the terms I use.

DIGRESSION ON TERMINOLOGY

The labels that have beguiled the controversies of recent decades over our (federal) judiciary and its role come in pairs. Aside from formalist/realist, there are activist/restraintist; interpretivist/noninterpretivist; clause-bound/non-clause-bound;and intentionalist/literalist.

A judicial activist is a judge who tries to do some good, whether doing good is defined by the Right or Left. A judicial restraintist is a judge who tries to help the country go to hell, if that is where the voters of the country decide that they want to go. A little reflection should show that this is a false opposition. A judge should be "active" in fulfilling her legitimate function and should "restrain" herself from doing anything more.

A noninterpretivist is a judge or, more likely, a legal scholar who believes that judges must go beyond the four corners of the Constitution in order to arrive at their "constitutional" decisions. This might seem a blatant contradiction, but it has serious and intelligent advocates, who make two arguments. Sometimes they argue (as do formalists) that there are a right and a wrong inherent in the nature of things and so conclude (as formalists do not) that nature, so understood, is a source of law to which judges must or may pay heed regardless of any precedent or text.

At other times noninterpretivists argue in the manner of the realists that since judges inevitably do draw on their own political views, they may as well do so openly. An interpretivist will reply to either argument that a noninterpretivist Court is a menace as soon as it disagrees with you. Since (whoever "you" are) there is no reason to expect life-tenured judges to agree with you in a predictable way over time, you are well advised to stick to the four corners of the constitutional text after all and to try to keep the justices within those bounds as well.

Yet how is interpretation to proceed? The clause-bound and nonclause-bound dichotomy arises here. A clause-bound interpretivist tries to understand the requirements of any particular clause of the Constitution in isolation from the rest. A non-clause-bound interpretivist, when not looking for a less awkward label, imports his understanding of the whole of the Constitution into his reading of any one of its provisions.[6] Yet even if some clauses must be understood through a broad "structural" reading, most will still have to be understood as if they stand on their own feet. So let us adhere to clause-boundedness for a moment, long enough to discover one more dichotomy.

An "intentionalist" judge or commentator tries to discern the meaning of a particular provision from a detailed historical inquiry into the original intention of its authors or of the authorities by whom it was ratified. One might collect all other possibilities, under a catchall negation, and call them nonintentionalist. A more interesting contrast pits intentionalism against literalism, the theory that a controversy may be resolved by the plain meaning of the words of a text, even if the authors of the text gave no thought to this controversy, had no clear "intention" on point, or would have opposed one of the clear implications of their text had it occurred to them. It was literalism in this sense, as applied to the clauses of the First Amendment, that Justice Hugo Black invoked in the defense of his renowned absolutism on questions affecting speech and the press.

What are the other sides of the First Amendment debate? What, for example, is the "balancing" that, absolutists warn us, threatens to undermine the protection offered by a literally understood text? Is balancing "restrained" or "realistic" or both? To answer that last question first: In First Amendment jurisprudence these two theoretical innovations of the New Deal period diverge drastically. Balancing can be either restrained or realistic. It cannot be both.

A "realist balancer" believes that the Supreme Court is competent to judge whether, in a particular case, free speech interests should prevail over the interest that the contested legislation or other governmental actions support. The judges at the trial level strike the first balance. The appellate judges review that balance for error, and yet another issue enters the gigantic maw of the judicial generation of policy.

A "restrained balancer," on the other hand, believes that the First Amendment simply orders Congress to take the importance of freedom of speech into account while drafting legislation. The first-order balancing, of the free speech interest against those other interests to which Congress may also attend, remains there, in the hands of the duly constituted legislature. Just as is the case with minimum wage laws or other commercial legislation, on the restraintist view, the balance Congress or state legislatures strike on free speech matters should not be overturned by the judiciary unless it proves unreasonable or its applications are shocking to a civilized conscience.[7]

An example of the application of these various theories is in order. In 1940 Congress passed the Smith Act, which declared that advocating, or joining a conspiracy to advocate, the forcible overthrow of the United States is a criminal offense. In 1951 several petitioners convicted of violations of this act by virtue of their active membership in the Communist Party, asked the Supreme Court to declare that act void as a violation of their rights under the First Amendment.

Chief Justice Fred Vinson wrote the opinion for the Court, Dennis v. United States (1951). This opinion is a splendid example of what I have just called realistic balancing, in which Vinson himself weighs the relative claims and makes his own policy decision: "Overthrow of the government by force or violence is certainly a substantial enough interest for the government to limit speech. Indeed, this is the ultimate value of any society, for if any society cannot protect its very structure from armed internal attack, it must follow that no subordinate value can be protected."[8]

Justice Felix Frankfurter concurred with the result, upholding both statute and conviction, but his own opinion expressed the views of a restrained balancer and explained that free speech claims are "not an exception to the principle that we are not legislators, that direct policy-making is not our province."[9] The balance must be struck, in the first interest, by those who *are* legislators.

Justice Hugo Black wrote a powerful dissenting opinion in which he complained that the First Amendment as construed by either variety of balancer is "not likely to protect any but those 'safe' or orthodox views which rarely need protection."[10] On that point, Black's loss in 1951 was to turn into a win after the Vinson Court became the Warren Court, which later Court in 1961 imposed evidentiary requirements on the prosecution of Smith Act cases so severe as, in effect, to invalidate the law.[11]

At the time of the Dennis decision, many expected that Chief Justice Vinson was about to leave the bench for the electoral arena. In a 1951 year-end review, U.S. News and World Report listed three possible Democratic nominees for president, should Harry S. Truman decline: the chief justice, General Dwight D. Eisenhower, and Governor Stevenson. Of course, the Republicans were also wooing Eisenhower. Vinson persuaded Truman that his health would not permit the rigors of a national campaign, and after that conversation, Truman's intention of anointing a successor led him to support Stevenson.[12]

Stevenson did receive that nomination, then lost the election to the Republican nominee, Eisenhower. Vinson did not live far beyond Eisenhower's inaugural, and the new president made a recess appointment of one of his political creditors, California governor Earl Warren, to the Supreme Court. So began what history calls the Warren Court.

A COLOR-BLIND CONSTITUTION

When Warren took his new office, several cases in the federal appellate system raised the issue of racial separation in public schools. It had been more than half a century since the Supreme Court first approved a scheme of state-mandated racial segregation and agreed with Louisiana that "the equal protection of the laws" requires only equally well furnished public facilities, not access to the same set of facilities. A law providing for separate but equal railroad cars, then, and requiring Homer Plessy to seat himself in the "colored" car leaves him with no constitutional grievance.[13]

It is important to recapture just what the arguments were in the notorious litigation known as Plessy v. Ferguson (1896). First, there was some controversy whether a sufficient number of Plessy's great-grandparents were "colored" to require the assignment of that label to him at all, under the Louisiana statute. Still, his counsel argue, "If Mr. Plessy be colored, and has tasted of the advantages of free American citizenship, and has responded to its aspirations, he abhorred the equal accommodations of the car to which he was compulsorily assigned."[14]

The key word in that passage is *compulsorily*. It does not matter that the benches were wooden in one car and likewise wooden in the other. It would not have mattered had the "colored" benches been cushioned, and the "white" benches wood. What matters is that if one man tries to walk from one car to another, an officer of the state will stop him, and if that man is insistent upon challenging these assignations, that officer and the law under the protection of which Plessy must live will put him in prison. This compulsory assignment, this coercion, is the evil that the vacuous opinion for the majority of the Court managed to find inoffensive, writing: "We consider the underlying fallacy of the plaintiff's argument to consist in the assumption that the enforced separation of the two races stamps the colored race with a badge of inferiority. If this be so, it is not by reason of anything found in the act, but solely because the colored race chooses to put that construction upon it."[15]

But one justice, to his undying credit, did not find Plessy's argument so fallacious. Justice John Harlan dissented in Plessy and wrote: "In the view of the Constitution, in the eye of the law, there is in this country no superior, dominant, ruling class of citizens. There is no caste here. Our Constitution is color-blind, and neither knows nor tolerates classes among citizens."[16]

Thirty years later, in Gong Lum v. Rice,[17] the Court formally extended the "separate but equal" doctrine of the Plessy majority to the public schools. It was there, in education and in 1954, that the same doctrine would receive its death strokes and old Harlan his vindication.

When Warren became chief justice, Thurgood Marshall, later to be an associate justice, was serving as chief counsel of the NAACP. In that capacity, Marshall argued the school desegregation cases before the court, which consolidated the batch of them under the heading of one from Kansas, Brown v. Board of Education.[18]

The unanimous opinion of the Supreme Court, announced May 17, 1954, after two rounds of arguments, held that "in the field of public education, the doctrine of 'separate but equal' has no place." The Supreme Court soon extended the same conclusion to other publicly owned places and used its revised conception of equal protection to strike down Jim Crow laws, which mandated racial segregation in privately owned places, and had grown up under Plessy's protective doctrinal wing.[19]

The Court's opinion in Plessy and Harlan's dissent in that case were within the tradition of what I have called formalism. The central doctrinal portion of Brown was likewise within, or at least consistent with, formalism.

The Court's opinion in Plessy was restraintist, in that it left the challenged state statute standing. The plaintiff had hoped to encounter a more activist court, as did Marshall's clients in Brown.

All decisions and arguments involved in the cases just described were interpretivist. Noninterpretivism is chiefly an academic position, not the way in which any large number of practicing lawyers and judges talk. One might describe the Harlan dissent in Plessy as non-clause-bound interpretivism, for as the previous quote from that dissent indicates, Harlan drew upon a general view of what the Constitution as a whole sees or what it does and does not "tolerate." The other opinions with which I have been concerned are clause-bound, in that they profess to explain specifically the meaning of the phrase "equal protection of the laws," which appears in the second sentence of the Fourteenth Amendment.

The Plessy Court is intentionalist, professing to know what the authors of that amendment would have said on the matter before the Court. The Brown decision is literalist. It allows the words of that phrase the meaning of their own implications.

The notions of literalism and formalism are akin. In formalist jurisprudence the function of a court is conceived after the model of logical deduction, as reasoning from the general to the particular. One form of deduction is syllogistic, and one form of syllogism is called the practical, because it ends not with a propositional conclusion but with an action. Here is an example:

Major Premise: Strawberries are good to eat.

Minor Premise: This object in front of me is a strawberry.

Conclusion: *The speaker plucks the object off the bush and pops it in his mouth.*

Simplifying a good deal, we can picture the plaintiffs in Brown asking the federal district courts to act on a similar practical syllogism:

Major Premise: This Court should order a school system desegregated if and only if its maintenance as a segregated system deprives some person of his or her constitutional rights.

Minor Premise: The maintenance of a segregated school system by the
                          Board of Education of Topeka, Kansas, deprives Linda
                          Brown of her constitutional rights.

Conclusion: *So ordered.*

The federal district court denied the validity of the minor premise and so
took no action. The plaintiffs appealed on that point of law. The central
doctrinal paragraph of Brown was a square affirmation of that minor
premise: "Separate educational facilities are inherently unequal. Therefore,
we hold that the plaintiffs and others similarly situated for whom the actions
have been brought are, by reason of the segregation complained of, deprived
of the equal protection of the laws guaranteed by the Fourteenth
Amendment."[20]

It is only after this paragraph that Brown takes a "realistic" turn. Given
normal appellate procedure, the Court should simply have reversed the
actions of the lower courts insofar as those decisions were inconsistent with
the legal conclusion just announced. It could then have awaited proceedings
in the lower courts consistent with the Fourteenth Amendment as now
understood, subject to further appeal of the decisions on remand. The issue
of remedy, as addressed by our major premise within the preceding syllogism,
in the normal course of events would have been left for first-instance
determination by a trial court.

But this was not an old-fashioned formalist court. This was Earl Warren's
Court, infused with realism and thinking itself competent to administer
schools directly, under a vaguely understood but enormously expansive
"equity" power, so Brown declared the issue of remedy one of "considerable
complexity" and requested another round of argument on point.

Now an act of God intervened in the deliberations of men. On October
9, 1954, Justice Robert Jackson, a Roosevelt appointee, died of a heart
attack after thirteen years of service on this bench. President Eisenhower
nominated John Harlan to fill the Jackson vacancy. This appointment was
a felicitous one, for this was the grandson of the John Harlan who had cast
the lone dissenting vote in Plessy v. Ferguson, the man whose ringing
endorsement of color blindness had just received its belated vindication. It
was precisely because of this beautiful bit of timing that the second Harlan's
nomination encountered some resistance, which delayed the Senate's vote
until March 1955 but then petered out into a lopsided seventy-one to eleven
vote to confirm.[21]

Two months after the ascension of the younger Harlan to his new office,
the Court issued Brown II.[22] This decision did, after all, remand the title
case and its companions to the district courts, but it gave them on remand
two unnecessary bits of baggage—an ambiguously worded instruction and an
irrelevant list of considerations. The instruction read as follows: "Enter such

orders and decrees consistent with this opinion as are necessary and proper
to admit to public schools on a racially nondiscriminatory basis with all
deliberate speed the parties to these cases."

How was a federal court or a school administrator to decide what velocity
was properly "deliberate," as distinct from improperly evasive? The Court
gave a list of the considerations that might justify delay "The courts may
consider problems related to administration, arising from the physical
condition of the school plant, the school transportation system, personnel,
revision of school districts and attendance areas . . . . During this period of
transition, the courts will retain jurisdiction of these cases."

The reference to a school transportation system may suggest to some
readers in 1992 the 'busing' controversy that erupted in 1970. But in the
context of this decision, 1955, when most of the black children whose families
had brought suit were seeking simply to get into the nearest and most
convenient public school, which school had been barred to them as a result
of the color of their skin, this reference to transportation was not a genuine
concern at all. It was a distraction. No bus costs any more or drives any
more slowly with Linda Brown on board than it would otherwise.

What is true of the concern for transportation is also true of the other
items on this much-quoted list. Not one of them has any close connection
with the real reason that the Court allowed "deliberate" speed. It suddenly
awoke to the reality of political resistance, which (had it proven effective in
scuttling the implementation of a desegregation order) would have left the
Supreme Court's role in the American system of law disastrously
undermined. The Court now hoped that it could defuse such resistance,
allowing for a slow pace of change as a sop to pro-segregation sentiment.

The following year brought a presidential election, and, perhaps because
of the political astuteness of Chief Justice Earl Warren, perhaps through
dumb luck, the Court's desegregation opinion did not become the hot
campaign issue it might have. The NAACP supported Estes Kefauver
against Adlai Stevenson in the contest for the Democratic nomination that
year.[23] Stevenson prevailed, nonetheless, and both he and the incumbent,
President Eisenhower, shied away from discussion of the matter during the
autumn election campaign, beyond bland assertions that Court orders must
be obeyed.

Those assertions became commitments in 1958, when Governor Orval
Faubus of Arkansas vowed to keep black children out of the schools of Little
Rock. In response, President Eisenhower federalized the Arkansas National
Guard, and in the midst of this crisis Governor Stevenson appeared on the
television news program "Face the Nation" to applaud the president's
firmness and so to present a bipartisan front in favor of law and against
demagoguery. Together, Eisenhower and Stevenson prevented in 1958 some

of the damage that the jurisprudential realism of <u>Brown</u> <u>II</u>, issued three years before, had invited.

The schools of Little Rock were opened to blacks. Soon after the crisis had cooled, the president, through Sherman Adams, invited Stevenson to become a member of the bipartisan Commission on Civil Rights, then in formation. The invitee declined.[24]

Two years later, in the nominating phase of the next presidential campaign, each major party adopted a civil rights plank for its platform. In the case of the Democrats, this was a necessary response to demographics, to the growing black presence in those northern cities that any nominee of that party must win, of which cities New York is the most prominent. In the case of the Republicans, the analogous plank was part of a "compact of Fifth Avenue," in which Richard Nixon, the vice president and nominee, made his peace with Nelson Rockefeller, an intraparty rival, and with the New York State delegation to the Republican convention.[25] So in each case New York, city and state, called the tune to which the platform committee of a major party danced. The effect was that civil rights, by then the firmly affixed code name for all issues of racial fairness, was no more than a minor theme of the second straight presidential campaign since the <u>Brown</u> decisions.

In the summer of 1962 President John F. Kennedy, victor in that 1960 campaign, sent three thousand troops to Mississippi to ensure that James Meredith could become the first black student at the University of Mississippi (Ole Miss). The following year two hundred thousand people marched on Washington. When they arrived (August 28) they heard Dr. Martin Luther King describe his dream, that "this nation will rise up and live out the true meaning of its creed." The lid was off. Civil rights would be <u>the</u> major issue on the congressional agenda for the following two years and the dominant domestic issue of the next two presidential campaigns.

In June 1964 Congress passed a comprehensive Civil Rights Act, which banned discrimination on the basis of race in hiring, in public accommodations, and in voting rights. In August, a year after King's famous address, the bodies of three missing civil rights workers were discovered in Mississippi. Before the investigation was complete, twenty-two white men were arrested for their murders.

The Voting Rights Act of 1965 added systematic prohibition of many popular mechanisms for the disfranchisement of blacks, and the Fair Housing Act addressed the question of the places to which one goes home after a day at the desegregated school or place of business. What may we say, even at the necessarily high level of abstraction, about this very complicated set of statutes?[26]

I think we may say that the term *civil rights* has come to refer to the rules that distinguish the public sphere of life from the private. In a principled system of law, short of the totalitarian, freedom of association prevails within a private sphere. If you wish to throw a party for your friends, and you exclude me because you do not like my appearance, that is your prerogative. Likewise, if members of one ethnic or religious group marry predominantly one another, they violate no one's rights, civil or other, by virtue of that habit.

The opposite of private is public, but the simple polarity of the two words gives us no indication of where the one named reality leaves off and the other takes up. It is clear that buildings created on the order of, and at the expense of, the state of Kansas are public. Thus, when I enter a courthouse or a public school in Topeka, I abandon much of the freedom of association that I take for granted at my dinner table. I must learn tolerance. If I have any business to do in such a place, I must do it without regard to the bigotries in which I engage in my home. This, on one reading of it, is the meaning of <u>Brown</u>.

It is pleasant to believe that the races will intermingle quite naturally, even in privately owned but publicly accessible commercial spaces, in the absence of coercive enforcement of Jim Crow laws designed to prevent that mingling. When <u>Brown</u> and the decisions that followed struck such laws, these decisions posed but did not resolve the question whether this pleasant belief is true.

It proved false, or at least untrue in any sense sufficiently automatic to preserve the pleasure. In the years after <u>Brown</u>, proprietors of a variety of commercial establishments sought to maintain segregated seating and service. The humble lunch counter became symbol and battlefield. Sit-in demonstrations flourished.

The Supreme Court faced a succession of sit-in cases, all with the same facts. A black man sat at the "white" lunch counter of a private restaurant. The owner or an authorized employee demanded he leave. The demonstrator refused, the police were called, and a trespass arrest was made. On appeal, NAACP attorneys asked the Court to strike as unconstitutional the pertinent state trespass statutes, as applied. Faced with this issue, the Warren Court hemmed and hawed and settled each sit-in case on the narrowest technical ground it could discover.[27] As the Court saw it, this issue very painfully blurred the line between private and public life, between the requirements of interracial tolerance, on one hand, and freedom of association, on the other. When Congress passed the Civil Rights Act of 1964, it rescued the Court from continued grappling with this quandary.

With the Civil Rights Act in place, a lunch counter becomes by fiat a piece of public space. Anyone waiting upon customers at such a counter is well advised to keep one's racial prejudice, if any, to oneself during business hours. The Supreme Court was relieved to receive this legislative guidance. Indeed, so relieved was the Court that, in <u>Hamm v. City of Rock Hill</u>

(1964),[28] it found that the new statute abated all trespass charges that would not have been brought had the act been in place at the time of arrest. This was a very imaginative reading of congressional intent, and it was very unkind to any remaining illusions of state sovereignty.

Does the Constitution give Congress any authority over the policies of the proprietor of a lunch counter in the city of Rock Hill, South Carolina, doing a predominantly intrastate business? Yes, at least according to constitutional doctrines that were old news by 1964, the narrow reading of property rights and the expansive reading of the interstate commerce clause. Even if only by buying his supplies from someone who bought them from someone who brought them in from out of state, this proprietor put himself into the unified flow of goods and services that "commerce" is now taken to imply.[29]

But does the commerce power give Congress the authority to "abate" cases pending within the state courts? I see no plausible reasoning to that conclusion. It is not purist formalism alone that conflicts with Hamm. No jurist or critic not fully imbued with realism can find this dish quite kosher.[*]

Allow me to pose a simple, even a naive, question. Were the developments in constitutional and statutory law just chronicled, from Brown I to Hamm, extending from 1954 to 1964, collectively a good thing or not? The doctrinal or formalist portion, or reading, of the first Brown decision seems to me the only *unmixed* good here. The subsequent developments are, at least, troublesome, in that they have bestowed upon federal district courts around the country a mandate for endless supervision in matters that once would have been considered well within the private realm. This has contributed to the great falling away from the system Publius envisioned in 1787–88, the falling away begun by the New Deal and sanctified in commercial contexts in 1937.

Nonetheless, one must recognize the defense of necessity.[30] The various branches of the government of the United States must do something more to check the inertial force of our long history of racial separation and domination than a mere declaration of its illegality can accomplish. A recognition of this necessity need not, and should not, make us uncritical of the particulars, but it must precede informed criticism.

Nor should the defense of necessity have the final word. Our clumsy and endless national grappling with the intractable has made any line between public and private increasingly indistinct, threatens to make all of life a matter for the political, partisan, arena, and threatens to dump us all (at least in principle, although mutual exhaustion may prove mitigating) into a fishbowl of a world.[31]

---

[*] Later discussions make it clear that I am not an advocate of purist formalism. At this stage of the argument, though, a distinction between varieties of formalist jurisprudence would be premature.

President Kennedy made two appointments to the Supreme Court, during what may be called the middle-Warren period. Kennedy's first was Byron White, best known to many Americans as "Whizzer" White, the all-American collegiate quarterback and National Football League rookie of the year for 1938. He was chairman of the national Citizens for Kennedy group in 1960 and was appointed deputy attorney general within the new administration in 1961, only to find himself a Supreme Court justice a year later.

Kennedy's second was his secretary of labor, Arthur Goldberg.* In 1948, when then-Senator Kennedy was at work on a bill addressing union corruption, incorporating recommendations of the McClellan Committee, the American Federation of Labor and Congress of Industrial Organizations (AFL-CIO) chief George Meany "lent" Goldberg, who was that federation's chief counsel, to the senator's office to assist in drafting what eventually became law under the name Landrum-Griffith.[32]

PUBLIC AND PRIVATE FIGURES

Perhaps the single best-known First Amendment decision of the middle-Warren period was <u>New York Times v. Sullivan</u> (1964).[33] This decision constitutionalized libel law and in the process compounded the confusion between public and private life previously noted. In order that I may describe that confusion, I must pass through some doctrinal preliminaries. Earlier, I defined three positions within the ongoing debate over the meaning of the First Amendment: literalism, restrained balancing, and realistic balancing. After Frankfurter's departure from the Court, the realistic balancing school became the clear majority position. The Court decided to decide the proper weight to be given, on one hand to the First Amendment itself and, on the other hand, to the various governmental interests against which it must be balanced.

But how is that balance to be struck? A talismanic reference to the "preferred position" of the First Amendment, although often encountered, means little.[34] Realistic balancers fall into two groups: the ad hoc and the definitional.[35] Ad hoc balancing weighs the government's interest in a particular regulation of speech against the speaker's interest in ignoring that regulation. It does this weighing on a case-by-case basis, unburdened (or unguided) by generally applicable rules. The objections to such an approach are obvious and devastating. Inequities are inevitable, as the ad hoc balance one judge strikes in one district proves very different from that his colleague strikes in another. Not all the cases involved in such discrepancies, not even any large share of them, can be expected to reach the Supreme Court, where

---

* White and Goldberg replaced, respectively, Charles Whittaker and Felix Frankfurter. Frankfurter had long been the Court's foremost advocate of a "restrained" view of the judicial role. After his departure, Justice Harlan took up that role.

they will not be resolved, anyway, in a fashion that gives future guidance. How is a would-be speaker to know how far her freedom of speech extends before opening her mouth and risking arrest? No one has ever suggested that law ought to be a wild guess at what some judge will do in fact.

Definitional balancing seeks to avoid chaos or unfairness, because when it weighs considerations on the side of both the government and the defendant, it proceeds by category, protecting or leaving unprotected not specific acts of speech but broad categories (sedition, obscenity, and press coverage of a criminal trial are all examples of controverted categories of speech). Through the first half of the 1960s, most justices did adopt some nonliteralist (and, not incidentally, nonformalist) variety of definitional balancing, but they did so in a scattershot manner that defeated the ostensible purpose of this approach. As they applied different definitions to different cases, uncertain always of the level of abstraction at which their discussions ought to operate, they came up with chaotic, unpredictable results that incurred all the liabilities rightly attributed to the ad hoc approach.

That observation brings me back to <u>Times</u> v. <u>Sullivan</u>. In 1960 four black clergymen from Alabama purchased a full-page advertisement in the <u>New York Times</u> soliciting contributions to defray the costs of civil rights protests. Both the protests and the ads were integral to ongoing attempts to change the racially discriminatory policies of the city of Montgomery. The commissioner of public affairs of that city, Louis B. Sullivan, brought an action in libel against the newspaper and the clergymen. He brought this suit in the state of Alabama (it would not have been a likely winner in New York), and a jury awarded him half a million dollars in damages. The Alabama Supreme Court upheld, but the Supreme Court reversed, this award.

Although there were some factual inaccuracies in the ad, the size of the award seemed to most observers disproportionate to any harm done to Sullivan's reputation by those errors and served on its face as evidence that the jury was punishing civil rights advocates for being civil rights advocates.

Justice William Brennan wrote for the Court. He explained the thinking of the majority thus: "We consider this case against the background of a profound national commitment to a principle that debate of public issues should be uninhibited, robust, and wide-open, and that it may well include vehement, caustic, and sometimes unpleasantly sharp attacks on government and public officials."[36]

Since Sullivan put himself in the public eye by becoming a commissioner of public affairs, he must expect to be the recipient of his share of contumely. In order that debate on matters wherein such persons shall inevitably figure may be kept "robust," Brennan announced that portions of the Alabama libel law are void as unconstitutional, and he announced a new rule, determining what other statutes shall survive judicial review, on their face or as applied: actions by a public official must fail, <u>unless</u> the plaintiff can show that the statements were made with actual malice—that is, that the statements were known to be false or were made in reckless disregard of their truth or falsity. Later litigation expanded this "public official" rule into a "public figure" rule.[37]

Without detailing the subsequent vicissitudes of this test, I observe that "public figure" and "reckless disregard" have each proven resistant to definition and that with such tests the purported distinction between ad hoc and definitional balancing collapses, leaving only the fact of realistic balancing, the fact of yet another broad accretion of power within the judiciary.

The opposite of a public figure is a private figure. Where does the one named reality end and the other begin?   Must one who desires the protection of defamation laws follow the old Cynic advice to "live unknown" in order to avoid forfeiture of any such cause of action? Is the spouse of a public figure also a public figure? Or, are the demands of robust debate in speaking of Geraldine Ferarro, onetime candidate for vice president, greater than those demands in speaking of her husband, John Zaccaro?

One might say that marriage itself is a voluntary act and that divorce these days is so easily granted that the decision to remain married as one's spouse moves into the center of public attention is still a voluntary act. On such reasoning, both members of the household are public figures if either is, and one strenuous standard of proof applies to a lawsuit brought by either member of the couple or perhaps by both as coplaintiffs. Yet this reasoning seems to make marriage not only a voluntary but an official act. If marriage is public, what remains within the sphere of the private?

However the public figures are defined, the constitutionalization of libel law, when the libel is aimed at such persons, raises still other quandaries. What are we to say of those persons whose character as public figures has no very close relationship to the robust "debate of public issues" of which Brennan wrote? Carol Burnett comes to mind in this connection. She was held to the "actual malice" standard during her litigation with the <u>National Enquirer</u>. But Carol Burnett is famous for her "Tarzan yell," which seldom arises in debates over national health insurance or gun control statutes. It is hard to see how this celebrity finds herself in the same constitutional boat as does Commissioner Sullivan as a fair target for the "unpleasantly sharp attacks" of which Justice Brennan warned.[38]

All balancing of competing interests becomes ad hoc in fact, however definitional in intention, so long as the judges who strike the balance retain the presuppositions of realism, especially the presupposition of their own omnicompetence. Any one arbitrary definition just introduces some new buzzwords, which become the subjects of equally arbitrary definition in the next landmark decision. Where one sort of right appears to conflict with another, as Burnett's right to an unsullied reputation appears to conflict with the right of the tabloids to sully her reputation for profit, realists call both purported rights "interests" and make a muddle of both in "balancing" them against one another.

It is enough to send one back for another look at literalism. From certain points of view, Black's First Amendment literalism may be seen as a partial, single-issue return of jurisprudential formalism. One can easily imagine the advocates of the line of decisions that struck minimum wage laws drawing courage from Black's writings, because "no deprivation of liberty means no deprivation," without due process of law. The cosponsor of the bill that became the Fair Labor Standards Act, Senator Hugo Lafayette Black, would not have joined them in that construction, but that is simply part of the mysterious obscurity of the human spirit.

If literalism is taken to imply absolutism, then the advocates of economic due process cannot employ Black's formula. The author of the Adkins opinion acknowledged that liberty cannot be an absolute, although he argued that the laws in question did not fall within the ambit of any of the recognized exceptions.

Furthermore, a look into the text of the main body of the Constitution discloses evidence that should make literalists very dubious about free-speech absolutism. For example, Congress is specifically empowered to pass laws protecting the exclusive rights of authors to their writings.[39] Copyright laws, enacted pursuant to this explicit grant of power, prohibit one person from unauthorized use of the work of another, even when that use is made by way of speech or through the press. In most cases, that is exactly how violations of these laws do take place. No one among Justice Black's warmest admirers really proposes that the Supreme Court should strike copyright laws. So "no law" in the First Amendment must mean something other than "no law." Perhaps the ideal for First Amendment law ought to be described as literalism plus a sense of context.

I summarize these comments on Hugo Black's view of the First Amendment: (1) absolutism in the law generally, as in this field specifically, is untenable and, (2) what is valuable in the Black approach—the recourse to the plain meaning of words, the discipline of a revived formalism with its independence of the factional lines of Right and Left—does not depend upon the absolutist trappings in which Justice Black wrapped it.

NOTES

1. Linde, "Judges, Critics, and the Realist Tradition," 82 Yale Law Journal 227 (1972).

2. O. W. Holmes, The Common Law (Boston, 1881).

3. B. Murphy, Fortas (New York, 1988) at 94.

4. Id. 613n.

5. Id. 95.

6. J. H. Ely, Democracy and Distrust (Cambridge, MA, 1980), 1–41.

7. Id. at 108.

8. 341 U.S. 494.

9. Id. 517, 539.

10. Id. 579.

11. Scales v. United States, 367 U.S. 203 (1961).

12. P. McKeever, Adlai Stevenson (New York, 1989), 374.

13. Plessy v. Ferguson, 163 U.S. 537 (1896).

14. Quoted in J. H. Wilkinson, From Brown to Bakke (New York, 1979).

15. 163 U.S. 537 at 551.

16. Harlan, dissenting, 163 U.S. 552, at 559.

17. 275 U.S. 78 (1927).

18. 347 U.S. 483 (1954).

19. State Athletic Comm. v. Dorsey, 359 U.S. 533 (1959); New Orleans v. Detiege, 358 U.S. 54 (1958); University of No. Carolina v. Frasier, 350 U.S. 979 (1956); Baltimore v. Dawson, 350 U.S. 877 (1956); Holmes v. Atlanta, 350 U.S. 879 (1955); Lucy v. Adams, 350 U.S. 1 (1955).

20. 347 U.S. 495.

21. H. Abraham, Justices and Presidents (New York, 1974), 242–244.

22. 349 U.S. 294 (1955).

23. Id. at 301.

24. McKeever, supra at 403.

25. T. White, The Making of the President, 1960 (New York, 1961), 202–204.

26. For the reasons to which the text alludes, I cannot concur with the argument for the repeal of one important component of the civil rights apparatus offered in 1992 by R. Epstein, Forbidden Grounds. I do believe that reform of that apparatus is in order, but my suggestions to that effect would have to arise in another context.

27. Lombard v. Louisiana, 373 U.S. 267 (1963); Peterson v. City of Greenville, 373 U.S. 244 (1963); Garner v. Louisiana, 368 U.S. 157 (1961).

28. 379 U.S. 306 (1964).

29. Heart of Atlanta Motel v. United States, 379 U.S. 241; Katzenbach v. McClung, 379 U.S. 294 (1964).

30. "Necessity" is the defense that protects an accused who, while dying from thirst, takes his neighbor's water without consent. Black's Law Dictionary defines necessity in the pertinent sense as "controlling force; irresistible compulsion; a power or impulse so great that it admits no choice of conduct."

31. Moose Lodge No. 107 v. Irvis, 407 U.S. 163 (1972).

32. P. Collier & D. Horowitz, The Kennedys (New York, 1984), 230.

33. 376 U.S. 254.

34. Kovacs v. Cooper, 336 U.S. 77 (1949).

35. Nimmer, "The Right to Speak from Times to Time," 56 Calif. L. Rev. 935, 935–936 (1968).

36. 376 U.S. at 270.

37. Gertz v. Robert Welch, Inc., 418 U.S. 323 (1974). The text simplifies a bit. Actually, for a moment the "public official" test seemed to have become a "public issue" test, in Rosenbloom v. Metromedia, 403 U.S. 29 (1971). Even an obscure and private person had to meet the Sullivan malice standard if that person had been defamed in a publication that addressed a matter of public concern. This line proved undrawable, and Gertz represented a partial retreat, hence, the "public figure" test.

38. Brill, "What if it wasn't the Enquirer?" 3 American Lawyer 5 (May 1981).

39. U.S. Constitution, Art. I, §8, ¶8. At the moment of transition between the Earl Warren and Warren Burger periods Thomas Emerson, describing the years just passed, wrote: "At various times the Court has employed the bad tendency test, the clear and present danger test, an incitement test, and different forms of the ad hoc balancing test. Sometimes it has not clearly enunciated the theory on which it proceeds. Frequently it has avoided decision on First Amendment issues by invoking doctrines of vagueness, overbreadth, or the use of less drastic alternatives . . . . The Supreme Court has also utilized other doctrines, such as the preferred position of the First Amendment and prior restraint. Recently, it has begun to address itself to problems of 'symbolic speech' and the place in which First Amendment activities can be carried on. But it has totally failed to settle on any coherent approach" (T. Emerson, The System of Freedom of Expression [New York, 1970], 15–16).

4

Warren Court, Final Years

In the final years of the Warren period (1965–69) "advice and consent" became a constitutional license for the ideological, polarized, and passionate confirmation campaigns with which the United States has since become familiar. There was a hint of this result during the Fortas confirmation hearing of 1965. The water was a bit hotter when Thurgood Marshall waded into his hearing in 1967, and it came to a furious boil at the second Fortas hearing, in 1968.

The vice president is an anomaly within the American system of government. When things go well, the occupant of this office is an idle "fifth wheel." But at moments of crisis, as in April 1945, that fifth wheel becomes a crucial spare.

A sentient wheel with a normal aversion to ghoulishness, however, finds this an unsatisfying occupation. The character of the vice presidential office is not the result of two centuries of tradition, nor of any recent deviation from the constitutional scheme. The original occupant of this office, John Adams, may have described it best. It is, he said, "the most insignificant office that ever the invention of man contrived or his imagination conceived."[1]

When Lyndon Johnson became vice president in 1961, he made one attempt to preserve the power base he had enjoyed as Senate majority leader. On January 3, 1961, the Democrats of the new Senate caucused informally. Mike Mansfield, the new majority leader, proposed to change the party rules to make the vice president the presiding officer at the caucus's more formal gatherings, that is, president of the Senate Democratic Conference. Several of those present argued against this plan, on separation-of-powers grounds. Mansfield quickly abandoned the idea.[2]

The proper application of the principle of separation of powers is, in this context, very murky. Publius insisted, in The Federalist Papers, that the principle is not absolute. Its excessively rigid enforcement would afford inadequate protection to the public weal from the dangers of legislative demagoguery. The Constitution that Publius defended and explained contains several clauses in which the personnel of the various departments have to act together to exercise their powers. One of these clauses pertains to the office now under discussion: Art. I, §3, par. 1, "The Vice President of the United States shall be President of the Senate, but shall have no vote, unless they be equally divided."

Johnson, then, became in January 1961 the presiding officer for the Senate, and held at least potential voting authority. The case could well have been made, had Mansfield wanted to push the point, that to make of him the president of the Democratic Conference within the Senate was simply to recognize his real constitutional role. It was not a violation of the principle of separation of powers to the degree to which the framers enacted that principle. One may with reason draw the inference that Johnson lost his power base in the Senate not because the Constitution so required but at least, in part, because Mansfield did not want to press the point, did not want his own opportunities as majority leader to be clouded over by Johnson's continuing presence.

Lyndon Johnson's abortive attempt to remain a quasi Senator was forgotten long before November 1963, when he was inaugurated president on the airplane carrying John Fitzgerald Kennedy's body from Dallas to Washington. Indeed, the nature of the "separation" between executive and legislative branches of government would arise again, soon. Early in 1964 the Senate opened a formal inquiry into allegations of influence peddling brought against Bobby Baker, Johnson's longtime friend and former aide. The Senate tried to subpoena Walter Jenkins, Johnson's "special assistant." Jenkins certainly knew in which closets Johnson's associates' skeletons hung, but, just as certainly, he did not want to have to choose between perjury and disloyalty. In a test of an issue that would achieve the status of a "constitutional crisis" in another context ten years later, the Johnson administration claimed that Jenkins could refuse to testify before a Senate committee on grounds of "executive privilege," a privilege alleged to derive from the constitutional doctrine of separation of powers. Abe Fortas wrote the twenty-six-page brief that espoused this theory.

In November 1964, President Lyndon Johnson received what was then the greatest popular landslide and second greatest electoral landslide in American history, topped in the lopsidedness of the electoral college vote only by Roosevelt's defeat of Alf Landon in 1936.

On July 14, 1965, the U.S. ambassador to the United Nations (UN), former presidential candidate Adlai Stevenson, died suddenly in London, England. Johnson persuaded Justice Goldberg to leave the Supreme Court and to take Stevenson's place at the UN. This left a vacancy that Johnson nominated Abe Fortas to fill. Fortas and Johnson had been close associates and allies since the ballot-stuffing litigation of 1948, and the president believed in the payment of such debts.

At 10:35 on the morning of August 5, 1965, the Senate Judiciary Committee, Chairman James Eastland presiding, met to consider this nomination. Since Fortas was a native of Tennessee, the committee heard first from the senators from that state, then from a representative of the District of Columbia Bar Association, all of whom spoke of Fortas's qualifications in glowing terms.[3] The first contrary witness was Marjorie Shearon, a onetime consultant to Senator Robert Taft. At the time of her testimony, Dr. Shearon was the publisher and editor of <u>Challenge to Socialism</u>, a weekly magazine devoted to the critique of welfare and regulatory legislation.[4]

Shearon charged that Fortas was a member of the National Committee for the International Juridical Association (IJA), the object of which committee was "to protect Communists when they get into trouble with the laws of the United States." In her view, the IJA was part of "the great network of Communist fronts which have operated and are still operating in this country."

Fortas appeared later that morning. Although the committee had responded to Shearon with open skepticism, her charges were considered sufficiently serious that the nominee had to be confronted with them. He did not deny that he had been a member of the National Committee for the IJA, but he did deny that he had participated in its activities in any way: "Joining was mighty easy, and we were all quick to do it, and I may have said, yes, and that is the totality of my connection with it."[5]

That statement precipitated the following exchange with the Committee chairman.

Eastland: You never attended a meeting?
Fortas: No, sir.
Eastland: You were not active at all?
Fortas: No, sir.
Eastland: Did you pay any dues?
Fortas: No, sir, not to the best of my recollection.

The committee adjourned at 1:15 that afternoon. That was the extent of the hearing. A favorable committee vote and full Senate confirmation followed quickly. The constituency for Marjorie Shearon and the activists who shared her convictions was a small one in 1965 and may have seemed to the Senate even smaller than it was, through the lens of the recent landslide defeat of Barry Goldwater. But the Johnson administration was on notice that its nominations would bear scrutiny not merely as to the contents of their résumés and the quality of their character but as to their associates and political philosophies as well.

Fortas, then, joined the post-Times realist muddle to which the previous chapter made reference, the slippery business of line drawing and balance striking.

Yet he continued to serve as an adviser to the president. On December 18, 1965, Johnson held a meeting for war policy review. The specific matter on the table was a proposed bombing pause. Although, as a sitting justice, Fortas would help determine the outcome of challenges to the war and war-related policies, and although he was to help determine the freedom or imprisonment of draft resisters, no one at the bombing-pause meeting questioned the propriety of a justice's presence at the formulation of executive branch military decisions. This is a far greater breach of the core of the doctrine of separation of powers than is the prospect of a vice president's participation in his own party's Senate Conference, yet the cacophony of objections in the one instance had no analog in the other. Such are the oddities of a political culture in which "legal formalism" has become a term of rebuke.*

THE BALANCE MODEL OF THE SUPREME COURT

In 1957, Time introduced the initials B,B,D & W into journalistic jargon.[6] These initials, composed in a parody of a prominent advertising firm, stood for Hugo Black, William J. Brennan, William O. Douglas, and Earl Warren. The idea behind the coinage was that these four men, two of them Eisenhower appointees, the other two Roosevelt holdovers, constituted a permanent liberal bloc. Although there were no other regular members of this bloc, there were "moderates," any one of whom might be won over on a particular issue to produce the liberal result. This way of understanding the Warren Court, the case-by-case search of Black, Brennan, Douglas, and Warren himself for a fifth vote, seems a peculiar conception to have arisen so soon after the unanimous and, in that sense, bloc-free decision in Brown v. Board. But people intent upon perceiving an evenly divided Court will ignore complicating facts and so ignored such facts in the 1950s just as they had in the 1930s and just as they do today.

There is a perennial conviction in the American public, or in a salient portion thereof, that the Supreme Court is balanced, that there is one swing vote between two blocs of four, or some similar condition, and that the most recent nominee is necessarily the next such swing vote. This conviction has produced the disturbingly divisive and polarized confirmation fights of our

---

* Fortas was the leading voice against a bombing pause, but his view did not prevail. The skies over Hanoi were empty of American bombers from Christmas Day 1965 to January 31, 1966.

time. In time, the most recent nominee, about whom so much noise is made today, will be on the bench or withdraw to the private sector to lick his wounds and write his memoirs. In either case, it will then be the next candidate or vacancy upon which the future of civilization depends, representing, as it will, the swing vote between two evenly balanced blocs.

Yet if this perception is responsible for much, what exactly is responsible for this perception? The dramatic convenience of journalists combines here with the polemical convenience of ideologues. Every journalist wants the latest piece of prose from his pen, or her next chance to stand in front of a camera to be *the* story, a *big* story, a front-page headline or the lead item of a broadcast. A routine change of personnel on a federal court, if one could but believe that there is such a thing, even on the highest of federal courts, as a routine change, would not satisfy this need. It just is not sufficiently dramatic to satisfy the demands of a thrill-sated age or its thrill-dispensing media. This alone goes far to explain why every appointment has to be seen as a knock-down-drag-out fight before it even gets under way. That expectation becomes a self-fulfilling prophecy.

The polemical convenience of ideologues, of Left or Right, is a different matter from the imperative of crisis journalism, but it works in the same direction. A common cliché to the contrary notwithstanding, a savvy leader always preaches to the church choir. The morale of the members of his choir is of paramount importance to the preacher. The choir wants to see its hopes for the future as if they are even now on the edge of attainment. Also, for purposes of morale, every preacher turns his congregation's fears into imminent danger. A fear that is a distant concern, "something to think about when you get the chance," does not get people out on the street ringing doorbells, which is where the leaders of the factions to which the doorbell-ringers belong think that they ought to be.

For the remainder of this book, the phrase "balance model" will stand for the whole way of thinking about the Court that these last four paragraphs have struggled to depict. There are other reasons for the endurance of this model among Supreme Court commentators, and these other reasons tie the endurance of that model to the personal power-wielding alliances of which the Fortas and Johnson connection is an example and to the jurisprudence of realism. The key point to remember is that the balance model portrays the Court as, in essence, a legislature.

Typically, in these United States, a representative enters the legislative body with a party tag. Each representative ran with that tag and with the support of that party. On certain issues, that party has taken a corporate position. When there is a vote on such an issue, each representative is expected to adhere to that issue, to "toe the line." The unpleasant term used in reference to the understudy of a party leader, the term *whip*, suggests a violent determination to keep the party members rowing the same galley with synchronized strokes.

Typically, also, the larger party in a legislative body, the "majority" where there are only two parties, finds that some of its members are less committed to the party line than are others, that some are susceptible to the blandishments of the minority. These "maverick" members of the majority inevitably become the swing votes who keep professional head-counters awake at night. All of this has become quite standard, the coin of common political discourse.

Though the restraintist would wish it otherwise, the realist revolution in jurisprudence has blurred distinctions between judges, on one hand, and politicians ("other" politicians?), on the other. Thus, realism has blurred the distinction between a legislature and a court. Indeed, restraintists bear some responsibility for the blurring. The language of restraint opened the floodgates for vast new interpretive responsibilities for the courts, and the resulting flood has left realism a natural, perhaps an inevitable, raft.

The individual states have fifty legislatures. The United States, as a single nation, has only one, though that one is bicameral. Democrats are the usual majority in each house, and there is always a swing faction, Democrats inclined to vote with Republicans on certain issues of enormous national visibility.

Since there is a general expectation, founded upon fact, that Congress will remain in balance with a small swing faction holding the crucial position between two hostile blocs, why should there not be a general expectation that the Supreme Court shall, at a particular moment, likewise find itself in balance? There is one annoying difference between the two expectations. The Court balance is always seen as precarious; the legislative balance is often recognized as stable. But that distinction one might attribute to a difference of scale, the difference between 9 and 535. The point remains: the country sees its national legislature and its legislatures in general as scenes of balanced opposing forces. Through the era of realism the country has come to see the Supreme Court as just another legislature. It is not surprising, then, that the country has come to see the Supreme Court as a scene of balanced opposing forces.

In 1965, eight years after Time's invention of the B,B,D & W bloc, popular wisdom had it that the Warren Court was still so divided. The second John Harlan and the only Potter Stewart were cast as conservative stalwarts. Tom Clark was treated as a frequent ally of theirs, and Byron White, appointed in the expectation that he would prove a predictable New Frontiersman, disappointed those expectations often enough to be considered the opposite. For those who believed in the reality of these blocs, then, Arthur Goldberg was the crucial fifth vote, the man whose general affinity with B,B,D & W kept the Warren revolution moving forward.[7] When

Goldberg resigned, breathing stopped in some quarters. When Johnson picked Fortas, breathing resumed with a sigh of relief. This was the appointment of a reliable "liberal" and would leave things as they had been.[8]

But the story that the opinions tell is often at odds with the story that newsweeklies tell, and an effort to understand the development of doctrine has far more predictive value than ages of head counting.

DOCTRINE: EQUAL PROTECTION

The two-tier theory of the equal protection clause is an example of the long, slow development of doctrine independent of the fluctuations of personnel.

What can the Fourteenth Amendment be thought to require, when it bars any state from depriving any person of "equal protection of the laws"? Every law makes a classification and, in that sense, imposes an inequality. A criminal code that punishes burglary discriminates between burglars and nonburglars. Likewise, any system of voter registration imposes an inequality between those who are qualified to vote (are of age and are citizens, to take the two least controversial points) and those who are not qualified to vote. It is clear, then, that the Fourteenth Amendment, which prohibits the states from depriving any person of equal protection of the laws, cannot mean that the states must treat all persons equally in all respects. As persons, their circumstances, their actions will vary and so will the state's reactions to those persons, circumstances, actions.

The Supreme Court distinguishes, then, between those classifications that are "suspect" and those that are not. As of the late Warren period the Supreme Court saw the equal protection clause as a license for strict judicial scrutiny of any laws that discriminate on the basis of a suspect classification—which means, primarily, by race, ethnic, or national origin or (perhaps!) alienage. A law might still discriminate on such a basis and survive strict scrutiny, but only if that law serves a "compelling state interest" and if the challenged classification is a "necessary" means to that compelling end.

As a thought experiment, one might ask oneself what result would have followed had Warren's Court, rather than Chief Justice Stone's Court, reviewed the actions of the United States and California in the internment of Japanese Americans in 1942 under the administrative authority of State Attorney General, later Governor, Earl Warren. The experiment is anachronistic, but it sheds some light.[9]

In this case there is a clearly suspect classification of persons by national origin. Strict scrutiny is required. There is, though, a compelling national and state interest to be served by this classification—nothing less than the defense of the Pacific coast of the United States against an aggressor. Was the means used necessary to that compelling end? One may make the argument that there was no quick and more reliable method available for identifying Japan's potential resident sympathizers, so that in the crisis following the attack on Pearl Harbor this obviously draconian means <u>was</u> necessary. One may make that argument and so seek to reconcile Warren with Warren. It is not necessary now to issue a ruling.

Such a case is an extraordinary one, and in virtually every actual controversy to come before the late Warren Court, that Court's decision to apply strict scrutiny to a statute was the death knell for that statute.[10]

This two-tiered model owes its origin to a footnote in an otherwise unremarkable case, <u>United States v. Carolene Products</u> (1938).[11] In that decision the Supreme Court upheld the constitutionality of a federal statute that prohibited the shipment of "filled milk"* in interstate commerce. Such discrimination among varieties of milk did not strike Justice Stone as offensive, nor did his opinion make for headlines, outside dairists' trade journals. But that inauspicious opinion did include the famous "footnote four," which explained that "prejudice against discrete and insular minorities may be a special condition . . . which may call for a correspondingly more searching judicial inquiry" than is required in meeting the complaints of milk shippers. This innocuously planted seed lay dormant until the litigation that followed <u>Brown v. Board</u> caused its germination into the "strict scrutiny" of all legislation that employs suspect classifications.

In the Warren Court's two-tier model of equal protection, the only alternative to strict scrutiny is minimal scrutiny. The imprisonment of burglars may serve, again, as an example. Burglars are a minority. But since anyone <u>can</u> be a burglar, they do not constitute a discrete minority. They are not "insular" either. Burglars come from, and strike all manner of, neighborhood and society. Burglarhood, then, is not a "suspect classification" in the sense suggested by the <u>Carolene Products</u> footnote, and the alleged discrimination against burglars warrants only minimal scrutiny, which requires only that the state show a "rational" relationship between this classification and a "legitimate" state goal. In this case, since law enforcement is a legitimate goal and the punishment of lawbreakers is a rational means to achieve that goal, the burglar-turned-plaintiff will lose his equal protection suit.

More generally, unless one is prepared to throw a majority of the members of some state's legislature into an asylum, one must acknowledge that virtually anything such a majority will decide to do will be "rational."

---

* "Filled milk" is a skimmed-milk product fortified by vegetable fats. Carolene Products shipped "Milnut," a blend of milk with coconut oil. The statute at issue put the company out of business on the (disputable) legislative determination that its product was unhealthy. The Supreme Court refused to be drawn into the issues of fact.

Just as the adoption of strict scrutiny is the death knell for a statute under investigation, so the adoption of minimal scrutiny is a pass through the pearly gates into eternal life.[12]

In the case of equal-protection doctrine, understanding (and predictive power) requires attention to the claims of <u>coherence</u>. The premises of the decision announced last session necessitate the conclusions of next session—or next decade, because formalism-as-practice has outlasted formalism-as-theory. Those who seek to understand the Court in this way must work a bit harder than do those who talk fashionably of "voting blocs" and "balances," but the effort is worthwhile.

In 1967 the president promoted Ramsey Clark to the post of attorney general. Tom Clark, Ramsey's father, resigned his seat on the Court in order to avoid the conflict of interest that would have arisen, otherwise, every time the United States appeared as a party before it. In filling the shoes of the elder Clark, Lyndon Johnson made history for black America, appointing the former chief counsel of the NAACP, the man who had argued the case of Linda Brown, as the new associate justice of the Supreme Court.

This proposal caused some consternation in the Senate, in part because Thurgood Marshall was considered a good deal more "liberal" than Tom Clark, so that the substitution of one for the other would tip the ideological "balance" of the Court in a manner some considered threatening.[13] The Judiciary Committee's questioning of Marshall ranged wide.

Senator Strom Thurmond (R.-S.C.) asked the following question: "What constitutional difficulties did Representative John Bingham of Ohio see, or what difficulties do you see, in Congressional enforcement of the privileges and immunities clause of Article IV, section 2, through the necessary and proper clause of Article I, section 8?"[14] The question was byzantine. Marshall's answer was simple: "I don't understand the question." Thurmond said that he thought it was as clear as he could make it.

There is an intelligible and intelligent inquiry buried in Thurmond's clauses. Article IV, section 2 of the Constitution reads: "The citizens of each state shall be entitled to all privileges and immunities in the several states." As a result of this clause my license to operate a motor vehicle, issued by Connecticut, entitles me to drive not in Connecticut alone but throughout the United States.

Why did Thurmond ask Marshall what difficulties John Bingham saw in congressional enforcement of this clause? Because in 1866 Bingham was instrumental in drafting what became the Fourteenth Amendment, itself part of a package of three constitutional amendments adopted in the aftermath of the Civil War. Bingham's name thus is associated with the second "privileges and immunities" clause, which appears in the first section of the Fourteenth Amendment and prohibits any state from making or enforcing any law "which shall abridge the privileges and immunities of citizens of the United States."

The likely significance of Thurmond's question, then, is that it presumes a narrow theory of Bingham's language. The senator was suggesting to Marshall that there was some unspecified "difficulty" with "enforcement" of the original privileges clause. The states did not respect one another's citizenry in the manner it required. Congress could not force them to do so. Bingham wrote language that helped Congress overcome these difficulties. The second "privileges and immunities" clause, then, if one accepts the premises of Senator Thurmond's question, has no new purpose. Its point is simply to reinforce the purpose of the first such clause. In asking his question in the way that he did, the Senator seems to have wanted to secure Marshall's consent to that historical and textual hypothesis. Marshall, with his simple-seeming reply, "I don't understand the question," refused to give his consent and so left open the possibility that the second privileges and immunities clause is something more than an awkward piece of patchwork. This was a classic moment in the history of the succinct.

It matters, because through much of the first two-thirds of the twentieth century, the U.S. Supreme Court was the scene of a sharp conflict over whether the Bill of Rights, especially amendments one through eight, constrains the actions of the several states as well as those of the federal government. The position that prevailed was that the bill does apply to the states, because its specific provisions are "incorporated" by reference in the Fourteenth Amendment, which specifically constrains state acts.[15]

Some of the advocates of incorporation argued that the best place to find this implication is, precisely, the "privileges and immunities" clause. Under this interpretation, the Fourteenth Amendment treats the first eight amendments as conveying privileges (i.e., to speak freely, to bear arms) and immunities (against compulsory self-incrimination or unreasonable searches). These privileges are now imposed upon the states, just as one's driving privilege is imposed upon all states by the unilateral action of the state that issued the license.

The Supreme Court adopted incorporation through its reading of another of the clauses of the Fourteenth Amendment, "due process," and the second privileges clause remains a dead letter. Still, Thurmond's question to Marshall was part of a personal campaign on the part of that senator against incorporation and so against the idea of any limit on the sovereignty of the states, whatever the clausal basis of the limit.

The next time Thurmond approached this subject, his meaning was clear:

Thurmond: Now, do you believe that the Bill of Rights has been made applicable to the States by way of the fourteenth amendment, and if so, through which clause of the fourteenth amendment?

Marshall: Well, I think individually, not as a whole, but sections of the Bill of Rights have been taken into the fourteenth amendment to be applied by the States. And, of course, it would be under article—I mean, section 1.[16]

This answer was perhaps still not as forthcoming as Thurmond would have liked, since both the "due process" and the "privileges and immunities" clauses appear within section 1.

Such selections from the Marshall hearings yield some perspective on the contemporary charges that David Souter won confirmation by "stealth" in 1990 or that Clarence Thomas, Marshall's successor, "walked away from his record" as a natural-law theorist in 1991. Nominees to judicial office have long sought to avoid discussion either of the cases that may come before them or of the specific, still-controverted, legal doctrines that would form the basis for their decisions, for fear that to engage in such discussion as a condition of confirmation would compromise judicial independence. The Democrats, who, for the most part, applauded such reticence from Marshall, have exhibited the convenience of their memories during the confirmation debates of more recent years.

On July 24 the Judiciary Committee approved Marshall's confirmation, eleven to five. On August 30, after a six-hour floor debate, the Senate gave its advice and consent to this appointment.[17] Marshall took his seat for the October 1967 term.

That term ended in June 1968, and during its closing days word of a Warren resignation letter leaked. On June 26, leaks became irrelevant. Lyndon Johnson announced that Warren had resigned and that he was nominating Associate Justice Abe Fortas to become chief justice and Homer Thornberry to fill Fortas's associateship. Thornberry, like Fortas, was a long-standing political ally of the president. Thornberry had inherited the Tenth District congressional seat, representing Austin and its environs, when Johnson vacated that seat to run for the Senate in 1948.[18] Perhaps in other circumstances Johnson could have persuaded critics that he nominated Fortas for chief justice not to reward a "crony" but to acknowledge merit. That job of persuasion became impossible once Fortas's name went out to the country teamed with the name of Thornberry.

On July 2, Senator Sam Ervin told aides to the president that he would oppose Fortas. Ervin believed that this justice's judicial philosophy would "permit a re-writing of the Constitution" to suit every passing fashion. This opinion of Ervin's was not the worst of the news he broke that day. He also told the Johnson aides that he had no scruples that would prevent his participation in a filibuster to block a vote on this nomination. This gave the White House its first clear indication of the trouble in which it had put itself.

Robert Griffin, a Republican senator from Michigan, had already made the argument that no president should make a "lame-duck" appointment and that Johnson's March 31 announcement that he would not be a candidate for reelection required him to leave this opening on the Court for the nominee of his successor. Now Ervin was suggesting a more dangerous line of attack, that the vote on Fortas or on the cloture of debate would be a vote on the whole Warren Court record. Meanwhile, the politics of this appointment had become intimately entwined with the politics of the presidential campaign.

Nelson Rockefeller, the governor of New York and then a candidate for the nomination of the Republican Party for president, announced support for the Fortas promotion.[19] Rockefeller was an example, at times the leader, of the faction within the Republican Party (often called the Ripon Society Republicans), which accepted the New Deal as an accomplished fact and sought to bring their party within the liberal consensus during its years of triumph. Governor Earl Warren had been one of the advocates of this position in the intraparty debates of the early 1950s. What better way was there for Rockefeller to prove that he accepted the transformation of the United States into a social democracy than to endorse the work of Earl Warren's Court? Or to do that, what better way than to announce his support for the elevation of an exponent and product of jurisprudential realism, Justice Abe Fortas, to the position of leadership on that Court?

While Republicans split along ideological lines familiar by 1968, Democrats split along regional lines, also familiar. Senator Ervin represented, indeed, he embodied, precisely the constituency to which Hubert Humphrey, Richard Nixon, and George Wallace would each make appeal in the general election campaign, the "new South." If Johnson could win him over, perhaps that act of persuasion would serve as a symbol that Humphrey could yet win over the South and reconstitute the New Deal alliance. But it was not to be.

The Judiciary Committee opened its hearings on the Fortas nomination on July 11, 1968.[20] Attorney General Ramsey Clark was the first witness. That afternoon Senator Griffin spoke on the Senate floor, denouncing the cronyism of the two nominations. The next morning Griffin appeared as a witness before the Judiciary Committee and rephrased his concerns in the language of separation of powers:

> It will be recalled that in April 1952, President Truman issued an Executive Order seizing the steel mills, and shortly thereafter, in June 1952, the Supreme Court ruled that he had no authority as President to take such action.
>
> Let us assume for a moment that several Justices of the Supreme Court had privately participated with President Truman in making the executive decision which culminated in the seizure of the steel mills.
>
> Is it in the public interest to assume that Justices who have engaged privately in such executive activity would disqualify themselves from consideration of resulting litigation?[21]

The nominee himself, in what was then a unique gesture for a sitting justice, accepted the invitation of this committee to appear as a witness. Almost twenty years later, when Reagan nominated Associate Justice William Rehnquist to the chief justiceship, Rehnquist appeared before the Judiciary Committee almost as a matter of course, so decisive was the Fortas precedent, so natural by now the assumption that any nominee must make such an appearance. In this way invitations become subpoenas.

But what were the senators to ask? Which of their questions should a sitting justice refuse to answer? The senators repeatedly asked Fortas about particular decisions. Why had he voted to strike the poll tax? Why had he helped handcuff police officers with his votes on exclusionary rule cases?[22] Fortas quite rightly refused to answer questions on such points. The senators asked anyway and often phrased their "questions" as lengthy speeches, only then inviting their guest to agree or disagree. Fortas sat still and respectfully attentive through their speeches and declined such invitations.

OBSCENITY AND OTHER CRIMES

Some of the speeches to which Fortas was subjected, barely veiled in this way as questions, attacked obscenity opinions in which he had voted with the majority.[23] Fortas found himself blamed as if he had single-handedly let loose a wave of smut upon a helpless nation. Before the hearings were through, some commentators, most notably the nationally syndicated columnist James J. Kilpatrick, were writing of the Fortas confirmation fight as if it were a single-issue referendum: those senators who favor smut ought to vote for Fortas as chief justice; those opposed to depravity should vote against.[24]

Fortas asked his friend, Edward Bennett Williams, to answer the Kilpatrick attack. On August 23 the Washington Star, the only paper in its market to carry the Kilpatrick column, ran Williams's letter, which described Fortas's jurisprudence as "middle of the road" on obscenity law, halfway between Harlan's restraintist view, which would let the states decide for themselves what is or is not obscene, and the Douglas absolutist view, which would ban any effort to prohibit the distribution of any material for reasons of morals or offense. The Williams letter invoked the balance model and worked it to Fortas's advantage. Williams portrayed Fortas as the fulcrum on whom the fortunes of the two factions swing and concluded that the public interest would be served by the elevation of this fulcrum.

Others of the speeches to which Fortas was subjected at the Judiciary Committee hearings attacked opinions in which he had joined that reversed criminal convictions in the courts below. Typically, such an opinion relies upon the unconstitutional character of the police procedure from which came evidence essential to the conviction. The "exclusionary rule," first adopted by the Supreme Court in 1914, and applied to state trials in 1961, bars the use of any material so obtained.[25]

The Fourth Amendment prohibits unreasonable searches and seizures; the Fifth Amendment, compulsory self-incrimination. These two provisions of the Constitution have generated most of the well-known exclusionary-rule precedents.

On March 3, 1963, the Metropolitan Police Department of Phoenix, Arizona, received a report of an abduction and rape. Officers Carroll Cooley and Wilfred Young arrested Ernest Miranda on the morning of the thirteenth. The victim viewed a lineup of four Mexican Americans and tentatively identified Miranda as the one of the four who looked most like her attacker. Shortly thereafter the officers in the interrogation room told the suspect that they had a positive identification from the victim. The suspect confessed.

Three months later, at trial, Miranda's court-appointed attorney, Alvin Moore, questioned Officer Cooley at some length about his interrogation techniques.[26] That line of questioning produced this exchange:

Q. I don't see in the statement that it says where he is entitled to the advice of an attorney before he made it.
A. No, sir.
Q. It is not in that statement?
A. It doesn't say anything about an attorney.

At the conclusion of the trial the judge gave the jury these instructions, among those deemed necessary before it could begin its deliberations: "The fact that a defendant was under arrest at the time he made a confession or that he was not at that time represented by counsel or that he was not told that any statement he might make could or would be used against him, will not render such a confession involuntary."

After five hours of deliberations the jury returned a "guilty" verdict. The defendant received a sentence of twenty to thirty years. Alvin Moore filed the necessary papers for an appeal to the Arizona Supreme Court.[27]

The Mallory case was one of the precedents that must have lent Attorney Moore some encouragement as he worked on the appeal. Mallory was a 1957 decision of the U.S. Supreme Court that carried the constitutional prohibition on compulsory cross-examination far beyond the obvious bans on the inquisitorial rack or the rubber hose. The Court there reversed a conviction because federal authorities obtained their confession during an illegally prolonged period between arrest and arraignment. According to the opinion of the great restraintist, Felix Frankfurter, violation of the requirement for a prompt arraignment (an in-court presentation of the charges against the accused) should have triggered the exclusionary rule at trial. That the rule was not triggered, the confession admitted, constituted reversible error.[28]

On April 22, 1965, the five justices of the Arizona Supreme Court affirmed the trial court's conviction of Ernest Miranda. With the decision of the state's highest court, the role of Miranda's state-subsidized attorney came to an end. The next step, a petition in forma pauperis to the U.S. Supreme Court, Miranda took on his own. A bare majority of that Court found for Miranda and reversed his conviction, in perhaps the most controversial decision between Brown v. Board and Roe v. Wade.

The majority in Miranda v. Arizona reasoned thus:

"Without proper safeguards the in-custody interrogation of persons suspected or accused of crime contains inherently compelling pressures which work to undermine the individual's will to resist and to compel him to speak where he would not otherwise do so freely. In order to combat these pressures and to permit a full opportunity to exercise the privilege against self-incrimination, the accused must be adequately and effectively apprised of his rights and the exercise of those rights must be fully honored."[29]

The Miranda warnings, so familiar to television viewers, are a mechanism by which a negative (the noncompulsory nature of a confession) may be established, and the statement that follows such a warning may be admitted at trial as a lawful piece of evidence.

Three years later, Senator Strom Thurmond shouted at a silent Associate Justice Fortas: "Mallory, Mallory, I want that word to ring in your ears, Mallory!" It hardly mattered to Thurmond that Mallory was decided seven years before the first day that Fortas donned black robes. Fortas wore such robes at the time of Miranda, voted with the majority, supported the exclusionary rule in general, and so was retroactively responsible for Mallory, a case where (according to the Thurmond summary) "a man raped a woman, admitted his guilt, and the Supreme Court turned him loose on a technicality."

The name "Mallory" and all that it implied from Thurmond's lips did ring in Fortas's ears. He did not reply to such "questions" about particular cases in the hearing room, but, before a friendlier audience, at a conference of the nation's lawyers, he asked his colleagues at the bar to work harder than they had, to make it clear to the public that constitutional rights are not "technicalities" and that it is the very business of the judiciary to defend them.[30]

A pattern was set. One charge after another was generated in the cloudy atmosphere of 1968, a year of racial tension, campus and urban violence, political assassination, countercultural defiance of middle America's way of life, increasing frustration over bad war news—one charge after another hit Fortas. He was described as a lame-duck appointment, a crony, a threat to the separation of powers, a friend of smut peddlars, a friend of rapists. By the end of July, with the name "Louis Wolfson" still unknown to public or Senate, it was clear to many in Washington, perhaps including the president, that Abe Fortas would not become chief justice of the United States. With both party conventions approaching, the Senate recessed.

In September the senators returned to work, and the Judiciary Committee asked Fortas to return for more questioning. He had had enough and refused. On September 17, the committee voted the nomination out favorably, eleven (eight Democrats and three Republicans) in favor, six (three of each party) opposed.[31]

One week later debate began on the Senate floor. On the twenty-seventh Senate Republican leader Everett Dirksen, formally a supporter of the nomination, announced his neutrality on the crucial issue of "cloture," the vote to end debate and so frustrate a filibuster. Perhaps Dirksen's announcement was the death knell for the Fortas nomination. Many senators had promised to vote for confirmation in the early days when Johnson's choice seemed likely to prevail as a matter of routine and Griffin's opposition was lonely and quixotic. If those senators now regretted the promise, they now had an honorable escape from its obligation. They could vote with the anti-Fortas side on cloture, following Dirksen and taking their stand on the impermissibility of limits on such an important debate. They might never have to reach the merits and never have to choose between keeping and breaking their earlier pledges.

By long-standing Senate rules, a motion for cloture must receive two-thirds of the votes cast. On October 1, 1968, twelve senators absented themselves. The cloture motion consequently required two-thirds of eighty-eight votes, or fifty-nine. The roll call was fifty-five "aye" and forty-three "nay." The Fortas supporters had managed a bare majority of the votes cast, far short of what they needed. Johnson withdrew the nomination of Fortas and the luckless Thornberry the following day.[32]

The precise wording of Warren's resignation letter acquired new pertinence. Warren had written in June to tell Johnson, "I hereby advise you of my intention to retire as Chief Justice of the United States, effective at your pleasure."[33]

This nontraditional phrasing had caused some confusion in the Judiciary Committee. Was there a vacancy on the Court, or not? The senators resolved their doubts by construing this letter as an actual resignation designed to take effect the moment that a confirmed successor should take the oath of office. Since there was, as yet, no successor, Earl Warren remained chief justice and took his seat in that capacity on the first Monday of October, which is always the start of the Supreme Court term and in 1968 fell on the seventh.

Nixon was elected president on November 5. Lyndon Johnson remained president, and Ramsey Clark remained attorney general until January 20, 1969. On November 11 Robert Morgenthau, U.S. attorney, southern District of New York, telephoned Clark, his superior, with disturbing news. His office had recently obtained the conviction of an investor, Louis Wolfson, for stock manipulation. Now it had discovered that, at a time when he knew himself to be the object of an investigation that would lead to this conviction, Wolfson paid Supreme Court justice Fortas twenty thousand dollars through a family foundation. The Internal Revenue Service (IRS) had no record that Fortas had ever reported this income. Even a mind not given to cynicism might have inferred that Wolfson thought he was buying under-the-table protection or at least a guaranteed friend in the event that he had to appeal a conviction.

Clark drove over to Fortas's house later that day to ask him about this discovery. Fortas assured Clark that the money had been payment for legitimate consultant services. Even so, this explanation continued, Fortas had himself realized that accepting such a payment, while Wolfson remained a defendant in a criminal proceeding, was improper. Fortas returned the money in the same year he received it. Because he had returned this money, he had not reported it as "income." Fortas showed Clark personal financial records supporting this account, and Clark decided that there would be no need for a formal Justice Department inquiry.[34]

As Nixon took office, Fortas continued to occupy his associate justiceship. Any threat that the Wolfson affair might pose to his continued occupation of this seat remained subterranean, a matter of whispers. But Nixon had one vacancy before him in any case, that of the chief justice, who was still awaiting a successor. Immediately, Nixon ordered an investigation of the credentials of Warren Burger, then a judge of the U.S. Court of Appeals for the District of Columbia.[35]*

On Sunday, May 4, 1969, <u>Life</u> went public with the story of Wolfson's payment of twenty thousand dollars to Justice Fortas. Within days of the

---

* In 1955, Thurman Arnold, who was then Fortas's law partner, represented Dr. John F. Peters, a man who had been fired from a federal post for suspected disloyalties after a hearing in which the identity of his accuser remained a secret. Arnold argued before the Supreme Court that the federal government has to respect constitutional considerations of due process at such a hearing. Warren Burger, then an assistant attorney general in the Eisenhower administration, argued to the Court that the Constitution does not apply to government personnel policies. Peters won the case on a narrow statutory ground. Burger won on the constitutional point, the issue of greatest importance to his superiors. At least, in part, as an expression of gratitude for this service, the Eisenhower administration appointed Burger to the court of appeals in 1956. He served there until Eisenhower's vice president resumed residence in Washington in 1969.[36]

appearance of this publication, Wolfson himself reported to authorities and began service of the prison sentence he may once have hoped that his relation with a man of Fortas's stature would prevent. Fortas's press release repeated the explanation he had offered Clark in November.

In the intervening months, the IRS had subpoenaed the files of the Wolfson Family Foundation and had discovered that that one check was only the beginning of what was meant to be a long-term, even a postmortem, relationship. In return for vaguely worded duties in the service of the foundation, Fortas was, by contract, to receive that amount, twenty thousand dollars, every year of his life. The same sum was to go to his wife for the rest of her life, should she survive him.

On May 7, John Mitchell, Nixon's attorney general, met with Earl Warren and showed him this contract, as well as the Fortas-Wolfson correspondence that the IRS had obtained through the same subpoena. One week later, Fortas submitted his letter of resignation to the president. Now Nixon, still in the early months of his term of office, had two vacancies to fill on the Supreme Court.

Fortas returned to the practice of law. There is some question why he did not return to Arnold & Porter, once known as Arnold, Fortas & Porter.[37] He died of a ruptured aorta at his home in Georgetown on April 5, 1982.

This tale of the defeat of Johnson and Fortas illustrates that confirmation debates can become bitter, ideological, and partisan, even if the same party that organizes the Senate occupies the White House. Such debates were on their way to all that they are today even before the era Nixon initiated, the era in which one party became accustomed to holding both houses of the legislature, the other accustomed to dominating presidential campaigns. President Clinton's election in 1992 may have brought an end to that period. Nonetheless, it is not ticket splitting, but some other cause, that produces the polarization of judicial politics. The best candidate for that other cause is the decline of principled deliberation, especially on the Supreme Court, but throughout the judiciary. This decline, in turn, is a consequence of the rise of result-oriented jurisprudence.

Once the habit of ticket splitting set in among the voters of the nation, though, it could only worsen what had begun in the late Warren period, the decline of advice and consent.

NOTES

1. D. S. Freeman, George Washington: Volume Six, Patriot and President (New York, 1954), 232.

2. R. Evans & R. Novak, LBJ (New York, 1966), 305–308.

3. Throughout these notes all quotations from Judiciary Committee hearings come from the volumes edited by Mersky & Jacobstein, and are cited thus: U.S. Congress, Senate, Committee on the Judiciary, Nomination of Abe Fortas, Hearings, 89th Cong., 1st Sess., August 5, 1965.

4. Id. 14.

5. Id. 39.

6. G. T. Dunne, Hugo Black and the Judicial Revolution (New York, 1977), 338, 461.

7. A. Schlesinger, A Thousand Days (Boston, 1965), 698.

8. Dunne, 404.

9. Korematsu v. United States, 323 U.S. 214 (1944).

10. In a concurrence of 1979, Justice Harvey Blackmun explained his own doubts about the continuing value of the strict scrutiny test. He wrote that if it "merely announces an inevitable result [the invalidation of the state action at issue it is] no test at all." Nevertheless, Justice Blackmun joined with the majority that employed that test to strike down a ballot access law, Illinois Elections Board v. Socialists Workers Party, 440 U.S. 173, at 188.

11. 304 U.S. 144 (1938).

12. McGowan v. Maryland, 366 U.S. 420 (1961) upheld Sunday closing laws. Most of the attention McGowan received at the time concerned the Court's rejection of the plaintiff's claim that "blue laws" constitute an establishment of religion. But plaintiffs also raised an equal protection claim, because the distinctions between products that could be sold on Sunday and products that could not be sold then struck them as irrational. Chief Justice Warren's response on that point illustrates just how cursory "mere rationality" scrutiny can be. See id. 425–428.

13. Robbins, "Apply Marshall's Principles to Clarence Thomas," Wall Street Journal, September 10, 1991, op ed.

14. U.S. Congress, Senate, Committee on the Judiciary, Nomination of Thurgood Marshall, Hearings, 90th Cong., 1st Sess., July 13–14, 1967, at 163.

15. "The controversy over the legitimacy of incorporation continues to this day, although as a matter of judicial practice the issue is settled" (R. Bork, The Tempting of America [New York, 1990], 94).

16. Hearings, Marshall, 167.

17. L. M. Kohlmeier, Jr., God Save This Honorable Court (New York, 1972), 70.

18. R. Caro, The Years of Lyndon Johnson: Volume II, Means of Ascent (New York, 1989), 367.

19. B. Murphy, Fortas (New York, 1988), 315.

20. U.S. Congress, Senate, Committee on the Judiciary, Nomination of Abe Fortas: Hearings, 90th Cong., 2d Sess., July 11—September 17, 1968.

21. Id. 49–50.

22. MacKenzie, "Fortas Berated for Two Hours," Washington Post July 19, 1968, p. 1.

23. Fortas Hearings, 1968.

24. Murphy, 459–462.

25. Weeks v. United States, 232 U.S. 383; Mapp v. Ohio, 367 U.S. 643.

26. L. Baker, Miranda (New York, 1983) 22–23 (quoting from trial transcript, Maricopa Cnty., Superior Court, June 20, 1963, Arizona v. Miranda.)

27. Baker at 24–25.

28.   Mallory v. United States, 354 U.S. 449 (1957).

29.   384 U.S. 436 (1966).

30.   Murphy at 455–456.

31.   Hunter, "Fortas Refuses to Appear Again in Senate Inquiry," New York Times, September 14, 1968, p. 1.

32.   Albright, "Fortas Bid Dealt Blow by Dirksen," Washington Post, September 28, 1968, p. 1.

33.   Fortas Hearings, 1968 at 365–388.

34.   Baker, Miranda, 261–262.

35.   This Court is often employed as a training ground for Supreme Court nominees. Its responsibility for review of the decisions of federal agencies gives it a visibility in the legal community second only to that of the Supreme Court itself (T. Phelps & H. Winternitz, Capitol Games [New York, 1992] at 3).

36.   Kohlmeier, 109–111.

37.   J. C. Goulden, The Superlawyers (New York, 1971), 112.

5

The Making of the Burger Court

On June 23, 1969, as the October 1968 term came to an end, Earl Warren performed his final act as chief justice, administering the oath of office to his successor, Warren Burger. But Fortas's empty associateship took another year to fill. The Senate and the nation first debated the qualifications of Clement Haynsworth of South Carolina, then those of G. Harrold Carswell of Florida, before President Nixon and the Senate finally agreed upon the appointment of Harry A. Blackmun, of Minnesota.

In some of its aspects, intellectual history is a matter of style, in which a complicated system of ideas may be said to go out of fashion for no better reason than that the new spring line is in. Literary theory is an example, in which the spring line always comes from Paris and in which structuralism gave way to deconstruction, which gave way, in turn, to Foucaultian countercanonicity, which will, in its turn, give way to something else. But in some of its departments, intellectual history is a matter of more weight. In jurisprudence the classroom is never very far from the courtroom, and the courtroom is never very far from the realities of street and shop, so systems of ideas come in and go out for better reasons than that such shifts are recommended to a handful of the residents of New Haven, Connecticut, by the denizens of the Left Bank.

With these thoughts in mind I take up again the contrast between realism and formalism, to acknowledge that formalism is guilty of most of the flaws with which realists have charged it.

In Chapter 3, I defined formalism by means of four propositions. A review of those propositions will yield the reasons for the fall of the house of Christopher Langdell:

1. The duty of a judge can be understood and must be exercised independently of all party affiliation or political ideology.

This might seem psychologically implausible to anyone. It must seem laughable to those who have actually argued at bar, before a real judge. Of course, judgment is rendered by a whole person, not by some duty-demarcated segment, and the whole person who receives appointment as a judge for a variety of affiliative and ideological reasons or who, in some states, is elected for such reasons will do what seems to that person right. In its recognition of this reality, Oliver Wendell Holmes's redefinition of law as a prediction of what the judge will do in fact may seem more healthy now than it did at first quotation.

2. There are a right and a wrong in the nature of things, which existed as such before they were declared by any authority.

The Founders of the United States declared that the separate and equal status of this nation among nations is decreed by the laws of nature and of nature's God. Since the time of that declaration, ever since so celebrated, Americans have found great appeal in the claim that right and wrong are natural facts, as immutable and as objectively ascertainable as the law of gravity. But this is a claim that can be taken in any of a number of ways, and in most of those ways, it is false. What are we to do, after all, with the obvious fact that one "natural lawyer's" self-evident truth is another's monstrous presumption?

3. The legal minds of earlier generations have already formulated this rightness for us, in easily understood and quite general terms.

It is true enough that they have tried. But the legal minds of earlier generations were not themselves infallible, unless one is willing to apply that appellation to the authors of the Dred Scott decision.[1] Sometimes Constitutions have to be amended, and sometimes the accepted interpretation of a Constitution has to be overturned, in acknowledgement of the fallibility of its authors.

4. The duty of a judge today is to apply those general terms to the particulars of the cases that come before her so that the conclusion, the necessary judgment, will appear of itself, as does the conclusion of a well-formed syllogism upon presentation of both the major and the minor premises.

This proposition suffers from the defects of each of the three upon which it rests and suffers from defects of its own, as well. As William James wrote, a "youth in the courtroom trying cases" with this notion of the law will cut a pathetic figure indeed, because "our rights, wrongs, prohibitions, penalties, words, forms, idioms, beliefs are so many new creations that add themselves as fast as history proceeds. Far from being antecedent principles that animate the process, law, language, truth are but abstract names for its results."[2] As to judges who take the syllogistic or deductive view of their own reasoning process, it must be said that this view goes hand-in-hand with arrogant certitude. One ought to hope, instead, for judges who will think of their decisions as hypothetical, probabilistic, and so, of course, subject to correction.

I have impaled myself upon the horns of a dilemma. I need formalism to save the legal system from the variety of evils to which, as I have tried to suggest, realism is heir. Yet I cannot have formalism, at least not with a good logical conscience and so not for very long. What, then, must I do? I propose to sketch a <u>minimal formalism</u>, scaled back to defensible frontiers yet containing everything pragmatically requisite for the development of a stable, predictable, comprehensible body of law. This sketch requires not four propositions, but six. Yet in order that it may be clear which of the new propositions modifies which of the old, I preserve the 1–4 enumeration.

1a.   As a consequence of the unity of the human personality, the duty of a judge can never be exercised independently of all party affiliations or political ideology.

1b.   Nonetheless, the duty of a judge can be *understood* in isolation from personal, affiliative, or factional considerations.

This is a claim about the utility of an act of abstraction. Just as one can abstract "adult human" from the particular men and women of one's acquaintance, so one can abstract features of the behavior and performance of judges from their various personalities and circumstances.

2a.   Logical consistency is an important element in the evaluation of any collection of authoritative pronouncements.

2b.   Within the development of a body of judge-made law, logical consistency requires that similar cases be similarly treated, that distinct cases and only distinct cases be distinguished.

This is an attempt to encapsulate one sense in which it is correct to speak of a right and a wrong in the nature of things. Any authority that presumes simultaneously to command and prohibit the same act is wrong. But to go further than that, one ought to introduce a historical context.

From time immemorial it has been the practice of judges among the English-speaking peoples to explain their decisions. These explanations set forth rules of law, and one of the functions of a rule of law is to tell future judges, or perhaps to remind the same judge at a later stage of her career, what facts are pertinent, what facts are irrelevant.

Suppose Jim's brown, black-spotted dog bites Jane's leg. Jane sues. A judge issues an opinion in her favor. In announcing this judgment, the court promulgates a general rule that "the person with custodial responsibility for a beast bears the liability for the harm that beast does to an innocent stranger." This rule, worded as it is, suggests that black spots on Jim's dog are not considerations. Even the fact that the "beast" that did Jane harm was a dog rather than a cow is not a consideration. If a cow does harm to an innocent stranger on the day following this judgment, the person with custodial responsibility for that cow may very well be liable for damages on the ground of this canine precedent. Recorded decisions, then, set forth rules of law, and these rules establish criteria by which one case is regarded as the same as, or as different from, another.

3.   The legal minds of earlier generations have formulated for us criteria by which the similarity of similar cases and the difference of different cases may be determined.

4.   Whatever may be a full description of the duty of a judge today, a partial description is this: a judge applies precedent along with the existing criteria of distinction to the cases at hand, or he refuses to apply precedent, explicitly overturns precedent, on reasonable and explicable grounds.

This wording recalls that of the old propositions 3 and 4, with appropriate changes as are required by the scaling back of the claims of the purer strain of formalism.

Simple as it seems, this minimal formalism imposes important constraints and ought to be accounted as an alternative view of the law, one distinct both from realism and from purist formalism.[3] Whether it is, on the whole, a better view than either of the alternatives is something the reader will have to decide, tentatively and hypothetically, for himself, until such time as this theory may be put to the test by a legal culture that instantiates these propositions.

That legal culture will be very different from what obtains in the United States now or from what did obtain in 1969, when the Haynsworth confirmation struggle demonstrated the enmity often directed at a judge who does his formalist duty.

THE BURGER COURT IS BORN

On Wednesday, May 21, 1969, President Nixon addressed the nation to tell it of his nomination of Judge Warren Burger as Chief justice of the United States.[4]

On June 3 the Senate Judiciary Committee convened to consider this appointment. Although Burger was there, the senators asked him little. At 12:20 P.M. this hearing ended with a unanimous vote to report the nomination favorably. Confirmation came within a week with a seventy-four to three vote.[5] On June 23, Earl Warren administered the oath of office to Warren Burger.

On August 18, Nixon nominated Clement F. Haynsworth, Jr., a judge on the Fourth Circuit Court of Appeals, to the remaining vacancy. As the Judiciary Committee opened its hearings, the two senators from South Carolina, Strom Thurmond (R) and Ernest Hollings (D), introduced their favorite son with praise. Senator Hollings, the junior of the two, expressed his confidence that "Judge Haynsworth will give balance where balance is needed" on the Court to which he was now to ascend.[6] The hearings went no further. After these introductions, the sudden death of Senator Everett Dirksen threw his colleagues into mourning and the Judiciary Committee into recess.

By mid-September, when the committee reconvened, the AFL-CIO, having studied Haynsworth's judicial record, announced reasons it considered sufficient for alarm at the prospect that Haynsworth would sit on the highest of courts. The reasons consisted of a single significant decision that took a position on a point of labor law contrary to that of the AFL-CIO and an alleged conflict of interest tenuously connected to that decision. If one hopes to understand Haynsworth's defeat, one must look at the unions's influence.

The statute that governs labor relations in most industries throughout the United States is the NLRA. Section 7 of this act vests in the employees of covered industries certain rights: to organize, to bargain collectively, and to strike. Section 8(a)(1) makes any "interference" with §7 rights an "unfair labor practice." Section 8(a)(3) prohibits employer "discrimination" against employees in hiring, job assignments, promotions, or firing on the basis of their union-related activities.

What result follows, under either of these clauses, if an employer closes its doors entirely, thus leaving unemployed its former workforce? Does this not "interfere" with the exercise of §7 rights? Of course, it does, in the direct sense that the former employees no longer have an employer with whom to bargain, collectively or otherwise, and against whom they might strike. But it is a settled principle of law and one widely endorsed by common sense, that the law will not try to force a business to stay open.[7] The reason for the closedown does not deflect the application of this principle. Whether the employer closes because creditors demand the sale of its capital assets or because management has decided it no longer wants to talk to pesty union officials, it is never an unfair labor practice to cease altogether one's employment of labor.

How far does this principle extend? Can an employer close a facility in the Northeast and open another in the Southwest to do much the same work, because nonunion labor is found more readily in the latter location than in the former? Is this discrimination against the unionized region and so prohibited under 8(a)(3)? Is it a prohibited interference in someone's §7 rights and so a violation of 8(a)(1)? If so, whose rights? Those of the old work site or the new? This issue of the "runaway shop" approaches, although it is not quite identical to, the question that raised the ire of AFL-CIO president George Meany at the expense of Judge Clement Haynsworth.[8]

In March 1956 the Textile Workers Union had begun an organized campaign at a textile mill in South Carolina. Darlington Manufacturing Co. owned this mill. A New York textile marketing firm named Deering Milliken owned a 40 percent interest in Darlington. The Milliken family, in turn, owned a controlling interest in Deering Milliken.

Darlington resisted the efforts of the Textile Workers Union. The company threatened to liquidate if the union won the representation election. This threat may have been an "unfair labor practice" itself under existing constructions of the loosely worded prohibition on "interference." If the union had lost the election, and if evidence had shown that its loss was an effect of the threat, it would have had a cause of action for the NLRB.[9] But this controversy took a different form. The union won.

In September, Darlington's board of directors voted to close. Stockholders approved in October. Work ended in November. The owners sold all machinery and equipment at auction in December.[10]

The NLRB, acting on a textile workers' complaint, found an unfair labor practice. It reasoned that Darlington was not the whole of a business but a part of a "single integrated employer group" controlled by the Milliken family. This wider entity had closed just part of its operations. Moreover, it was animated in so acting not by legitimate business considerations but by antiunion animus. The board ordered Deering to offer back pay to all Darlington employees and to restore all terminated workers to the payroll until they obtained substantially equivalent work or were placed on preferential hiring lists at the other Deering Milliken mills.[11]

Deering Milliken appealed. The Fourth Circuit Court of Appeals, Haynsworth voting with the majority, enjoined enforcement of the NLRB decision.[12] The Fourth Circuit took the view that just as an employer has a right to go out of business, so that employer has a right to decide upon a partial closing and that neither enforcement agencies nor the courts ought to look into motivation in the one case anymore than in the other. The action of the employer was legal, whether that employer was Darlington (as Deering maintained) or Deering (as the NLRB held).

The union appealed. The U.S. Supreme Court reversed the Fourth Circuit and remanded the case for further proceedings before the NLRB.[13] Justices Stewart and Goldberg took no part in this decision. The other seven members of the Court all joined an opinion by Justice Harlan that reasoned:

> While we thus agree with the Court of Appeals that viewing Darlington as an independent employer the liquidation of its business was not an unfair labor practice, we cannot accept the lower court's view that the same conclusion necessarily follows if Darlington is regarded as an integral part of the Deering Milliken enterprise.
>
> ...A discriminatory partial closing may have repercussions on what remains of the business, affording employer leverage for discouraging the free exercise of §7 rights among remaining employees.[14]

Observe that Harlan's disagreement is not with the Fourth Circuit alone. It is with the board as well, for the board considered the employees at the closed mill victims of an unfair labor practice whereas in Harlan's view only the workers at the other mills, the workers who may be cowed into submission by the Darlington closing, might be found to be victims. That is why this opinion remanded the case to redirect the attention of the NLRB to the closing's possible non-Darlington effects.

On reconsideration the NLRB again found that Deering Milliken was guilty of unfair labor practices. This time it phrased its findings in the language that the Harlan opinion required. George Meany employed this case in lobbying the Senate to stall the confirmation of Judge Haynsworth. Since Haynsworth had voted with the majority of the Fourth Circuit in a decision in which that circuit ruled against a union, and especially since he had ended up on the losing side of that issue, Haynsworth was obviously actuated by an antiunion animus of his own.

Given their own polemical needs, it is understandable that Haynsworth's detractors seldom mentioned the outcome of this litigation. After the second

NLRB ruling, the defendants took a second appeal. This time, the Fourth Circuit, Haynsworth again voting with the majority, upheld the union and the board position. This vote is strong evidence that, at each of the two moments when he had to adjudicate this case, Haynsworth made a conscientious attempt to make sense of the law as it applied to the facts before him.[15] The law was different the second time, made different by Harlan's opinion. Haynsworth's switch reflected the difference. What it did not reflect was an injudicious temperament or an antiunion bias.

The minimal formalist principles previously outlined or any variant of formalism may serve as a standard by which to measure the law of labor relations in the United States, as that body of law bears upon the Darlington litigation. The board and the courts were struggling with two rules of law. The first distinguishes actions taken as a consequence of an "antiunion animus" from actions that have a "legitimate business purpose." This distinction is untenable and leaves unions and managers with an enigma instead of a rule. Is the containment of labor costs a legitimate business purpose, or not? The courts generally recognize that it is.[16] Can an employer reasonably expect an increase in labor costs as a result of unionization? Does such anticipation itself imply antiunion animus? If so, the distinction disappears. If not, what more is needed? It seems unlikely that the two phenomena (concern about increased costs as a result of unionization, on one hand, and some additional spite toward
unions, on the other) are sufficiently distinct to render it rational for a legal system to draw its lines of tolerance or punitive prohibition there.

There is a second rule of law at issue; that a complete closing down of a business is lawful but that a partial closing down may be judged unlawful. This rule seems to function as an exception to the first rule. If the antiunion action is found to be animated by an illegal motive, it may still be lawful if it amounts to a complete closing down of the business. The scope of this rule seems to depend upon its purpose. Is it thought tyrannical for the state to order a business to keep its doors open? Is the prevention of such tyranny, thus, the rationale for the rule? If so, then how does it apply to an order that merely seeks compensatory payments from the owners of the closed business for the costs (it is alleged) their closing has imposed on others? Or is it deemed impractical to locate and enforce an order against former owners, so that this rule is justified by the need for an efficient allocation of administrative resources? Or is there some broad, free-market argument that favors the unimpeded closing down of a business, in order that resources may find their most profitable use? The way in which one ought to extend, or refuse to extend, this tolerance to closings that are or seem to be less than complete depends upon what one understands to have been the purpose of the rule, and the authorities do not seem to have examined themselves in this matter with any persistence.

The AFL-CIO and its chief senatorial ally, Birch Bayh, soon realized that the mileage they could get out of the Darlington decision alone was limited. If every controversial vote cast by a federal judge becomes a political litmus test, then no judge with any length of service on the bench will ever be confirmed to the Supreme Court. Senator Bayh would have to combine this decision with something else, with a "conflict of interest." He found one.

The nominee was a man of substantial wealth, the consequence of some fortunate investments. In 1950 Haynsworth had been one of a group of friends in Greenville who invested the necessary capital to incorporate Carolina Vend-A-Matic, a company formed to operate automatic food and coffee vending machines. As new industrial plants came to South Carolina in the 1950s Carolina Vend-A-Matic did quite well for its investors. By 1964 (when he sold his interest) Judge Haynsworth's initial investment of $3,000 was worth 14,566 percent of that amount, or $437,000.[17]

The Senate itself was (and still is) a haven for millionaires. Neither the fact nor the source of Haynsworth's wealth would have counted against him, but for the revelation that Carolina Vend-A-Matic did business with Deering Milliken. In 1963 Vend-A-Matic was leasing its machines to forty-six plants and mills throughout South Carolina. Three of those sites belonged to Deering Milliken, one of the defendants in the Darlington case. This was a consequence of no decision of Haynsworth, who was an investor, not a manager.

Did Haynsworth vote as he did on the Darlington appeal in order to curry favor with a customer of one of the firms in his portfolio? Nobody could quite bring himself to say that. Yet some such implication had to hang in the air if this discovery was to have the effect the Meany-Bayh strategy required. Should the judge have recused himself from every case in which any party owned a facility that used or that could at some time in the future use a vending machine? Nobody could bring himself to suggest that, either. Haynsworth's critics were left with an old substitute for intelligent criticism, the charge that the "appearance" of impropriety is impropriety enough.[18]

On October 9, only three days after the start of the Supreme Court's term, the Senate Judiciary Committee voted ten to seven in favor of Haynsworth's confirmation. Debate commenced in the full Senate on November 13.

Although the AFL-CIO continued to carry the lobbying, it had by now picked up partners, notably the NAACP. The coalition strategy required a shift of focus away from Haynsworth's alleged antiunion bias, toward the insufficiency of his ardor for civil rights. There was never any charge of active opposition to the implementation of Brown v. Board or of a pro-segregation ideology. There was, instead, what Tom Wicker has since called a "rather vague contention" that the nominee was insufficiently sensitive in such matters.[19]

RACE AND RELIGION

This is how that vague contention sounded from the mouth of New York Republican Jacob Javits. Javits thought Haynsworth "so consistently insensitive to the centuries-old injustice which we as a nation have caused our black citizens to bear that I could not support the introduction of Judge Haynsworth's philosophy into the nation's highest court."[20]

What stood behind such charges was evidence that Haynsworth continued to take the Supreme Court at its word even after that Court under the direction of Chief Justice Warren had begun sub silento to shift the ground of its school desegregation decisions. From 1954 until 1968 the Supreme Court repeatedly spoke of the constitutional imperative of eliminating dual school systems, that is, the de jure discrimination between races. During that same fourteen-year period the Court refused to give the federal district and appeals courts any explicit mandate to oppose de facto discrimination; that is, to reshuffle school systems that had become mostly white, black, or Latino due to housing patterns or "white flight" from cities.

The abstention was appropriate. The equal protection language of the Fourteenth Amendment on its face bars discriminatory state action but creates no mandate for judicial orders to buffer the effects of housing markets.

Haynsworth followed the instructions of this period. He voted with the majority of the Fourth Circuit to uphold the action of a county that had closed all of its public schools without regard to their racial composition.[21] He voted, again with the majority, to uphold a "freedom of choice" plan adopted by another county despite the nonintegrated character of the choices that parents employed that freedom to make.[22] The Supreme Court reversed each of these decisions, although in so doing it was untrue to its own words. Haynsworth's conscientious attempt to apply the law as the Court above him had expounded it exposed him to the enmity of politicians and lobbyists, who can not distinguish between interests and principles.

Although seldom mentioned, the matter of religious balance on the Supreme Court was much on the minds of many senators in 1969.[23] Fortas was a Jew. So was his predecessor in that seat, Arthur Goldberg. It began to be argued in about 1969, and has become an accepted principle since, that no deliberative body can be said to be properly representative of the population at large unless its members constitute a demographic cross-section of that population as to race, religion, sex, age, nation of origin, and an expanding list of other particulars. On this premise, if the nation is roughly one-ninth Jewish and if a particular deliberative body has nine members, a "Jewish seat" necessarily renders that body more representative than it would otherwise be. Would two Jewish justices, as sat on the bench in the 1930s (Louis Brandeis and Benjamin Cardozo) be excessive? The theory of demographic representation is never very clear on such points. Its proponents talk often of inclusion while hiding the fact that their arguments necessarily imply exclusion as well.[24]

On November 21 the nomination of Judge Haynsworth came to a vote. Vice President Spiro Agnew exercised his constitutional prerogative of presiding over the Senate that day because a tie vote was considered possible. But all of those senators whose votes appeared in the undecideds columns of the head-counters around Washington went into the nay column of the count that mattered most, and the roll ended with a vote against confirmation, forty-five to fifty-five. Seventeen of the senators in opposition were Republicans. Nixon's defeat was more complete than Johnson's. This was not a vote on cloture but a direct refusal of consent, the first such refusal since 1930, when the Senate blocked Hoover's appointment of John Parker.[25]

NIXON: DEFEAT AND REVENGE

The day after that vote Nixon invoked the balance model of the Supreme Court: "I deeply regret this action. I believe a majority of the people in the nation regret it . . . . The Supreme Court needs men of his legal philosophy to restore the proper balance to that great institution."[26] Attorney General Mitchell was, as was his habit, a good deal more blunt than his boss: "If we'd put up one of the Twelve Apostles, it would have been the same."[27] Given the great Democratic need for a Republican scalp in this hour of the Chappaquidick scandal[28] and of what Rowland Evans and Robert Novak called the atmosphere of "gloom and defeatism" in the Democratic Party that summer, there was much truth to Mitchell's observation.

On January 19, 1970, President Nixon announced the nomination of G. (George) Harrold Carswell. The simplest way to understand this action is the best. Nixon avenged himself upon the Senate, which had rejected a perfectly qualified appointee, by offering an utterly unqualified appointee for the same post.

Carswell had an eleven-year record as District Court judge in the Northern District of Florida. But he had only the most nominal record at an appellate level—eleven months on the Fifth Circuit Court of Appeals. What was most important to Nixon and Mitchell was that the Fifth Circuit of that time lay to the south of Haynsworth's Fourth and encompassed Florida, Georgia, Alabama, Mississippi, Louisiana, and Texas.[29] Judiciary Committee hearings began on January 27.

By January 30 attention focused on one speech from Carswell's pre-judicial electoral career. In 1948, while running for a seat in the Georgia legislature, he told an audience, "I yield to no man as a fellow candidate, or as a fellow citizen, in the firm, vigorous belief in the principles of white supremacy, and I shall always be so governed." The senators may already have yearned for Haynsworth's return. They had traded a man alleged to be inadequately zealous in his support of civil rights for a man who had demonstrably boasted eternal fidelity to the hegemony of the white race.

Carswell acknowledged the speech and the sincerity of its sentiments when uttered. But, as he observed, twenty years can mean a great deal in the evolution of one's sentiments, and as of 1970, "I do not harbor any racial supremacy notions." Later that day Professor William Van Alystyne of Duke University Law School asked the committee whether the conviction expressed in the 1948 speech "can be significantly discounted by clear and reassuring events of more recent date?" If not, Alystyne continued, it would be "uniquely inappropriate" for the Senate to vote to confirm.[30]

Carswell could perhaps have survived the disclosure of his 1948-era segregationist philosophy. But matters were worsened by a country club issue. The city of Tallahassee opened an all-white municipal golf course in 1935. After Brown v. Board and largely out of concern that the municipal facility would have to be desegregated, Tallahassee officials decided to sell it, instead. At this time Carswell was U.S. attorney for the Northern District of Florida (1954–59). In 1956 he became one of several prominent white citizens of Tallahassee, many of the others also public officials, who organized the Capital City Country Club, Inc., bought the golf course, and so preserved its all-white status. This episode shows a mingling of private and public roles for the clear purpose of evading the law that blacks and whites concerned with racial fairness quite rightly considered offensive.[31] To state the problem in the words of Van Alystyne's test: The events of a more recent date not only did not discount the convictions of the 1948 speech but confirmed it.

Still, owing to the reluctance of some senators to leave the Supreme Court any longer shorthanded, Carswell found defenders. John Sherman Cooper, who had voted against Haynsworth, explained to a journalist why the country club issue would not lead him to vote against Carswell: "I would have to be convinced that the golf club was made into a private corporation solely to exclude Negroes. That wasn't it at all. The place was bankrupt, and they were trying to keep it open."[32] This is not convincing. Why must an act be performed solely for the purpose of excluding blacks in order to give offense? Is an act performed only predominantly for that reason outside the ambit of senatorial disapproval?

The alternative explanation Cooper accepted is implausible. Although a municipality can indeed become bankrupt, a particular municipal asset (whether a golf course or a firehouse) cannot. Perhaps Cooper meant that the country club was not meeting its own expenses as hoped and that the city understandably wanted to rid itself of this drain upon its finances. But would such a consideration have led city officials to sell to themselves and their associates rather than hold a public auction and sell to the highest bidder (which might have been the NAACP, for all it would have mattered to municipal finances)? There was no such auction.

Senator Cooper's comment demonstrates the great advantage that Judge Carswell still held. Many senators wanted to find a reason to vote for him. Carswell was not a wealthy man, certainly not on Haynsworth's scale, and, in part as a result, there was no allegation of a judicial impropriety arising from a financial conflict of interest weighing on the side of opposition to this appointment. Had Carswell made a creditable showing at the Judiciary Committee hearings, he might have overcome the suspicion of past and continuing racism, which did weigh in that scale.

But his performance was poor. The word it most often inspired was "mediocre." Bryce Harlow, a longtime associate of Richard Nixon, told the president that the senators had come to see Carswell as "a boob, a dummy. And what counter is there to that? He is."[33] Senator Richard Russell put the best possible construction on the facts and argued that the Senate should prefer: "a 'b' or 'c' student who was able to think straight, compared to one of those 'a' students who are capable of the kind of thinking that winds up getting us a 100% increase in crime in this country."

Nonetheless, by March the Justice Department's own lobbyists on Capitol Hill were noticeably acting pro forma in their presentation of Carswell's case. Senator William Saxbe (R.-Ohio) noticed the diminution of administration enthusiasm and wrote the president to ask whether this was a policy shift or simple sloth. President Nixon could not admit to either. His answer was that there is a matter of high principle at stake, "the Constitutional responsibility of the President to appoint members of the Court."[34]

Was Nixon right? No and yes. As Carswell's opponents were quick to observe, the Constitution splits that responsibility. The Senate did not encroach upon the president's prerogative to nominate by exercising its own prerogative to grant or withhold confirmation. Yet the president was right that there had been an important change. In Chapter 1 I reviewed the intentions of Publius, indicative of those of the Founders. The expectation of those who wrote the advice and consent clause was that *in the normal course of events* the Senate would grant consent. Refusal to confirm would be an extraordinary event, and its mere possibility would serve to remind the president of the great responsibility inherent in his appointive power. Through the years 1968–70, in the midst of controversies over Fortas, Haynsworth, and Carswell and impeachment of William O. Douglas, what had been meant as an extraordinary contingency became a normal part of our politics. Nixon was right to suggest that this was a lamentable descent from the Publian scheme.

But Carswell was not a felicitous vehicle for reasserting the original balance. On April 6 the Senate voted on a motion to recommit (an informal burial). This motion failed, forty-four to fifty-two. On April 8 the vote on confirmation was nearly identical, forty-five ayes to fifty-one nays. Carswell, in the end, received as many votes as Haynsworth had, and four fewer votes were cast in opposition to Carswell than to Haynsworth. This proves nothing about the quality of the two nominees. It does prove that it is easier for a senator to vote nay once than twice.[35]

On April 9 Nixon issued an angry statement: "I understand the bitter feelings of millions of Americans who live in the South about the act of regional discrimination that took place in the Senate yesterday."[36]

The president was wrong. There had been no act of regional discrimination in the Senate the previous day. But the rejections of Haynsworth and Carswell were hardly examples of judicious weighing of merit, either. If there were any real nonpartisan standards left, any consensus as to what "merit" means, Haynsworth would never have been rejected and Carswell would never have been named. The whole process of judicial appointment had become, by 1970, an exercise in bare-knuckled factional power. With the abdication by the Supreme Court of anything like its real and crucial constitutional role long accomplished, can the decline and fall of the advice and consent clause be wondered at?

A TRUCE, NOT A PEACE

On April 14, Nixon announced the nomination of Harry Andrew Blackmun of Rochester, Minnesota, to fill the long-unfilled Fortas vacancy. Blackmun was a graduate of Cambridge University and Harvard Law School. As a boy, he had attended elementary school in St. Paul, where one of his schoolmates was Warren Burger.[37] That much of his biography received attention at the time of his nomination. What received no attention but has had a great impact on the subsequent development of constitutional law is that Rochester is the home of the Mayo Clinic, a center of medical practice and research with an international reputation. Blackmun served as that institution's resident counsel from 1950 to 1959. When the Supreme Court heard the abortion case three years later, this former physicians' counsel, more than any of the other eight, saw abortion as an unremarkable medical procedure and saw its prohibition by the states for any reason other than the strictly medical as an intrusion upon the confidentiality of the doctor-patient relationship.

On April 15, Gerald Ford (R.-Mich.), House minority leader, took to the floor of that chamber to present what he called a "preliminary statement . . . of the law of impeachment and the facts about the behavior of Mr. Justice Douglas." His view of the law was as follows:

What, then, is an impeachable offense? The only honest answer is that an impeachable offense is whatever a majority of the House of Representatives considers it to be at a given moment of history; conviction results from whatever offense or offenses two-thirds of the other body considers to be sufficiently serious to require removal of the accused from office. Again, the historical context and political climate are important; there are few fixed principles among the handful of precedents.[38]

Here realism has come to the law of impeachment. Realism in jurisprudence is precisely the rejection of "fixed principles," a rejection that Ford considers "honest." Oliver Wendall Holmes, in a dictum that has long defined realism, said that the law is a prediction of what the judge will do in fact. Gerald Ford claimed in 1970 that an impeachable offense is whatever the House finds it to be in fact.

One of the implications of these remarks is that William Douglas need not have done anything "wrong." He was out of step with "historical context and political climate"—that is enough.

On Wednesday, April 29, at 10:45 a.m. the Senate Judiciary Committee began its hearings on Blackmun. The close conjunction between the Douglas impeachment inquiry in the House and the Blackmun hearings in the Senate allows for a reasoned suspicion, although not for more, that the Republicans now offered the Democrats a deal: "We will leave Douglas alone if you let Blackmun pass unchallenged." If the offer was made, it would seem to have been accepted. The NAACP, which had sent witnesses to testify against both Carswell and Haynsworth, took no position on Blackmun.[39] The AFL-CIO likewise kept silent. On May 9th the Judiciary Committee voted unanimously to recommend Blackmun's confirmation to the Senate.[40] On May 12 came the vote to confirm, ninety-four to none.

NOTES

1. Scott v. Sandford, 19 How. 393 (1857).

2. W. James, Pragmatism (New York, 1907), 158–159.

3. As applied to constitutional litigation, this minimal formalism might also be called a "moderate textualism." That is what Professor Leslie Friedman Goldstein calls it. Those of my readers who want to argue with my sometimes schematic comments on constitutional and jurisprudential theory ought to turn first to that more complete explanation, In Defense of the Text (Savage, MD, 1991).

4. Baker, Miranda at 243–244 (quoting Nixon speech).

5. U.S. Congress, Senate, Committee on the Judiciary, Nomination of Warren Burger, Hearings, 91st Cong., 1st Sess., June 3, 1969.

6. U.S. Congress, Senate, Committee on the Judiciary, Nomination of Clement Haynsworth, Hearings, 91st Cong., 1st Sess., September 16, 1969, at 35–39.

7. National Labor Relations Board v. Adkins Transfer Co., 226 F.2d 324 (6th Cir. 1955).

8. International Ladies Garment Workers' Union v. NLRB, 374 F.2d 324 (6th Cir. 1955).

9. NLRB v. Rapid Bindery, Inc., 293 F.2d 170 (2d Cir. 1961).

10. Textile Workers Union v. Darlington Mfg. Co., 380 U.S. 263 (1965).

11. Id. 267.

12. 325 F.2d 682 (4th Cir. 1963).

13. 380 U.S. at 277.

14. 380 U.S. at 274–75.

15. Darlington Mfg. Co. v. NLRB, 397 F.2d 760 (4th Cir. 1968) cert. denied 393 U.S. 1023 (1969).

16. NLRB v. Lassing, 284 F.2d 781 (6th Cir. 1960) cert. denied 366 U.S. 909 (1969).

17. Haynsworth Hearings, 39–54.

18. L. M. Kohlmeier, Jr., God Save This Honorable Court (New York, 1972), 130–132.

19. T. Wicker, One of Us (New York, 1991), 496–497.

20. Kohlmeier, 139.

21. Griffin v. Prince Edward County, 377 U.S. 218 (1964).

22. Green v. New Kent County, 391 U.S. 430 (1968).

23. S. Ambrose, Nixon, The Triumph of a Politician, 1962–1972 (New York, 1989), 316.

24. In June 1972 the Chicago Sun-Times printed an open letter from columnist Mike Royko to the leader of an Illinois reform slate then contending for credentials to the Democratic National Convention. It was high tide for the demographic theory, and Royko saw the exclusion implicit in the talk of inclusion: "About half of your delegates are women. About a third of your delegates are black. Many of them are young people. You even have a few Latin Americans. But as I looked over the names of your delegates, I saw something peculiar . . . . There's only one Italian there. Are you saying that only one out of every 59 Democratic votes cast in a Chicago election is cast by an Italian? And only three of your 59 have Polish names . . . . Your reforms have disenfranchised Chicago's white ethnic Democrats, which is a strange reform . . . . Your co-leader, Jesse the Jetstream, didn't make it to his local polling place. He's being hailed as a new political powerhouse, and he couldn't deliver his own vote. Now they are delegates, having been declared so by themselves . . . . Anybody who would reform Chicago's Democratic Party by dropping the white ethnic would probably begin a diet by shooting himself in the stomach."

25. Kohlmeier, 139–140.

26. Id. 140.

27. Id. 141.

28. R. Evans & R. Novak, Political Report, August 13, 1969, No. 57, p. 1.

29. Congress has since revised the circuits for the U.S. Courts of Appeal. The new Fifth contains only Louisiana, Mississippi, and Texas. The newly created Eleventh contains Georgia, Florida, and Alabama.

30. U.S. Congress, Senate, Committee on the Judiciary, Nomination of George Harrold Carswell: Hearings, 91st Cong., 2d Sess., January 27–February 3, 1970, at 21–23 (Carswell's address) and 136 (Alystyne's testimony).

31. Id. 156–157.

32. R. Harris, Decision (New York, 1971), 136.

33. Wicker, 498.

34. Id.

35. Kohlmeier, 159–160.

36. Public Papers of the Presidents: Richard Nixon–1970, No. 108, "Statement about Nominations to the Supreme Court," April 9, 1970, 345, 346.

37.   U.S. Congress, Senate, Committee on the Judiciary, <u>Nomination</u> of <u>Harry</u> <u>A.</u> <u>Blackmun</u>: <u>Hearings</u>, 91st Cong., 2d Sess., April 29–May 9, 1970, Letter from Richard G. Kleindienst, Deputy Attorney General, to the Honorable James Eastland, Chairman, 12-18.

38.   W. Douglas, <u>The</u> <u>Autobiography</u> of <u>William</u> <u>O.</u> <u>Douglas</u>: <u>The</u> <u>Court</u> <u>Years</u> (New York, 1980), 359.

39.   <u>Blackmun</u> <u>Hearings</u>.

40.   Kohlmeier, 176–177.

6

The Unraveling of an Administration

In any system founded on the separation of powers among three branches there are two ways in which these branches can manage coexistence. First, each branch may accept its own limits and refrain from intrusions upon what is understood to be the "turf" of the other. Second, the three branches may coexist in a continual tug and push, their respective turfs always contested, always subject to revision. The Pentagon Papers case was a symptom, as American government slid toward the latter condition. Watergate gave this lamentable transition a sharp forward push.

In 1970, in the midst of a dispute over the use of public money for the development of a supersonic transport (SST), several private citizens brought suit in the U.S. District Court for the District of Columbia. The first-named plaintiff, Gary Soucie, and his associates, asked that the court compel the director of the Office of Science and Technology (OST), Edward David, to release documents pertaining to that aircraft. The Freedom of Information Act (FOIA), which provided the statutory ground for this action, states: "On complaint, the district court . . . has jurisdiction to enjoin the agency from withholding agency records and to order the production of any agency records improperly withheld from the complainant."[1] The FOIA also sets out "exemptions," that is, circumstances wherein an agency shall not be required to produce its records to private persons.

The district court dismissed Soucie's complaint. The trial judge held that the OST is not an "agency" within the meaning of the language just quoted, so the act does not grant to Court jurisdiction.

The court of appeals reversed and remanded.[2] Chief Judge David Bazelon wrote for the court and settled the issue of the definition of an agency in favor of the appellant/plaintiff. Circuit Judge Malcolm Wilkey concurred but in a separate opinion. Wilkey's opinion noted that since the district court had found that it had no jurisdiction, it "quite logically did not

proceed to consider the exemptions" from information requests provided for
by the FOIA.[3] If this case is remanded, the court below will have to treat
of such exemptions, and in particular with the fifth, which protects from
disclosure: "interagency or intra-agency memorandums or letters which
would not be available by law to a party other than an agency in litigation
with another agency."[4]   In offering the district court some guidance on
remand, Judge Wilkey observed that this opaquely worded exemption five is
a codification of executive privilege, and he proceeded to offer one of the
most elaborate discussions of the basis and character of that privilege to be
found in the federal reports.

Wilkey sees it as just one-third of a "tripartite privilege," possessed by all
of the branches of the U.S. government against each of the others and, by
extension, against the public as well. He offers two arguments for the
existence of this privilege. On one hand, he wrote, there is a "common
sense-common law principle" that operates even "apart from the
Constitution . . . that not all public business can be transacted completely in
the open." One of the many good reasons behind this principle is the fear
of disclosure, which could chill the willingness of a subordinate to offer
advice that might later prove unpopular or otherwise damaging in the harsh
light of partisan debate. On the other hand, Wilkey's analysis continues, a
constitutional component of the tripartite privilege "arises from the principle
of separation of powers among legislative, executive, and judicial branches
of our government." This consideration was especially important in the
instant case because Judge Wilkey suspected that the demand for disclosure
was brought at the instigation of the congressional opponents of the SST.[5]

Much of Wilkey's concurrence could serve as a brief for any executive
agency that might decide to fight any demand for FOIA disclosure. The
great omission in Wilkey's opinion is any discussion of the limits of executive
privilege. Is it absolute? So far as one can discern from his discussion, the
answer to that question is yes. Yet facts are seldom kind to absolutes, and
though the victory of the stop-the-SST forces in Congress soon rendered this
particular application of that privilege moot, the underlying issue would arise
again. On June 13, 1971, the New York Times began to publish excerpts
from the "Pentagon Papers," a Department of Defense study that traced the
origins of American involvement in the war in Indochina. The United States
filed suit to enjoin the further publication of this material.

On June 19, district court judge Murray Gurfein denied the government's
motion for an injunction. But he continued a temporary restraining order,
so that the United States could seek relief from the Second Circuit Court of
Appeals. In that court the vote was five to three to reverse Gurfein, on the
theory that theft and its fruits are not protected by law.[6]

A PRIVILEGED STUDY OF THE WAR?

On June 30, the U.S. Supreme Court voted six to three that the president has no authority to impose restraints on publication, given the facts at issue. Accordingly, that Court reversed the court of appeals and reinstated Gurfein's denial of the government's motion for injunctive relief. But the vote of six represents only this holding, not any reasoned jurisprudential position. Indeed, there were no two justices united on any position. In an extraordinary development, the Pentagon Papers case produced nine written opinions.[7]

It is unfortunate that each justice saw the Pentagon Papers case as a controversy over the First Amendment. None saw it as a question of the extent of the president's authority in Article II. The nine opinions exhibited every possible attitude toward a First Amendment issue: realistic (both ad hoc and definitional balancing), restraintist, formalist.

William J. Brennan was the realist ad hoc balancer for the majority.[8] He allowed that injunctive relief might be appropriate to prevent publication of the sailing dates of troop ships. But even in such a case, the government must tell the judges to whom it applies for an injunction that the sinking of certain identified ships is the particular threat that justifies the action demanded. In the case at hand, Brennan complained, the government had left the specific threat quite vague.

Realists have always believed in the omniscience of the judicial branch. This is one of the distinguishing planks in their platform. Brennan's argument that an exercise of prior restraint, as against a newspaper, may be proper but must pass judicial examination on its military-strategic merits is a perfectly clear-headed conclusion from Brennan's premises.

Yet an opposing conclusion is possible from the same premises, and Harry A. Blackmun, the realist ad hoc balancer for the minority, drew it. Blackmun thought that the government had made its case and that the release of information contained in the Pentagon study would bring about "the death of soldiers, the destruction of alliances, the greatly increased difficulty of negotiating with our enemies."[9]

Byron White and Thurgood Marshall voted with the majority and were realist definitional balancers in their separate opinions. The United States may forbid the publication of information injurious to its own national security, but this decision must be a decision of the sovereign United States, not of the commander in chief alone. For these two justices, the decisive consideration was that President Nixon had invoked no legislative ground for his request for an injunction.[10]

Potter Stewart was the restraintist for the majority. He began his discussion with the premise that the Supreme Court should never make policy. The justices should apply and interpret the "specific regulations" and "specific laws" emanating from the popularly elected branches. Here there was neither law nor regulation.[11]   The government, in asking for an injunction, was also requiring the judiciary to pull from thin air the pertinent standards for such an injunction. Such an invitation and requirement ought to be refused.

John Harlan was the restraintist for the minority. He, too, believed that justices must be wary of a policy role. Harlan concluded that such wariness required deference to the judgment of the president of the United States, the constitutional custodian of our national security and foreign policy apparatus.[12]

Justice Hugo Black was the formalist for the majority. Black took the position that the president has no authority to restrain the publication of any information, whether legally or otherwise obtained, about sailing dates or other information and that even if there were an act of Congress purporting to convey such authority, that act would be void.

With prose as emphatic as ever, in what proved to be his final written opinion, Black made his view of the role of a free press unmistakable: "Paramount among the responsibilities of a free press is the duty to prevent any part of government from deceiving the people and sending them off to distant lands to die of foreign fevers and foreign shot and shell . . . the New York Times, the Washington Post, and other newspapers should be commended for serving the purposes that the founding fathers saw so clearly."[13]

Black's insistence that his own understanding of the First Amendment was the only straightforward, literalist reading encounters some difficulty here. The text of that amendment begins with the word *Congress*. Congress alone is explicitly enjoined to make no law abridging freedom of speech or of the press. Any limit on the executive is inferential. In the passage just quoted, Black expands the word *Congress* to mean "any part of government." This is a reasonable expansion, and it is, as Black observes, in accord with the motives that impelled George Mason and other antifederalists to insist upon a Bill of Rights in the first place. Still, it shows that literalism by itself is never enough. If *Congress* does not quite mean Congress, then what of "no law"?

William O. Douglas joined Black's opinion and wrote his own. Douglas's opinion reads like a paraphrase of Black's.[14]

Chief Justice Burger was the formalist for the minority. He agreed with the Second Circuit that the decision should turn on the simple fact that government property had been stolen: "Interestingly, the Times explained its refusal to allow the Government to examine its own purloined documents by saying in substance this might compromise *its* sources and informants! The Times thus asserts a right to guard the secrecy of its sources while denying that the Government of the United States has that power."[15]   The analogy is inexact. Imagine that some rival newspaper were to discover the "sources and intermediaries" of the New York Times through an individual intermediary in the Times's employ. The editors of the untrustworthy Times man might learn of this "leak" before the damaging information appeared in the morning edition of their hypothetical rival. If so, though, they will have no power or right, nothing but an appeal to the collegial courtesy of their fellow journalists, by which to intervene in the rival's editorial decisions or to stop the rival's presses. In the most important sense, then, the Times was not asserting the power itself that it would deny to the government.

Only two of the nine justices made a formalist argument, and both such arguments are flawed. So let me dispense with doxography or textual exegesis and look at the case with my own eyes. There were three distinct issues:

1. Does the President possess a general prerogative to control information or opinion generated within the executive branch?

2. If such a prerogative exists, does it survive its first failure? That is, can the president act in some way to stop the distribution of "leaked" information after the fact, after such information has passed to persons outside the executive branch? This issue was not raised in the SST litigation and so not addressed by Judge Wilkey's concurrence in Soucie v. David.

3. If such a prerogative exists and survives the leak, then and only then does one really arrive at a First Amendment issue: is the exercise of the president's prerogative in the case at hand constrained by the protection offered in the Bill of Rights to speech and to the press?

The analogy of a game of bridge illustrates the priority of the first two questions over the third. If one's analysis ends in a yes answer to each of the first two, one might say on this analogy that the president's hand contains the high card for the Article II suit, for that article constitutes and empowers the executive branch. Only then ought one to consider whether the New York Times has a winning card from outside that suit, a trump card, in its invocation of the First Amendment.[16]

So let us look at Article II. It contains a list of such presidential powers as command of the armed forces, negotiation of treaties, pardon or reprieve of criminal suspects or convicts. There is also a broad enabling clause, Art. II, §1, par. 1—"The Executive Power shall be vested in a President of the United States of America"—which does not parallel language from Article I on legislative power. That is, it does not say that "executive powers herein listed shall be vested." It says simply that the executive power—in the singular—shall be vested. The breadth of this wording allows for such unenumerated powers as may be essential to the efficient use of those powers that are enumerated. The control of intrabranch information is a natural example of this inherent authority.

That textual case is strengthened by an appeal to the controversy over Jay's Treaty, in the days when the founding generation governed the United

States. Late in 1794 Chief Justice John Jay, special envoy for the United States to Britain, concluded negotiations with the ministry of William Pitt. The resulting treaty, which settled outstanding maritime and boundary disputes between the two nations, was immediately unpopular at home, and the House of Representatives demanded that the president provide information on the negotiations. Early in 1795 President George Washington sent the House the following message, which evidences the view of the founding generation on executive confidences: "It is essential to the due administration of the Government that the boundaries fixed by the Constitution between the different departments should be preserved. A just regard to the Constitution and to the duty of my office, under all the circumstances of this case, forbids a compliance with your request."[17] The best answer to the first of the three questions previously listed, then, is yes.

But what is to be said about the specific sort of control that President Nixon tried to assert in the Pentagon Papers case? It was the control of information after it had passed into the hands of persons not themselves public authorities, persons such as (but not uniquely) newspaper editors. My own view is that the Washington and Jay precedent does not stretch that far. The president's prerogative ends with the occurrence of a leak, subject only to his pursuit of enforcement of the law against the persons responsible. Anything more seems an unconscionable expansion of the straightforward phrase "executive power." If I am right, it follows that in the case at hand, the plaintiff did not have the high card in the suit it led. Therefore, no question of the defendant's possession of a trump card need arise.

Between the Pentagon Papers case and the great test of executive privilege in the summer of 1974, there were to be two more changes in the composition of the high Court.

PASSING OF TWO GIANTS

On August 16, 1971, Justice John Marshall Harlan entered Bethesda Naval Hospital in great pain. He was soon diagnosed as suffering from spinal cancer.[18] On the twenty-eighth, Justice Black entered a room down the same corridor of the same hospital. As a consequence of the inflammatory condition of his blood vessels, Black sent the president a letter of resignation dated September 17. In accepting that letter, Nixon praised Black's "independence, tenacity, and integrity of mind" and predicted that his "imprint on the Court and our nation will be indelible."[19] On the eighteenth Black suffered a stroke. On the twenty-third Harlan tendered his resignation.[20] Black died on the morning of the twenty-fifth; Harlan died late that December.

By early October, Nixon seemed to have nearly made up his mind to name Senator Robert C. Byrd, a West Virginia Democrat, to one of those vacancies. Byrd would have been a difficult nominee for his fellow senators to oppose, as even Senator George McGovern of South Dakota, who was then a candidate for the Democratic Party's nomination for president, acknowledged.[21]

Within the administration, though, there was opposition. Attorney General Mitchell argued that a West Virginian would not satisfy southern allies who would insist that a native of one of the states of the old Confederacy be appointed to the Court in satisfaction of Nixon's long-standing commitment. There was another problem: Mitchell had given assurances to the American Bar Association (ABA) that the organized bar would have an opportunity to screen any future Supreme Court nominees before a public announcement. He expected that Byrd, a nonlawyer, would encounter trouble in the screening committee.[22] In due course Mitchell's warnings prevailed, and talk of Byrd stilled.

The next front-runner in the internal councils of the administration was Herschel Friday, an experienced trial attorney with a practice in Little Rock, Arkansas. Since Friday counseled the Little Rock School Board in its opposition to desegregation in the course of the litigation that led to Faubus's infamous defiance, his nomination would have touched off another vigorous confirmation contretemps.[23] To buffer that expected obstacle, Nixon planned to link the nomination of Friday to a historic first—the nomination of a woman to the Supreme Court. The name of Mildred Lillie, judge of the District Court of Appeals of Los Angeles, would go forth with Friday's.[24] But on Monday, October 18, newspapers around the country carried stories of the research of Harvard Law School Professor Laurence H. Tribe, then an enfant terrible aged twenty-nine. Tribe alleged that Judge Lillie's decisions had been overturned with "extraordinary frequency" by the California Supreme Court. Some people might see that as a distinction. Tribe did not.

Neither did the ABA screening committee, which met on the twentieth to discuss the qualifications of Friday and Lillie. Shortly after 5 P.M., the chairman of the committee, Lawrence Walsh, later to acquire fame as the prosecutor of Oliver North, called Attorney General Mitchell to tell him that the vote was for a "not qualified" rating of both.

On the following day, John Mitchell informed the ABA that the administration was bringing to an end its practice of providing nominee names to that association in advance of their public announcement. But because the story of the not-qualified ratings appeared at once in the Washington Post,[25] the names of Friday and Lillie, damaged goods, dropped out of sight.[26]

At 7:30 on the evening of October 23, the White House announced the nomination of Lewis Powell of Richmond, Virginia, a former ABA president, and William Rehnquist of Phoenix, Arizona, a political protégé of Senator Barry Goldwater.[27] In his explanation of these nominations Nixon struck again the law-and-order theme from his campaign: "I believe the peace forces must not be denied the legal tools they need to protect the innocent from criminal elements."[28] The members of the ABA's screening committee heard this announcement as it aired or read it in their morning papers and felt the abolition of their earlier role as something of a sting. But, unasked, they proceeded to review the qualifications of Powell and Rehnquist.

On November 3, the Senate Judiciary Committee opened its hearings on the two nominees. Lawrence Walsh testified that the ABA found Rehnquist qualified, Powell highly qualified.[29] Rehnquist was bound to be the more controversial figure. He studied political science at Stanford and law at Harvard. He practiced law in Phoenix for years until his appointment to head the office of Legal Counsel in 1969, where he worked closely with Attorney General Mitchell. In that capacity Rehnquist wrote a memorandum that approved of the legality of a controversial wiretapping program, a program that many scholars believed then, and believe now, ran afoul of the constitutional prohibition on unreasonable searches and seizures.[30] The Judiciary Committee questioned him on that memo. Rehnquist defended his conclusions. The committee also asked him about the mass arrests of antiwar protestors in Washington, D.C., on May 1, 1971. Rehnquist replied that he could find no fault with any of the actions of the authorities that day, except that they should have had more adequate detention facilities, so that the persons under arrest might not have been so crowded.

On November 10, the committee voted to confirm both nominations. The vote on Powell was sixteen to none. Many senators were as happy to find a well-qualified southern jurist for whom they could vote as President Nixon was to have sent them one. But Rehnquist, who, despite Phoenix's southern-latitude relation to Richmond, is a westerner in the topography of American politics, not a southerner, benefited from no such wave of relief, and the committee's vote in his case was twelve to four.

Still, the two names went to the full Senate together, and on December 6, that body voted to confirm Powell eighty-nine to one. Senator Fred Harris of Oklahoma cast that lone negative vote.[31] In the full Senate, as on the committee, Rehnquist had the turbulent passage. On December 10, the Senate also confirmed his nomination, sixty-eight to twenty-six. Thirty Democrats voted to confirm; only three Republicans voted against—Edward Brooke, Jacob Javits, Clifford Case.

Widespread journalistic opinion now described the Supreme Court as split among three blocs. There were the three liberals: Douglas, Brennan, Marshall. Next were the four Nixon appointees, all considered men of the Right: Burger, Blackmun, Powell, Rehnquist. Then there were the moderates, or "swing votes": Stewart and White.

By election day, 1972, the New Deal coalition was dead, the long story of its dissolution complete. The "Wallace Democrats" of 1968 did not return home; their votes entered Republican columns in their respective states. But what would replace that deceased coalition? How would America be governed in its absence? The realignment (a word made familiar in political science departments around the country by the works of Walter Dean Burnham[32]) created a split. The United States thereafter witnessed a solid "lock" on the office of the chief executive by the Republican Party. President Jimmy Carter's one term was a brief exception to this rule. President Clinton's first (?) term may represent the end of the operation of this rule or just another brief exception. Meanwhile, the Democratic Party continued, up until November 1994, to dominate the legislative apparatus.

I neither praise nor lament the split (or "gridlock") except to say that there is no reason to believe that any patchup job on the old Democratic coalition would have governed the country more ably over those twenty years than it was governed throughout the enforced cohabitation of parties.

PRIVILEGED EVIDENCE OF A CRIME?

The unraveling of the scandals lumped together under the label "Watergate," through the years 1973–74, arose out of abuses of power by the Nixon administration. The first stage of the affair occurred during the spring and summer of 1972 and consisted of various "dirty tricks" or "plumbing operations." The second stage, later in the campaign and into 1973, consisted of ham-handed efforts to hinder investigation and prosecution of the tricksters and plumbers.

There is little consensus on the particulars that lie behind those general assertions, only an endless controversy and a gargantuan bibliography.[33] One might wish to avoid engaging in the one or reading much of the other, but there are compelling reasons for some discussion, not the least of which is that Watergate marked the first appearance of Robert Bork, solicitor general in 1973, into public attention.

Further, without Watergate there would be no such decision as U.S. v. Nixon.[34] In what follows, I concern myself with neither of the two phases of the abuse of power previously distinguished but chronicle the unraveling of an administration, the unsuccessful cover-up of the cover-up.

In the spring of 1973 Richard Kleindienst, John Mitchell's successor as attorney general, resigned. Kleindienst was implicated in the spreading scandal and eventually pleaded guilty to a misdemeanor. Nixon appointed Elliot Richardson, a lifelong civil servant, in his stead. Richardson promised the Senate that he would appoint a special prosecutor and would defend the independence of that office. Once confirmed, Richardson chose Harvard law professor Archibald Cox for this post.

In August Cox sought to subpoena tapes made in the White House and crucial to his investigation. Nixon refused the subpoena on the ground of executive privilege. On August 29, district court judge John Sirica issued an order commanding the president to obey Cox's subpoena. Nixon petitioned the court of appeals to correct Sirica's alleged error of law. On October 12 that court, by a vote of five to two, upheld Sirica and Cox.

Its per curiam opinion (not credited to any individual judge, hence "by the court") relied on the authority of U.S. v. Burr.[35] In 1806 Aaron Burr was arrested for treason. In the trial that followed, Burr's counsel sought to obtain letters addressed to the president from one of Burr's coconspirators. Jefferson resisted this subpoena. Chief Justice Marshall ruled that a subpoena may be directed to the president in order to acquire papers pertinent to a criminal defense.[36] The appeals court, in 1974, thought it an appropriate extension of that principle to uphold a subpoena directed to the president in order to acquire tapes pertinent to a criminal prosecution. Judge MacKinnon dissented and argued that the two cases were distinct: upholding a defendant's subpoena may be essential to that defendant's right to a fair trial; upholding a prosecution's subpoena serves no such constitutional principle.[37]

Judge Wilkey, the same judge whose opinion in the SST case gave an unusually incisive explanation of the tripartite evidentiary privilege relied upon by the appellants in U.S. v. Sirica, also wrote a dissent. But the reasoning of Wilkey's dissent was oddly weak. He relied upon a precedent that he had not even mentioned in his 1970 concurrence, U.S. v. Reynolds (1953).[38] In Reynolds the secretary of the air force refused to provide information on the design of an aircraft to a private litigant in a lawsuit arising from an aviation accident. The Supreme Court upheld that refusal on the basis of the privilege of the executive to keep military secrets.

But the executive privilege that derives from the need for candid policy discussions within any one of the three branches is very different from the national security interest in the secrecy of airplane design. The latter, founded upon the president's explicit authority as commander in chief, is only a distraction in cases such as Watergate, where the pertinent authority is that implicit in the vesting of "the executive power." Wilkey's change of ground undermined the credibility that a firm and broad restatement of executive privilege on his original grounds might have had in the events to follow.

Soon after Nixon heard of the court of appeals's per curiam decision, he ordered Attorney General Elliot Richardson to fire Archibald Cox. Richardson refused. Nixon fired Richardson and ordered the second in command at the Justice Department, Deputy Attorney General Ruckleshaus, to fire Cox. Ruckleshaus also refused. Nixon fired him. The third in line at that department, and thus the new acting attorney general was Solicitor General Robert Bork. Bork did consent to fire Cox, which brought this

"Saturday Night Massacre" to an end. The uproar that followed brought Nixon a good deal closer to impeachment than he had stood at the end of the business day Friday. Bork hired former ABA president Leon Jaworski to continue Cox's work and prepared a regulation, on his own authority as acting department head, that formalized Jaworski's independence.

On October 24 Peter Rodino announced an impeachment inquiry. Nixon soon faced subpoenas from the House, in addition to those he already faced from the Cox-Jaworski office within his own branch of government. On October 30 he released several of the recordings under demand—not all.

On March 1, 1974, a grand jury acing on evidence presented by Special Prosecutor Jaworksi indicted seven former White House officials for conspiracy to obstruct justice. The same grand jury named Nixon an "unindicted coconspirator." On April 18, Jaworski issued a subpoena for additional recordings pursuant to these indictments. On May 1, the president's counsel, James St. Clair, in the district court before Judge John Sirica, moved to quash this subpoena, again on the ground of executive privilege. Sirica denied St. Clair's motion and ordered that the tapes be delivered to the court for in camera (in chambers) inspection. The judge intended to direct the preparation of a transcript that the parties could then introduce in any further proceeding in lieu of the unedited tapes.[39] Both sides appealed this ruling.

In order to expedite their appeal, the litigants decided to consolidate this dispute with the pending appeal of the circuit court's decision in Nixon v. Sirica. The Supreme Court heard arguments on July 8. Such is the procedural history of the litigation that became known as U.S. v. Nixon.

Before the Supreme Court, St. Clair argued that this was an intrabranch dispute (Nixon was Jaworski's superior) and thus it was "not subject to judicial resolution."[40] Chief Justice Burger's opinion for the Court rejected that argument, reasoning that the acting attorney general's regulation assuring Jaworski his independence was the law of the land until officially revoked, as it had never been; "Indeed, the United States as a sovereign composed of the three branches is bound to respect and to enforce it."[41] With that regulation as legal foundation, the special prosecutor had raised precisely "the kind of controversy courts traditionally resolve."[42]

St. Clair also made a broad argument, indeed, one absolute in its implications, "that the separation of powers doctrine precludes judicial review of a president's claim of privilege."[43] The Court found the unqualified preclusion of _any_ review implausible. It responded that the confidentiality of executive communications, although important, is subject to balancing when "a confrontation with other values arises." Sirica's solution to this confrontation, an in camera inspection with "all the protection that a district court will be obliged to provide," struck the eight participating justices as a judiciously balanced accommodation of the interests invoked on each side.[44]

St. Clair's remaining claim, though, was that even if executive privilege is not absolute, it is at least presumptive. The tapes are presumed privileged on the president's authority. The burden of rebutting that presumption must rest on the prosecutor. Burger, for the Court, accepted, at least _arguendo_, this placement of the burden. But Burger found that the presumption of privilege had been rebutted by Jaworski's successful showing that the material requested was relevant to the just resolution of a criminal proceeding.[45]

On that ground, then, the Supreme Court upheld Sirica's original order. President Nixon, in turning over the contested materials, confessed that one of the tapes would show that he tried to steer the Federal Bureau of Investigation (FBI) away from an investigation of the burglary at the Watergate Apartments. This was the "smoking gun" that led almost immediately to the erosion of Nixon's support in the House, which was scheduled to take a vote shortly on three articles of impeachment drafted by the Judiciary Committee. Nixon resigned, August 8, 1974, effective at noon the following day.

What jinxed St. Clair's case was his insistence on the _absolute_ character of that privilege. The justices felt compelled to prove that the United States is not a Filmer-like monarchy,[46] that _none_ of the privileges or powers of our presidents are absolutes. Of course, they were right in their distrust of the unlimited. The president and his counsel should have acknowledged bounds on the operation of the principle they tried to assert, and they would have been well advised to do so without phrasing that acknowledgment in the slippery language of a rebuttable presumption.

St. Clair might have admitted that the only system of law that can accommodate an absolute would be one in which that absolute is the only principle, that is, "do what the chicken entrails say!" In any system with many principles, they will of necessity jostle and so delimit one another.

St. Clair might then have set about ascertaining the limits of the principle of the confidentiality of intrabranch communications. He might have acknowledged the propriety of the Court's holding in the Pentagon Papers case, to the effect that confidentiality ceases with the first leak—as soon, that is, as the communications are no longer intrabranch.

But in this instant case, I imagine St. Clair continued, there has been no leak. Indeed, this would seem to be the _core_ case of intrabranch information. The tapes sought by subpoena at issue were made entirely at the personal discretion of the president, were for his own reference, and in every case contained conversations between the president himself and his immediate subordinates. Even the location of the taping confirms its privileged character. These talks took place in the Oval Office, which is more akin (to draw an analogy between the executive and the judicial branch) to a judge's private chambers than to an open courtroom.

Counsel might have concluded with a flourish, "If there is to be any principle of intrabranch confidentiality, however qualified it must be in other applications, it must apply here."

I make no claim that such an argument would have prevailed. It would have required St. Clair to persuade the Court that he understood the Pentagon Papers case better than did any of the nine justices who wrote opinions on it, seven of whom sat before him during the new case. But this argument does seem to me cogent, and its success in preserving the Nixon presidency could hardly have been less than that achieved by the absolutist argument actually employed.

In a sense one can say what almost everyone except a few die-hard Nixonians do say, that this president lost his office as a consequence of his overreaching ambition. But the overreach that counted most in the end was not that of the campaign year 1972 nor that of the cover-up of 1973. It was the overreach of the litigation of 1974.

NOTES

1. 5 U.S.C. §552(a)(3).
2. Soucie v. David, 448 F.2d 1067 (1971).
3. 448 F.2d, 1018–1081.
4. 5 U.S.C. §552.
5. "It puts the matter in a different focus to know that originally Congressman Henry S. Reuss had sought to obtain this Report over a period of months" (448 F.2d at 1081).
6. H. E. Salisbury, Without Fear or Favor (New York, 1980), 311–343.
7. New York Times v. United States, 403 U.S. 713 (1971).
8. Id. at 724.
9. Id. at 759.
10. Id. at 730, 740.
11. Id. at 727.
12. Id. at 752.
13. Id. at 714, 717.
14. Id. at 720.
15. Id. at 748, 751, n. 2.
16. R. M. Dworkin, Taking Rights Seriously (Cambridge, MA, 1977), xi.
17. J. Richardson, Messages and Papers of the Presidents (New York, 1896), I, 186.
18. "Now the Nixon Court and What It Means," Time, Vol. 19, No. 14, p. 15 (October 4, 1971).
19. Dunne at 434.
20. Time, supra, at 16.
21. S. Ambrose, Nixon: The Triumph of a Politician, 1962–1972 (New York, 1989), 469.
22. Id.
23. Kohlmeier, 229–230.

24. Id., 230–237.

25. Id. 239.

26. Id. 240.

27. Public Papers of the Presidents: Richard Nixon—1971, No. 337, "Address to the Nation Announcing Intention to Nominate Lewis F. Powell, Jr., and William H. Rehnquist to be Associate Justices of the Supreme Court of the United States" October 21, 1971, at 1053.

28. Id. at 1055.

29. U.S. Congress, Senate, Committee on the Judiciary, Nominations of William H. Rehnquist and Lewis F. Powell, Jr.,: Hearings, 92d Cong., 1st Sess., November 3–10, 1971.

30. Amsterdam, "Perspectives on the Fourth Amendment," 58 Minn. L. Rev. 349 (1974). Professor Anthony Amsterdam suggests, rather sardonically, that the government might announce "half-hourly through television . . . that we were all forthwith being placed under comprehensive electronic surveillance." According to one reading of post-Katz Fourth Amendment law, he continues, such broadcasts would constitutionalize any surveillance of anyone, by abolishing the subjective "expectation of privacy" (Id. 384).

31. Kohlmeier, 246.

32. W. D. Burnham, Critical Elections and the Mainsprings of American Politics (New York, 1970).

33. Still essential, after all these years, is C. Bernstein & R. Woodward, All the President's Men (New York, 1974) and The Final Days (New York, 1976). Another contemporary journalistic account is that of J. Breslin, How the Good Guys Finally Won (New York, 1975).

For a more recent, more scholarly account one might turn to L. Colodny and R. Gettlin, Silent Coup (New York, 1991); S. Kutlet, The Wars of Watergate (New York, 1990); or J. Hougan, Secret Agenda (New York, 1984).

The best of the many tellings by participants of the events following that infamous break-in is from J. Sirica, To Set the Record Straight (New York, 1979).

R. Berger has written two very polemical discussions of the legal issues involved: Executive Privilege (Cambridge, MA, 1974) and Impeachment (Cambridge, MA, 1973). Raoul Berger believes that the Founders intended to create a government of legislative supremacy, the executive and judicial branches possessing only such functions as Congress may decide to award them. From this premise, Berger concludes in these two books that Nixon possessed no such executive privilege as he claimed and that Congress would have been justified in impeaching him simply for making that erroneous claim.

That is an extreme argument and one at odds with the views of Publius, who feared the legislature as the most dangerous branch, the breeding ground of factionalism.

34. 418 U.S. 683 (1974).

35. U.S. v. Burr, 25 Fed. Case 30, 34–35 (D. Va., 1806). The decision has acquired authority beyond that usually accorded to a trial court ruling, because Chief Justice Marshall, riding circuit, presided.

36. Ex Parte Bollamn and Ex Parte Swartwout, 4 Cranch 75 (1807); Appendix, "Wilkinson's First Affidavit," 4 Cranch 455.

37. Nixon v. Sirica, 487 F.2d 700 (2d Cir. 1973).

38. 345 U.S. 1.

39. J. Sirica, To Set the Record Straight, 121–123.

40. U.S. v. Nixon, 418 U.S. 683 at 692.

41. Id. at 696.

42. Id.

43. Id. at 703.

44. Id. at 706.

45. Id. at 707–14.

46. When John Locke wrote his classic <u>Two</u> <u>Treatises</u> <u>on</u> <u>Government</u> (1690), it was Sir Robert Filmer's work, <u>Patriarcha</u>, that Locke employed for his polemical target. In that book Filmer presented the theory of the divine right of kings and of the celestial character of the Stuart family in particular, in very uncompromising terms. But Nixon's conception of executive privilege, if taken seriously, claimed nothing less for himself than Filmer claimed for the patriarch he favored, Cox, "Executive Privilege," 122 <u>U.</u> <u>Pa.</u> <u>L.</u> <u>Rev.</u> 1383, 1389 [1974].

7

The Meaning of the Burger Court

In 1973, the Supreme Court decided in <u>Roe</u> <u>v.</u> <u>Wade</u> that most state restrictions upon abortions are unconstitutional in that they violate a right to privacy unenumerated, but implicit, in the Bill of Rights. In 1975, President Ford appointed John Paul Stevens to the Supreme Court. The eleven years that followed, until the retirement of Chief Justice Burger, represent in many respects a halt in the declines both of the Supreme Court's exercise of its constitutional role and of the Senate's exercise of this advice and consent responsibility.

On first reading the due process clause seems simple. No state shall "deprive any person of life, liberty, or property, without due process of law." Only after rereadings and some efforts at application do complications appear. Is due process required only when a state applies a penalty to some individual (death, imprisonment, or a fine), and does the clause only ensure that the process through which such a penalty is assessed is fair? Or is due process also a limit upon state enactment of policies that have the effect of depriving the individual of some right? For example, does this clause protect the owner of a piece of property who is deprived of its use and enjoyment by an arbitrary statutory "wetlands" designation? In order that a distinction may be made between these two issues, lawyers and constitutional scholars call the former "procedural due process" and the latter "substantive due process."

Many scholars believe that all claims of substantive due process are inappropriate and observe that the label is an oxymoron, just as "procedural due process" is redundant. But the sound of a phrase should not require a prejudgment about the thing that phrase is meant to describe. Due process is a very easily circumvented barrier unless it has a substantive component. Should an individual defeat the state's attempt to take away his property as punishment and find that the state is free to take the same property, or more, just as arbitrarily, even vindictively, under the label "policy" or "tax"? Such an absurdity, naturally enough, cannot long survive as law. In our constitutional history, substantive due process is always ushered out the front door and always sneaks back in through the servants' entrance. This has happened often enough to encourage the conclusion that substantive due process is a permanent member of the household and that the charade of eviction ought to cease.

By what standards, then, may the substantive fairness of a policy be determined? At least since <u>Griswold</u> <u>v.</u> <u>Connecticut</u> (1965),[1] part of the answer has been that the level of review depends upon the nature of the right allegedly infringed by the policy under challenge. Certain interests are more "fundamental" than others. Neither as a "liberty" nor as a "property" interest, for example, is the profitable use of land to which one holds title considered a fundamental right. The due process review of a state law restricting one's use of that land, even destroying its profitability, is minimal.* The state need only point to some plausible reason for its action. On the other hand, one's freedom to procreate or to use birth control devices in avoidance of procreation is deemed fundamental, and due process review of a state law restricting that interest is strict, analogous to the high level of scrutiny given under the equal protection clause to statutes that distinguish among persons on the basis of race or national origin.

Five years after the publication of <u>Griswold</u> a plaintiff known as "Jane Roe" brought suit in a federal district court to have the Texas antiabortion statute declared unconstitutional and the state attorney, Henry Wade, enjoined from any action in its enforcement. The district court granted the declaratory, but not the injunctive, relief requested. Both sides appealed. The case was first argued before the Supreme Court in December 1971 and reargued in October of the following year.[2] By the time the Court issued its opinion, in January 1973, <u>Roe</u> had acquired a companion case, <u>Doe</u> <u>v.</u> <u>Bolton</u>, a challenge to the antiabortion statute of Georgia.[3]

The plaintiffs offered three theories from which the Court was invited to choose in striking such state laws:

1. That they violate liberty rights as embodied in the due process clause of the Fourteenth Amendment.
2. That they violate the zone of privacy protected by penumbras of the specific clauses of the Bill of Rights, which penumbras, as incorporated into the Fourteenth Amendment, apply to the states.

---

* Recent renewed discussion of the "takings" clause of the Fifth Amendment has been instigated by the desire to restore judicial protection to property values and commercial liberty. The distinction between "takings" analysis, on one hand, and an economic application of substantive due process, on the other, is not crucial to the above discussion. But see Chapter 11.

3. That they violate the rights reserved to the people by the Ninth Amendment.[4]

In response to this doctrinal smorgasbord, the crucial passage in Blackmun's opinion for the Court seems to give the answer: "all of the above." Justice Stewart wrote a brief concurrence, in which he opted for the first of the plaintiff's theories and rejected Roe's attempts to explore the mysterious territory of the Ninth Amendment.[5]

Rehnquist dissented. He argued that the only proper substantive due process scrutiny is minimal scrutiny, and that here, since, as Blackmun's opinion concedes, some legitimate state interests are served by a prohibition on abortion, such a law survives such scrutiny. The strict examination of Blackmun's opinion, the "conscious weighing of competing factors" for and against the law, is "far more appropriate to a legislative judgment than to a judicial one."[6]

Justice Douglas, concurring in Doe, proved more comfortable than any of his brethren with the plaintiff's second theory, the emanation of penumbra from the Bill of Rights.[7] This is not surprising, since that theory was inspired by his own Griswold opinion.

Justice Byron White, dissenting in Doe, adopted an indignant tone absent from the Rehnquist dissent in Roe: "As an example of raw judicial power, the Court perhaps has authority to do what it does today; but in my view its judgment is an improvident and extravagant exercise of the power of judicial review that the Constitution extends to this Court."[8] This is where the law on abortion stood when Nixon's resignation made Gerald Ford president of the United States.

WHO IS JOHN PAUL STEVENS?

Early in November 1975, Ronald Reagan, former governor of California, telephoned Gerald Ford to inform the president that he, Reagan, was about to announce his candidacy for the Republican nomination for president. On November 12, Justice Douglas retired. Ford was gracious, as presidents invariably are at such moments, and wrote Douglas to express "great gratitude for your more than thirty-six years as a member of the Supreme Court. Your distinguished years of service are unequalled."

For a replacement, Ford considered Carla Hills. Hills is a lifelong public servant and was then secretary of housing and urban development (HUD). But Ford, thinking both of his rival within the party and of the crowded field of Democratic candidates for president, sought a nominee who would not become an issue in the campaign. Whatever benefit Ford might have obtained from naming the first woman justice, he feared he would lose from charges of cronyism in naming Hills, a member of his own administration. In December Ford announced the nomination of John Paul Stevens, a fifty-five-year-old federal judge of the Seventh Circuit Court of Appeals, which sits in Chicago, and encompasses Illinois, Indiana, and Wisconsin.

Stevens, who graduated first in his class at Northwestern Law School in 1947, clerked for Supreme Court justice Wiley Rutledge through the following term. Stevens was already at this time a Republican, but Justice Rutledge was a Democrat, and a Roosevelt appointee and, in the balance-model theorizing of his day, was always counted as a member of the "liberal wing" of the Court. This one fact goes far to establish the genuinely nonpartisan character of authentic legal reasoning, as does the further fact that Stevens is, to this day, profuse in Rutledge's praise.[9]

The Senate Committee on the Judiciary opened hearings on Stevens's confirmation as associate justice on December 8, 1975, and closed them on the following day. On the tenth the full Senate voted, ninety-eight in favor, none opposed. The least favorable evaluation of the nominee that one can find among the press clippings of the time came from Garry Wills, to the effect that President Ford, in making only a good appointment, had lost an opportunity to make a great one. Wills did not suggest names.

Stevens quickly became the intellectual leader of the Burger Court, and his leadership improved the quality of the decisions of that Court, both statutory and constitutional.[10] Indeed, Stevens is committed to a jurisprudence akin to what I have described in Chapter 5 as "minimal formalism." His respect for stare decisis is genuine, as are his belief that rules established by precedent are nonetheless subject to improvement and correction; and his eagerness to see and draw such distinctions as real factual differences warrant.

Precisely because the virtues of minimal formalism are not flashy, Stevens has long suffered from underestimation. Stevens, more than any other justice, sought to turn the Burger Court into a formalist Court, and in some respects he succeeded. The minimum wage serves as one example of Stevens's influence to the good and leads me into a discussion of the "right to privacy," first, in criminal trials as a ground for the application of the exclusionary rule; and next, as a broad principle of substantive due process.

In Stevens's first term on the Court he and his colleagues decided National League of Cities v. Usery.[11] This decision struck at Congress's efforts to extend the Fair Labor Standards Act and impose the federal minimum wage on state and local governments. The majority in Usery, by Rehnquist, reasoned not from due process but from state autonomy. A state's power to determine the wages of its own employees is an "undoubted attribute of state sovereignty." Stevens doubted the undoubted attribute, and his dissent repays study.

He acknowledges the imprudence of a minimum wage, for "the proposition that regulation of the minimum price of a commodity—even labor—will increase the quantity consumed is not one that I can readily understand."[12] But he reminds his brethren that the issue before the Court is not wisdom but power. If the power of Congress is limited, there must be a constitutional principle that explains why the limit is where it is. Can Congress prohibit the governor's limousine from traveling at more than fifty-five miles an hour? Can it require that a state-employed janitor observe safety regulations identical with those observed by the private-sector janitor working down the street? Since Stevens did not imagine that the Usery majority's members would answer no to such questions, he did not believe that they had stated a rule that could survive many efforts at application.

In 1983 the issue of state autonomy in personnel policy arose again, this time over the applicability of the Age Discrimination Employment Act to the mandatory retirement ages decreed by the state of Wyoming for its servants.[13] The Equal Employment Opportunity Commssion (EEOC), brought an age discrimination lawsuit against the state. The district court, in reliance upon Usery, dismissed that suit. The Supreme Court reversed that dismissal. In upholding EEOC authority, the Court implicitly repudiated Usery, but Brennan, writing for the majority, refused to make that repudiation explicit. He wrote that the two cases are distinct, because the "tangible consequential effect" of the application of federal law to state wage scales is a much greater threat to the autonomous hiring practices of those states than is the ban on mandatory retirement involved here.

That attempted distinction does not wash. It is a difference of degree only, not a matter of principle, and, as John Paul Stevens noted in concurrence, one does not advance the principle of stare decisis when one follows an earlier decision in form that one cannot follow in substance. A simple retraction of error is more respectful of the structure of precedent and doctrine than this, especially if the error is itself so recent that little has been built upon it, other than Brennan's ad hoc distinction.[14]

Stevens had his way. Usery was overturned explicitly, just one term later, in Garcia v. San Antonio.[15] There were now five votes for that result, because Justice Blackmun had changed his mind in the year since Wyoming. Appropriately, then, Blackmun wrote the opinion for the new majority. His reasoning echoed the two earlier Stevens opinions. Labor law, as it pertains to such matters as wage floors and antidiscrimination policy, must be all of one piece, from coast to coast and throughout both private and public employments, given the unitary nature of the nation's labor markets. Congress has supreme authority to create this unitary system of rules.

One might hope that Congress will someday use its preemptive authority to enact a laissez-faire labor policy. One might even hope that the Supreme Court will someday see fit to push Congress in that direction. But if that ever comes to pass, the handhold for the push will be found in the due process clauses of the Fifth and Fourteenth Amendments, not in the Tenth Amendment's reservation of sovereignty to the states. In helping to clear away the Usery debris, Stevens performed a service for which the friends both of free markets and of an effective judiciary must be grateful.

Stevens also took the lead in the Burger Court's slow movement toward the restoration of formalism in the interpretation of the Fourth Amendment's "search and seizure" clause. The key formalist precedent in this field is Olmstead v. United States.[16] In that decision, in 1928, the Supreme Court rejected Roy Olmstead's appeal from his conviction for a violation of the Volstead Act. At trial the prosecution had introduced tape recordings of the defendant's private telephone conversations. Officers of the United States had made a wiretap on the telephone wire in the street near the defendant's home. Olmstead asked that the Court find that this wiretap violated the Fourth Amendment's ban on compulsory self-incrimination.

Chief Justice William Howard Taft wrote for the majority. The crucial point, for him, was that there had been no trespass. The tap was not on the phone within the defendant's residence but on the wire outside and so in the public domain.

Holmes and Brandeis, known in that era as "the great dissenters," dissented. Brandeis's dissent, the more thorough of the two, introduced the phrase "right of privacy" into the language on constitutional law:

> The makers of our Constitution undertook to secure conditions favorable to the pursuit of happiness. They recognized the significance of man's spiritual nature, of his feelings and of his intellect. They knew that only a part of the pain, pleasure and satisfactions of life are to be found in material things. They sought to protect Americans in their beliefs, their thoughts, their emotions and their sensations. They conferred, as against the Government, the right to be let alone—the most comprehensive of rights and the right most valued by civilized men. To protect that right, every unjustifiable intrusion by the government upon the privacy of the individual, whatever the means employed, must be deemed a violation of the Fourth Amendment. And the use, as evidence in a criminal proceeding, of facts ascertained by such intrusion must be deemed a violation of the Fifth.[17]

As always, Brandeis's prose is memorable and lofty. As is often the case, though, the distinctions that he employs are slippery and impractical. Where does "man's spiritual nature" leave off and the "satisfactions of . . . material things" begin? How, except by reference to the particular language of the Bill of Rights, can one decide which governmental intrusions upon privacy are "justifiable" and which are not? Finally, when Brandeis asserts that privacy is the right most prized by "civilized men," is he placing his colleagues in the majority into some other, uncivilized category?

Chief Justice Taft, in his plodding, and mundane manner, announced a rule of law that would have developed into a coherent body of search and seizure decisions, capable of adequate flexibility in response to technological change. For in the natural meaning of the English-language terms involved, a search does not take place unless there is a physical intrusion upon a private enclosure, and a seizure does not take place unless there is an equally physical taking and carrying away of some object.

It was not technological change that destroyed Taft's rule but the arrival of realism. Olmstead was overturned by the Warren Court in 1967.[18] What has replaced it? That is hard to say. Ever since 1967 the courts have struggled to define what they call the "reasonable expectation of privacy" that a suspect possesses and to describe conditions in which these expectations have been violated. The violation of a reasonable expectation is now held to constitute a search or seizure. In the course of the struggle to decide cases under this new dispensation, the law of the Fourth Amendment has become a maze wherein every rule has twelve exceptions, and each exception has twenty-four qualifications. This maze is inescapable, since the test that has replaced Olmstead is viciously circular. What one's reasonable expectations are, in any place, depends largely upon what one knows of the law in the jurisdiction where one lives. The justices and lower court judges trying to follow their authority have struggled to make the law follow the public expectations, which, in turn, follow from what the public knows or thinks it knows about the law. That is not a situation conducive to clarity.

Stevens took the lead on the Burger Court in the effort to extricate the law from this mess and to return it to something akin to Olmstead. His opinion for the Court in U.S. v. Ross, a 1982 automobile stop-and-search decision, demonstrates a scholarly mind hard at work on this problem.[19]

In lieu of a detailed study of the pertinent decisions, the point to retain is that in the application of the exclusionary rule to the Fourth Amendment, the Warren Court abandoned formalism for realism, and subsequent justices, Stevens prominent among them, have sought to undo that work.

On the other hand, in the application of the exclusionary rule to the Fifth Amendment's ban on compulsory self-incrimination, the reverse is true. The Warren Court, in Mallory and Miranda and beyond, developed a line of precedent in commendably formalist fashion, resulting in a coherent and predictable set of rules; and subsequent critics have used the argumentative style of realists in their efforts to undo that work. Here again one finds Stevens on the formalist side to good effect.[20]

The law of criminal procedure illustrates the independence of the formalist conception of law from political or partisan labels. It is neither "liberal" to defend Miranda on the preceding grounds nor "conservative" to defend Olmstead for the same reason.

These cases, on state employees and criminal procedure, demonstrate the strengths of Stevens's jurisprudence. What follows, however, qualifies the high opinion I have expressed. Stevens is, to put it bluntly, confused in some of the particular applications he has made of the formalist principles that he and I share. His confusion contributed to the failure, in the end, of the

Supreme Court's retrograde movement in the Burger years; it brought an end to the halt in the decline of the Court.

In what follows, we find that Stevens has adopted the two-tier theory of due process of Stewart's concurrence in Roe. On the other hand, he emphatically rejects the two-tier theory of equal protection. When we have evaluated these two sets of "tiers" for ourselves, we shall have a good view of the limits on Stevens's contribution to the law of the land; for his positions on these two clauses are mutually inconsistent and severally untenable.

THE BURGER COURT AND PRIVACY

In November 1976, James Earl Carter was elected president. Since his opponent was closely associated with Richard Nixon in the public mind, and since Nixon had left office just days ahead of removal, what was most striking about the result of this campaign was that it was close—Gerald Ford won twenty-seven states, and some of the more populous (California, Illinois, his home state of Michigan) were among them. In retrospect, Carter's one term in office was an interregnum, squarely within, and an exception to, a period of Republican dominance of presidential politics. Carter had no opportunity to make an appointment to the Supreme Court. The Burger period rolled on.

After Potter Stewart's retirement in 1981, Justice Stevens became the Court's foremost defender of the "substantive due process" justification for the decision in Roe v. Wade. In order to illustrate his tenacity in that role, jump three years into the Rehnquist period and treat the 1989 decision Webster v. Reproductive Health Services.[21]

In Webster the Court was faced with a challenge to a Missouri statute that regulated, but did not prohibit, abortion. The most restrictive of the regulations at issue required the operating physician to determine the viability of a fetus before performing an abortion on any woman more than twenty weeks' pregnant. In upholding this twenty-week rule the Court implicitly overturned at least one aspect of Roe. Blackmun's Roe opinion had divided the balance of interests into three trimester periods and had indicated that state laws would have to incorporate the same division into any permissible scheme of abortion regulation. The twenty-week rule of Webster split pregnancy into two halves, oblivious of the Roe system.

But how much of Roe survived the new holding? The five justices who voted to uphold the challenged regulations split three ways in answering that question. The plurality, or what garners the most votes among the opinions in the majority (Rehnquist writing for himself, White, and Kennedy), announced that in their view: "This case affords no occasion to disturb Roe's holding that a Texas statute which criminalized all non-therapeutic abortions unconstitutionally infringed the right to an abortion derived from the Due Process Clause. Roe is distinguishable on its facts, since Missouri has determined that viability is the point at which its interest in potential human life must be safeguarded."

That language seemed to leave Roe alive, but on an artificial respirator. Scalia would have pulled the plug on any "right to an abortion", which, he said, was "constructed overnight" in 1973 and should be just as summarily abolished.[22] O'Connor thought Roe was still alive and well:

> Unlike the plurality, I do not understand these viability testing requirements to conflict with any of the Court's past decisions concerning state regulation of abortion. Therefore, there is no necessity to accept the State's invitation to reexamine the constitutional validity of Roe v. Wade . . . . Where there is no need to decide a constitutional question, it is a venerable principle of this Court's adjudicatory process not to do so.[23]

The four dissenters also split. Blackmun wrote for himself, Brennan, and Marshall—all of those members of the original Roe majority who were still on the Court. Blackmun's opinion was concerned chiefly to defend the trimester scheme:

> The trimester framework simply defines and limits [the] right to privacy in the abortion context to accommodate, not destroy, a State's legitimate interest in protecting the health of a pregnant woman and in preserving potential human life . . . . Fashioning such accommodations between individual rights and the legitimate interests of government, establishing benchmarks and standards with which to evaluate the competing claims of individuals and government, lies at the very heart of constitutional adjudication.[24]

Stevens wrote for himself. He made two points. On the one hand, he was concerned that certain provisions of the Missouri law, not the viability testing requirement, seemed to enact a particular theology into official status and so violated the First Amendment's prohibition on an establishment of religion. (Into the coils of Church-State argumentation we shall not follow him.) On the other hand, Stevens offered with approval a lengthy quotation from Justice Stewart's concurrence in Roe, taking a frankly substantive view of due process and of the liberty interest it protects.

Beyond its impact upon the transient political debates of its time, what was important about the split in Webster was the trend in jurisprudential theory that it displayed. Four justices, Scalia along with the three in the plurality, believed by 1989 that the only proper standard for judicial review of a law challenged under substantive due process is the minimal standard, the review for mere rationality. That was Rehnquist's argument in dissent in 1973, and it remained his view sixteen years later. One justice, O'Connor, was then in search of an intermediate level of review that would demand more of legislators than that they be rational but that would not demand that they be wise. (See Chapter 12 for a later, 1992, milestone in that justice's search for this level.) The four dissenters in <u>Webster</u> continued to accord strict scrutiny to abortion statutes under some variant of the two-tier system. Justice Stevens understood the clausal basis of that position with greater clarity or was in the habit of stating it with greater vigor than were the other justices of his side of the argument. That is to his credit. But, insofar as Stevens's position on abortion rights accepted and preserved the two-tier view of liberty that derives from Brandeis's <u>Olmstead</u> dissent, it was untenable.

Implicit in the foregoing narrative is my view that there should be no tiers in due process law. No portion of the liberty interest is more fundamental than any other. Since the phrase "right to privacy" has come to stand for this allegedly fundamental and so strictly protected variant of the right to liberty, I have no hesitation in declaring that this "privacy right" is a compound of confusion and caprice. My liberty as a landowner deserves no less protection than does my liberty as a sexually active adult. I do not take off my right to due process when I put on my clothes, nor do I walk away from the Constitution when I walk out of my home into the workaday world.[25] There is only one standard for substantive due process.

That single standard should not be a minimal standard. It is an abdication of the Court's responsibility to reason that the legislators were not lunatics or utterly thoughtless, and that therefore they <u>must</u> <u>have</u> respected the liberties of the individuals coerced by their statutes. No. If individuals are to preserve liberty against the majoritarian pressures that operate within popular assemblies, the standard for substantive due process review must have considerable bite.[26]

<u>Roe</u> can be saved, then, only if its advocates are willing to become across-the-board libertarians, as to business as well as to sex, and are willing to read a large portion of the libertarian platform, as applied to judicial review, into the due process clauses of our Constitution.

I think <u>Roe</u> should be saved, at exactly that cost. What is more important is that if <u>Roe</u> is lost, it will be a casualty of the compounding of confusion and caprice, especially on the part of America's intellectuals of the Left, whose untenable argument has been that only the liberties about which <u>they</u> care count under the Constitution.

To restate: Justice Stevens is a staunch upholder of the two-tier theory of due process, and as such he defends an indefensible position. He worsens that predicament by the contrast between his due process jurisprudence and his equal protection jurisprudence, to which I now turn.

THE NEW EQUAL PROTECTION[27]

In 1971 the Court decided Reed v. Reed, striking an Idaho law that had favored men over women as estate administrators.* The law, reasoned the Court, bore no "fair or substantial relation to the object of the legislation."[28] Presumably the "object" of legislation pertaining to the administration of estates is the orderly execution of the lawful wishes of the deceased. But from where comes this talk of a fair or substantial relation? That seems to require more than a "rational" relation to a legitimate end. It also seems to require less than a necessary relation to a compelling end. With Reed v. Reed, the Court began the creation of an intermediate level of equal protection scrutiny. This was to lead not to the elimination of the other two tiers and the establishment of a unitary test but to a sum of three tiers and to a quarrel, which continues today, over which classifications ought to be examined under which of these three lenses.

One of Stevens's first opportunities to expound his view of sex discrimination arose when the Court heard a challenge to an Oklahoma statute that regulated the sale of one variety of beer (3.2 percent beer): Craig v. Boren.[29] The legislation prohibited the sale of the alcohol at issue to males under twenty-one or to females under eighteen.

Justice Brennan wrote the opinion for the Court. The state had argued that it has a very urgent interest in highway safety and that young intoxicated men are a far greater threat to that safety than are their female counterparts. It follows, thought state's counsel, that the age and sex differential in question is warranted and constitutional. Justice Brennan thought not.

The Court's opinion opens with a clear statement of the intermediate tier: "Gender must serve important governmental objectives and must be substantially related to achievement of those objectives."[30] The equal protection clause may now be represented graphically as follows:

Sample Grouping	Connection of Ends to Grouping	Status of Ends	"Tier"
Burglarhood	rational	legitimate	minimal scrutiny
Sex	substantial	important	intermediate scrutiny
Race	necessary	compelling	strict scrutiny

---

* Many jurists use the label "gender discrimination" for Reed-like cases. Since the discrimination is against people, not words, that is improper. I use "sex discrimination" in what follows.

Reed, Craig, and several similar lawsuits represented the self-assigned workload of the Woman's Law Project of the American Civil Liberties Union (ACLU). Ruth Bader Ginsburg chaired that project throughout the early Burger period. The ACLU and the Court, of course, conceded Oklahoma's point as to the end for which it had classified young men and women differently. Brennan wrote that "the protection of public health and safety represents an important function of state and local governments."[31] But he did not concede that the connection between maleness, on one hand, and proneness to drunk driving, on the other, is substantial: "The principles embodied in the Equal Protection Clause are not to be rendered inapplicable by statistically measured but loose-fitting generalities concerning the drinking tendencies of aggregate groups."[32] The law failed.

Stewart's concurrence called the disparity in the treatment of men and women a "total irrationality" that would be vulnerable even under minimal scrutiny.[33]

Powell's concurrence expressed distaste for the term *middle tier* as a label for the analysis in which the Court was now engaged. Powell thought it enough to say that the lower tier (of two) "takes on a sharper focus when we address a gender-based classification."[34] This distinction between a "higher tier" and a "sharper focus" is one of metaphor, not of result or method.

Stevens's concurrence in Craig is worth quoting at length:

There is only one Equal Protection Clause. It requires every State to govern impartially. It does not direct the courts to apply one standard of review in some cases and a different standard in other cases. Whatever criticism may be levelled at a judicial opinion implying that there are at least three such standards applies with the same force to a double standard.

I am inclined to believe that what has become known as the two-tiered analysis of equal protection claims does not describe a completely logical method of deciding cases, but rather is a method the Court has employed to explain decisions that actually apply a single standard in a reasonably consistent fashion. I also suspect that a careful explanation of the reasons motivating particular decisions may contribute more to an identification of that standard than an attempt to articulate it in all-encompassing terms. It may therefore be appropriate for me to state the principal reasons which persuaded me to join the Court's opinion . . . .

The legislation imposes a restraint on one hundred percent of the males in the class allegedly because about 2% of them have probably violated one or more laws relating to the consumption of alcoholic beverages. It is unlikely that this law will have a significant deterrent effect either on that 2% or on the law-abiding 98%. But even assuming some such slight benefit, it does not seem to me that an insult to all the young men of the state can be justified by visiting the sins of the 2% on the 98%.[35]

Chief Justice Burger's dissent denied that there is either "independent constitutional basis supporting the right asserted" or any principled rationale for "disfavoring the classification adopted."[36]

Justice Rehnquist's dissent defended the two-tier theory but took a narrow view of which classifications merit strict scrutiny.[37] By a process of elimination, then, Rehnquist concluded that the sex and age classification at issue warranted only a minimum rationality standard, and he voted to uphold the law under that test.[38]

I am not especially concerned that my reader should evaluate the rights and wrongs of Oklahoma's liquor laws. I _am_ concerned that he or she understand the weakness of Stevens's position as displayed in the previous lengthy quotation.

That quotation began with the incontestable assertion that there is only one equal protection clause. It is just as true that there is, as applied to the states, only one due process clause. If a restriction upon the "privacy right" warrants strict due process scrutiny, why cannot the use of a suspect classification warrant strict equal protection scrutiny and, by implication, at least two "tiers" in the application of that clause? Stevens's Webster reasoning is plainly at odds with his Craig reasoning.

But forget that inconsistency. Even on its own terms, the Stevens argument is unpersuasive. Apply the principle that there is no difference that does not make a difference.[39] What is the difference between Stevens's reasoning in Craig and Brennan's, for the Court? Each justice voted to overturn the statute at hand. There is no difference in the result. Nor is there any difference in the reasoning most proximate to that result. Brennan referred to Oklahoma's statistical arguments as loose-fitting generalities, and Stevens says much the same. The difference is that Brennan applied a test, which he formulated in general terms involving both ends and means. Stevens refused to endorse that test or to formulate an alternative, because that would require "an attempt to articulate it in all-encompassing terms." That is the difference between Brennan and Stevens.

What difference does it _make_? To a state legislator trying to draft a new liquor law, it makes a very important difference. She can look at Brennan's test and ask herself whether the statute she proposes will pass by that standard. Stevens's decision gives no such guidance. All it says is that the one equal protection clause "requires every state to govern impartially." Impartial as to whom or what?

This question of guidance, of Supreme Court decisions that allow legislators and potential litigants a good chance to predict "what the judge will do in fact," is behind the tiered structure of equal protection law. Because Brennan accepts the tiered structure, he is able to enunciate standards that give guidance. This is true because of the logic inherent in the phrase "equal protection of the laws," whereas it is not true of the phrase "due process of law."

Stevens has the implication of the Constitution's language exactly wrong. Tiers are irrelevant to due process but irreplaceable for equal protection. It is perfectly appropriate that a state should be required to justify its legislation with ever higher burdens of persuasion as the invidiousness of the classifications used in its legislation increases. Perhaps a continuous "sliding scale of invidiousness" would serve the purposes of equal protection better than three discrete tiers can. But the three-tier scheme is easy to formulate and apply. No continuous scale would share that trait. The tiers, then, may be taken as an acceptable approximation of the ideal.

POSTSCRIPT

In June 1988 the Senate rejected President Reagan's nomination of Bernard Siegan to a federal judgeship.[40] Siegan is the author of Economic Liberties and the Constitution (1980), a work on which much of the foregoing has been based. It appears to be the position of the Senate that any scholar who does not support the distinction between fundamental and nonfundamental liberty for purposes of due process analysis or who does not regard economic liberties as nonfundamental is, by virtue of those views, unfit for the federal bench. An objective observer would have to conclude that what began as the voluntary incoherence of the judiciary has become an enforced incoherence.

NOTES

1. 381 U.S. 479.
2. Roe v. Wade, 410 U.S. 113 (1973).
3. 410 U.S. 179 (1973).
4. 410 U.S. at 129.
5. Id. 167. See Caplan, "The History and Meaning of the Ninth Amendment," 69 Va. L. Rev. 223 (1983): "The historical evidence . . . suggests that the ninth amendment is not a cornucopia of undefined federal rights, but rather that it is limited to a specific function, well-understood at the time of its adoption: the maintenance of rights guaranteed by the laws of the states" (227).
6. 410 U.S. at 173.
7. Id. 209.
8. Id. 221.
9. Stevens, "Mr. Justice Rutledge," in Mr. Justice, A. Dunham & P. Kurland, eds. (Chicago, 1956) at 177.
10. R. J. Sickels, John Paul Stevens and the Constitution (University Park, PA, 1988).
11. 426 U.S. 833 (1976).
12. Id. 880.

13. Equal Employment Opportunity Commission v. Wyoming, 460 U.S. 226 (1983).

14. Id. 246.

15. 469 U.S. 528 (1984).

16. 277 U.S. 438.

17. Id., 478–479.

18. Katz v. United States, 389 U.S. 347 (1967).

19. 456 U.S. 798.

20. Rhode Island v. Innis, 446 U.S. 291 (1980). But should the Supreme Court even find its way to a unitary, practicable theory of the "search and seizure" clause of the U.S. Constitution, the analogous clauses of the several state constitutions will remain up for grabs (McGushin, "High Court Narrows Auto Search Exception Under State Constitution," Connecticut Law Tribune [August 30/September 6, 1993], 1).

21. 492 U.S. 490 (1989).

22. Id. 532.

23. Id. 522.

24. Id. 549.

25. See Chapter 2.

26. B. Siegan, Economic Liberties and the Constitution (Chicago, 1989): "In a society that extols private property and private enterprise, those who engage in economic activities in reliance on existing laws are entitled to be secure against arbitrary and confiscatory government actions . . . . This is one of the major reasons that we have a Supreme Court."

27. In cases regarding race discrimination, the Burger Court preserved strict scrutiny, and as to remedies it went further than had the Warren Court (Swann v. Charlotte-Mecklenburg Bd. of Education, 402 U.S. 1 [1971]).

28. 404 U.S. 71.

29. 429 U.S. 190 (1976).

30. Id. 197.

31. Id., 199–200.

32. Id., 208–09.

33. Id. 214.

34. Id. 210, n.

35. Id., 211–214.

36. Id., 215–17.

37. Id. 217.

38. Id. 228.

39. W. James, Pragmatism (New York, 1907), 45.

40. P. McGuigan & D. Weyrich, Ninth Justice (Lanham, Md., 1990), 283–284.

8

The Making of the Rehnquist Court

In 1981, at the start of a one-term period of Republican control of the Senate, President Reagan appointed Sandra Day O'Connor to the Supreme Court. In 1986, near the end of that period of control at a time when Reagan could still muster majorities only though strict party discipline, his administration and the Democratic minority became embroiled in three confirmation controversies—over Jefferson Sessions, nominee for a district judgeship; Daniel Manion, for the Seventh Circuit Court of Appeals; William Rehnquist, for chief justice.

Much of this book has told the story of a decline—the dissipation of the ability and the willingness of the Supreme Court to meet its constitutional responsibilities. The Court abandoned the defense of property rights in the 1930s, adopted realism as a working creed in the course of the 1940s, awarded itself an indefinitely expansive equity power in the 1950s, and lost all ability to make coherent, defensible distinctions of principle in the 1960s, as displayed especially in the defamation and search-and-seizure decisions of that decade. In the early and middle 1970s the Court fumbled two opportunities to expound the law on executive privilege and the separation of powers in a definitive and intelligible manner. Its decline, when viewed as a whole, is not merely enormous but an enormity.

One of the most fashionable phrases of the journalism of 1980 was "the gender gap." The phrase conveyed the theory of feminists that Reagan's inability to attract the votes of women would prove fatal to his presidential aspirations. Instead, his success in the campaign of that year eliminated at least one cliché. (The division of the sexes revealed by exit polls showed that the "gap" was a Democratic men deficit, not a Republican women deficit. Reagan received the votes of 54 percent of the men asked, 46 percent of the women. Carter received the votes of 37 percent of the men, 45 percent of the women. Independent candidate John Anderson received 7 percent, men and women.[1])

But before that success was assured, Reagan promised that he would appoint a woman justice to "one of the first Supreme Court vacancies in my administration."[2]   The following summer Justice Potter Stewart, an Eisenhower appointee and one of those treated by the balancing model as a swing vote, weighing impartially the claims of the blocs to his left and right, announced his retirement.   Reagan nominated Sandra Day O'Connor, a fifty-one-year-old judge on the Arizona Court of Appeals, to this vacancy.

Although it is tempting, one should not infer from the facts just stated that the appointment of a woman was forced on the president by public memory of his campaign pledge. That promise had contained an important hedge, allocating not the first but "one of the first" of his appointments to the female sex. William P. Clark, a onetime justice of the California Supreme Court and a longtime confidant of the former governor of that state, in 1981 newly minted as deputy secretary of state but an influential adviser in matters judicial, told journalist Lou Cannon that he came away from a discussion of this appointment convinced that the president was compelled more by his "sense of justice" than by the expediency of political tactics to name a woman to the first available high Court vacancy.[3]

Congressman Morris Udall immediately praised the nomination, writing that it showed a "flexibility" he had not associated with this president.[4] One ought to be reluctant to attack any expression of agreement that unites Reagan and Udall, but the warm consent, by all our factions, to the use of sex as a qualification for such an office is troubling. The very language in which it is praised tells against this criterion. Justice must be tempered, now and then, by demonstrations of flexibility.   But the Clark and Udall comments show that flexibility and justice have come to be regarded as synonyms, which is lamentable.

The O'Connor appointment, which no one ever even pretended to have been made on merit or qualification alone and which was avowedly demographic, cannot, strictly speaking, be said to test what I have earlier called the demographic theory of representation—which would require four and one-half female justices. But it does exemplify one of the arguments often employed in defense of that theory, the diversity principle.[5] This principle holds that a group defined by biology or class has a distinctive "point of view" to contribute and that the effort to include that point of view within any decision-making council contributes to the legitimacy, the wisdom, and the virtue, in that council's decisions.

The talk of diversity attaches a stigma to the persons it presumes to aid.

Or two stigmata. First, there is the presumption of inferiority on the merits. Nothing in the foregoing should be taken to imply that Justice O'Connor was not the best or among the best available jurists for the post to which she was elevated in 1981. I cannot know that. But what I do know is that if she was qualified by tests indifferent to sex, then all the to-do about her sex, insofar as it implies otherwise, is unfair to her. If she was not so qualified, the talk still creates a presumption unfair to women jurists generally.

Second, there is the presumption of a uniform "point of view" within the group that the appointee is intended to represent. If a woman is expected to bring a woman's perspective to the Court or to any other body where such reasoning is thought to apply, then there must be only one such woman's perspective in the matters with which that body deals. If Justice O'Connor rules against that one perspective (by whom defined?), then she is likely to be treated by those inclined to such arguments with the special revulsion reserved, for their turncoats, by persons who see themselves as righteous, besieged, and battered by battle.

Whether the motive for O'Connor's appointment was wise or foolish, whether or not it was flexible in a praise-worthy or blame-worthy sense, the nominee's confirmation was never in doubt. The election of 1980 had done more than change the occupant of the White House. It had installed a Republican majority in the Senate. In the wake of a sweeping and coattail-offering victory, there was no intraparty opposition to Reagan or Reaganism, any potential opposition of that sort having been discredited with John Anderson's departure from the nomination process in the spring of 1980, when Anderson decided to wage an independent campaign under the banner of National Unity. No opposition to this first Supreme Court appointment of the new president seems to have been either considered or feared.

The internal politics of the Republican Party has a regional character. It bears upon the nature of the electoral coalition in 1980 and upon the nature of the presidency that was to follow and is worth discussion here. The following table shows regional patterns in the Ford and Reagan delegate commitments at the 1976 National Republican Convention. The figures represent the percentage of delegates from each region aligned with each candidate:[6]

	REAGAN	FORD
SOUTH	73	27
WEST	82	18
MIDWEST	32	68
NORTHEAST	12	88

President Ford's support may be described, roughly, thus: (1) people long active within the Republican Party who found this opportunity appropriate for the repayment of a debt owed to the president, a man who had accumulated many such credits during his long service in the Congress; (2) people, often conservative, who either feared another Goldwater-style defeat in the event of Reagan's nomination or proved susceptible to the blandishments available to an incumbent; and (3) people comfortable with what, in Chapter 4, I called Ripon Society Republicanism.

Outside California, where Reagan also had political debtors, the ex-governor's support consisted of the only bloc that was left, that of conservatives who had been neither induced nor frightened away. The political scientist E. J. Dionne, the source of the delegate percentages in the previous table, ended his discussion of Ripon Society Republicanism with Ford's defeat that fall, a defeat that left the party that Ford had led as the inheritance of Reagan's southern and western constituencies. This shift to the sunbelt was also a shift to the Right, where "all the energy of the Republican Party" has dwelt ever since.[7]

So runs Dionne's analysis. It is not complete. One might further say that the nearness of the Carter-Ford contest, the avoidance by Ford of what in the aftermath of Watergate could have been a Democratic landslide, at a moment when the death of the Republican Party was widely reported, not only saved the party but gave new vigor to its more moderate and northeastern components. This is why there was an Anderson campaign four years later, why he came in second in a crowded field in the Massachusetts primary and became a factor in the November tally. Still, he was just the final flicker of the Ripon torch, and, with a four-year revision in chronology, Dionne's larger points hold. The Republican Party in the Reagan years and since has been a party of the South and West, a party where a president from Connecticut would assume the airs of a Texan, and it has become just as firmly the party of the political Right.

It is emblematic of this shift that Sandra Day O'Connor became the second sitting justice from Arizona. Arizona does not have a large population. Its double representation on a nine-member Court might offend geographical conceptions of "balance" if anyone still adhered to such conceptions against the crush of ideological and demographic considerations. As it is, the double presence of that state may be said to represent the sunbelt character of the coalition that won the presidency and temporarily changed the organization of the Senate in 1980.

THE BURGER COURT AT WORK

O'Connor's appointment was the last during Burger's chief justiceship and provides an observer with an opportunity to pause and compare the Burger Court with its predecessor. How much has changed in the jurisprudence of the Supreme Court? Did anything change, in regard to the dominance of "realism," between, say, 1965 and 1983? In my remarks on this point, the doctrine of the separation of church and state serves to make a case for an answer of no.

Both federal and state actions come under frequent challenge from plaintiffs who believe that many such actions violate the First Amendment separation of church and state.[8] The Warren Court developed a three-part test for the evaluation of such challenges. An act under challenge will fail unless the authority by whom it was enacted can show a secular purpose (part one) and a predominantly secular effect (part two). The act will fail, despite a successful showing on both of these points, if it is adjudged an "excessive entanglement" of church and state.

The third part is the most severe, in the sense that its wording erects no limit to judicial fiat. To call an entanglement "excessive" is no better than to call an invasion of privacy "unwarranted." What are the standards? Without much more, any decision founded on this part of the test in particular is a blatant petitio principi.

An unwieldy doctrinal structure produces erratic results. A legislature cannot so much as mandate a moment of silence during school hours, a moment to be employed in whatever thoughts an individual student may deem appropriate.[9] A legislature may mandate the provision of "equal access" to public school facilities for prayer groups (a guarantee of access equal to that available to such secular groups as chess clubs) and may in this sense support honest-to-God, outright prayer, so long as it is offered at the right time of day, as an extracurricular event.[10] The public treasury cannot pay for the visual aids employed by the teachers in parochial schools. But the public treasury may pay for the textbooks used by those same teachers in those same schools.[11] An atlas would constitute a permissible textbook, but a freestanding map would constitute a prohibited visual aid.

It is not just the involvement of church and state in the common task of educating the young that produces such constitutional confusion. A crèche standing alone on public land is unconstitutional. A crèche, standing on the same land but surrounded by plastic reindeer and as part of an inducement to shop downtown is constitutional. Is it the plastic of the reindeer or the credit cards that has this magic curative effect upon the infection of transcendence?

However that facetious question may be answered, the historian must note that the Burger Court, which inherited this rickety structure, this awkward three-part formula that is not even a rule of law but the straightforward promotion of some preferred and quite partisan results by "realist" judges, did nothing to replace it. Reference to just two of these "establishment clause" cases will suffice to illustrate that Court's nonfeasance both before and after the appointment of Justice Sandra Day O'Connor.

In Marsh v. Chambers (1983) Chief Justice Burger, writing for the Court, upheld the practice of Nebraska, which employs a chaplain for its legislature. The function of this state official is to open each day's session with a prayer.[12]

The result in Marsh, that the chaplain can continue in the state's employ, is inoffensive. What ought to offend, though, is the Court's refusal either to employ or overturn the tripartite test for an "establishment of religion." The opinion for the majority mentioned the words *purpose, effect, entanglement* only in its paraphrase of the reasoning of the appellate court below. In their own reasoning, the justices substituted metaphor for judgment, stating that chaplains have become "part of the fabric of our society."

In a (potentially) important footnote, the chief justice cites the pretrial deposition of the chaplain whose continued service was at issue, Robert E. Palmer. In that deposition, Palmer characterized his own prayers as nonsectarian and indicated that he abandoned references to Christ in 1980 after a complaint from a Jewish legislator. Palmer also referred to his prayers as "Judeo-Christian" and stated that they include "elements of the American civil religion."[13]

The Court's opinion is maddeningly silent on the obvious questions this footnote raises. Were Palmer's prayers unconstitutional before the deletion of references to Christ in 1980? Did they become part of the fabric of American society before or after that year? Does the Court now recognize that there is, as the deponent believed, such an entity as the American civil religion? What are the implications of that recognition?

Justice Brennan wrote in dissent. This is not surprising. Justice Brennan was instrumental in the creation of the traditional test the majority here ignores.[14] In his general jurisprudence, Brennan was always a realist ad hoc balancer, and it is likely that he helped to develop such a complicated constitutional doctrine precisely because he saw it as sufficiently flexible to allow judges and justices to do what they see as best case by case.

I review only one other Burger Court decision here, Stone v. Graham (1980).[15] In Stone the Court considered a Kentucky statute that required the posting of the Ten Commandments in the classrooms of Kentucky's public schools. The state responded to challenge by arguing that there is a perfectly secular purpose for such a law. Those commandments have helped to shape the legal codes of numerous countries through the ages, our own among them. Perhaps this argument would have prevailed had Kentucky also required the posting of an excerpt from the Code of Hammurabi alongside this excerpt from the Code of Moses, on the reindeer-with-crèche analogy. But on the facts before the Court, Justice Brennan wrote for the majority that the preeminent purpose for the mandate is "plainly religious in nature" and so forbidden.[16]

Rehnquist dissented and wrote that "the fact that the asserted secular purpose may overlap with what some see as a religious objective does not render [the act] unconstitutional."[17]

Stone demonstrates the infinite flexibility and so the worthlessness of the test that both the majority and the dissent professed to apply. Does any jurist have a firm grasp on the dichotomy between "secular" and "religious" on which two-thirds of the test rests? As to the first third, can a Court select any one purpose as the purpose? There are many purposes at issue even in the case of the prayer of a legislative chaplain: invoking the favor and protection of a God, formally opening a session, quieting the membership, impressing on the representatives the solemnity of their responsibilities, and so on.

There is even a crucial ambiguity about what the word *purpose* means in this context. Are the justices looking for the purpose most evident on the face of the bill under challenge? Or for the motives of its supporters? What of the "purpose" of securing reelection? Is that religious or secular? These are some of the questions with which the Court in Marsh would have had to grapple had it squarely confronted the existing body of constitutional doctrine with the facts of the legislative chaplain controversy. But the grappling in Stone, although less blatantly evasive than the silence of Marsh, is unimpressive. Each side simply attributed to the legislation at issue the "purpose" required to produce the result it desired—the majority attributing a religious, the minority a secular, purpose to the same legislative text.

If the Burger Court left the law of church-state relations no clearer for such efforts, and if its inertness on this matter left "realism" unchallenged, what would the Rehnquist Court do?

CREATION OF A REHNQUIST COURT

The midterm election of 1982 reduced the size of the Reagan majority in the Senate. The president's reelection in 1984 did nothing to restore that margin, because the American electorate knows how to split its tickets and does so increasingly to bar either party from becoming the governing party. The next midterm election, 1986, returned the Senate to Democratic control, restoring the split government of the Nixon-Ford years.

The confirmation debates to which I now turn took place during the election campaign of 1986 and so in the final months of the Republican majority in the Senate. The first-term senators who created the majority with their entry into that body would have to preserve it by winning reelection. This fact was on the mind of every participant in the judiciary debates of that spring and summer.

On May 27, Chief Justice Burger advised the president that he would retire at the end of the current term in order to spend all his time over the following two years as the chairman of the Commission on the Bicentennial of the United States Constitution. In a letter dated June 17, the president accepted this decision.[18]

As these two men exchanged notes, the Senate Judiciary Committee considered two lower-court appointments. On June 5 a majority of that committee voted against Reagan's nomination of Jefferson Sessions to the Federal District Court for the District of Alabama. Sessions, the U.S. attorney in Mobile, had prosecuted three civil rights activists the year before on charges of fraud. The defendants were acquitted. Many senators came to the conclusion that they should never have been charged, and from that inference, in turn, they inferred opposition to civil rights on Sessions's part.

Some questions come to mind as soon as the matter in controversy is explained. If Sessions acted improperly in prosecuting these people, why was no effort made to discipline him? If he was motivated by opposition to civil rights, should he have been allowed to continue as U.S. attorney? If, on the other hand, Sessions had exercised his prosecutorial discretion in a manner that did not merit discharge, what exactly was the barrier to confirmation? Are political activists immune from criminal charges? Or should these activists be considered an improper object of prosecution simply due to the result of the trial? If so, does it not follow that a prosecutor must win every case of his that comes to trial in order to remain eligible for higher office? These questions never received the full airing of a debate on the Senate floor, because the Sessions nomination came to an end with the unfavorable committee vote.

On June 17 President Reagan, outgoing chief justice Burger, chief justice nominee Rehnquist, and associate justice nominee Antonin Scalia held a joint press conference. The first question concerned abortion: "Mr. President, what impact do you think they will have on the abortion issue.?"

The second question also concerned abortion: "Are you satisfied that the Judge [Scalia] agrees with you on the abortion issue?" Reagan refused to answer either question.[19]

In a June 21 radio address, Ronald Reagan defended the credentials of his nominee to the Seventh Circuit appellate bench, Daniel Manion:

> Partisanship in the Senate has pushed fair play by the boards, which is why I've sent a letter to the Senate expressing my strong opinion about the prerogative of the President to make qualified appointments to the Federal judiciary and what I feel has been the partisan use of the confirmation process . . . . I believe the Senate should consider only a nominee's qualifications and character, not his political views. Now, I would welcome a national debate on those political views and how we're going to keep up the attack on this nation's crime problem. In the meantime, however, I intend to keep right on appointing tough, responsible judges to the courts.[20]

The president was correct in his opinion that the Senate should not employ tests that the Founders and the framers of our Constitution would have called "factional" in offering its advice and giving its consent to judicial appointments. For this reason, the use of a single-issue criterion, such as a justice's willingness to affirm Roe v. Wade, the criterion that instigated the first two questions at the press conference previously cited, is inappropriate. On the other hand, the president could have made that point more forcefully if he had not immediately turned to equally factional considerations in order to defend the same choices. For this reason, the invocation of Manion's presumed "toughness" against crime was also inappropriate.

The most frequently invoked doctrinal ground for opposition to the appointment of Daniel Manion did not involve crime or a right to privacy. He was accused of insufficient respect for the separation of church and state. While a state legislator in Indiana, Manion introduced a bill analogous to the Kentucky statute discussed before, authorizing public schools to post the Ten Commandments on their classroom walls.

Manion drafted this bill two months after the publication of Stone v. Graham.[21] He obviously intended it as an immediate challenge to that decision. This challenge is reminiscent of Abraham Lincoln's contention, in the course of his debates with Stephen Douglas, that the Supreme Court's authority in Scott v. Sandford (1857)[22] extended no further than to its disposition of the matter before it, and so bound no one but the litigants.[23]

In a letter released to the press on June 24, more than twenty deans of law schools urged Manion's rejection, asserting that the nominee had insufficient "scholarship, legal acumen, professional achievement, fidelity to the law and commitment to our Constitution" to serve in such a responsible capacity.[24] The first three alleged incapacities amounted to a "mediocrity" argument of the type once made against Carswell. It may have been appropriate in that earlier instance as in this one. But the last two deficiencies on the list were utterly inappropriate and in the nature of a slur on a man's character. There was no evidence, then or later, that as an attorney Manion had ever conducted himself in a manner unfaithful to the law or inconsistent with a commitment to the Constitution.

What may have been most important in building such suspicions against Manion is that he is the son of <u>Clarence</u> Manion, one of the founders of the John Birch Society, a political organization given to surreal conspiracy theories.[25] Even were one inclined to visit the peccancy of a father upon his son, though, one would have to acknowledge that this datum is double-edged. Clarence Manion seems to have served as something of a moderating influence within that society, a check upon the megalomania of master-dogmatic Robert Welch.

After much debate on such facts and their significance, the Senate voted on Manion's nomination on June 26. This vote ended (or seemed to end) in a tie at forty-seven. Vice President Bush would have broken that tie in favor of confirmation but for a bit of parliamentary maneuvering. Minority Leader Robert Byrd changed his vote from nay to aye. This left Manion confirmed but gave Byrd the right to move for reconsideration—something only a member on the winning side of a vote can do. Byrd made that motion immediately.

On June 30, <u>Newsweek</u> published a cover story, "Reagan's Law." The reader will be ready for the revelation it contained, that the Supreme Court was evenly balanced and that the appointment of Scalia could have a decisive effect upon that balance. The cast is familiar ("right," "left," and "center" blocs), but some of the names have changed—Justice White, always before counted as a member of right-ward blocs, now appears in the center.[26] The tilting of the delicate balance of the Court is, like the Apocalypse, every day just a day away for those who participate in the pertinent interpretive labors at all.

Early in July, Senator Alphonse D'Amato of New York announced his opinion that Manion did not have "outstanding" legal qualifications, and he expressed his hope that Ronald Reagan would not press the fight on this point.[27]

July was also marked by the shocking suicide of Senator John East, who left behind a note that criticized, by name, a physician at Bethesda Naval Hospital whose ministrations, East believed, "ruined my health."[28] No one drew a connection between this grievous death and the ongoing arguments over President Reagan's judicial appointments, but a connection there would prove to be.

As the final week of July began, the Senate voted on Byrd's motion to reconsider Manion's confirmation. Ninety-nine senators were present for the vote. Manion's opponents could have carried this motion fifty to forty-nine, if they had taken advantage of the illness and consequent absence of Manion supporter and Arizona senator Barry Goldwater. But in a striking instance of collegiality, Goldwater's Democratic counterpart, Dennis DeConcini, declined to cast his vote, balancing the effects of Goldwater's illness. The result was another tie. This time no maneuver intervened to prevent a tie-breaking vote by the vice president, and Manion now sits on the Seventh Circuit.

On July 29 the Judiciary Committee began its hearings on the nomination of William Rehnquist as chief justice. On the same day, Senator Edward Kennedy announced his opposition. On July 30 the American Bar Association released the decision of its screening committee, which gave Rehnquist the highest possible rating. It was also on the thirtieth that Rehnquist testified on his own behalf. He was asked if he had "harassed or intimidated" minority voters when he was a Republican poll challenger in Phoenix. He said that he had not. He was asked if he was aware that there was a restrictive covenant in the deed to his property that barred its sale or lease to nonwhites or nonChristians. He said that he was not.

Harassment is not a matter of observational fact; it is a legal conclusion. What seems a legitimate challenge to the credentials of a voter in the eyes of the pollworker designated for that task will almost invariably seem harassing in the eyes of the person challenged.

The matter of the restrictive covenant (a restriction that no Court in America would enforce, as Rehnquist explained to the Senate), seemed at first likely to give considerable difficulty to the administration and the advocates of this appointment. But one such advocate, James McClellan of the Center for Judicial Studies, soon discovered a restrictive covenant with very similar wording in the deed to a house once owned by Senator Joseph Biden, ranking minority member on the committee.[29] The threat to Rehnquist's advancement from that quarter soon faded.

Judge Scalia appeared before the Committee on August 5 and 6. The most widely noted fact in the press reports on that appearance was that Scalia, if confirmed, would be the first justice of Italian descent. It seems that the theory of demographic representation had at last come to the aid of a white ethnic.[30]

Through the early days of August, sentiment built in the Senate for a demand that the executive turn over to the committee copies of all memoranda that Rehnquist wrote while working in the Nixon administration. The demand posed a dilemma for the president. If he refused to disclose this material, then the "cover-up" itself would become an issue useful to those who wanted to stop Rehnquist's confirmation. On the other hand, if he complied with the demand, it was likely that there would be some ammunition concerning some of the same issues that had been aired when Rehnquist was confirmed for the associate justice post fifteen years before.

Or so those senators pushing this issue may have thought. In the event, the White House provided these materials to the Senate on August 5 and no bombs went off. On the ninth, Reagan spoke of the Rehnquist and Scalia nominations in another radio address:

> There were many serious allegations by political opponents of Justice Rehnquist and Judge Scalia. One Democratic Senator announced that he would vote against Justice Rehnquist even before the hearings started. There were dark hints about what might be found in documents Justice Rehnquist wrote while a Justice Department official many years ago. To deal with these unfounded charges, I took the unusual step of permitting the Senate committee to see the documents themselves. Of course, there was nothing there but legal analyses and other routine communications. The hysterical charges of coverup and stonewalling were revealed for what they were: political posturing.[31]

As that excerpt from the speech illustrates, President Reagan turned his own release of materials into a charge against those who had "hysterically" asked for it and so into an argument for the confirmation of the appointment. It was an effective piece of political judo, but the opposition was not quite overcome. On August 13 the Washington Post reported that Justice Rehnquist had been for a time dependent upon a powerful drug that he had been using for the alleviation of a painful back condition. This leak was an extraordinary move away from the public career of a nominee into such a personal, indeed private, matter as illness, medication, and alleged addiction. The fact that such a tactic spurred no outrage even when employed against a sitting justice illustrates how far the Supreme Court had fallen by 1986 from its once-Olympian position in the public esteem. The absence of outrage over the leak of personal medical information also accounts for the subsequent repetition of such planned leaks in the Thomas matter five years later. One attendant irony is that the person or persons responsible for providing this datum probably thought of themselves as acting to protect the "right to privacy."

Nonetheless, on August 14, the committee voted in favor of confirmation, thirteen to five for Rehnquist and eighteen to none for Scalia. As August lingered, the medical consideration redounded to Rehnquist's favor among still-undecided senators. For the public learned that Rehnquist's dependency began while he was under the care of the same physician named in Senator East's suicide note. On the supposition that Rehnquist was a victim of inappropriate medical practice, a supposition undemonstrated but natural, East's colleagues appear to have rejected the attempt to use Rehnquist's burden as a disqualification for the office of chief justice.

The best that the anti-Rehnquist senators could do with the nominee's record in the Nixon administration was to play up a "Brief in Opposition" to the Equal Rights Amendment (ERA), dated May 4, 1970, prepared by

Rehnquist for the benefit of Nixon counsel Leonard Garment. Senator Howard Metzenbaum alluded to this memorandum during the floor debate and placed it in the <u>Congressional</u> <u>Record</u>.[32]

This document reveals nothing about William Rehnquist's own views on that subject, as a voter or a citizen. He responded to a request that he "summarize objections to the adoption of the amendment, in order that both sides may be available to"[33] Garment's review of administration policy. (Another attorney in the Justice Department had already prepared a memorandum in favor of the proposed amendment, as part of the same review.)

Senator Metzenbaum, ignoring the advocate's role that it was Rehnquist's duty to perform, treated this memo as one link in a chain of evidence that the nominee was deaf to the just cries of women and minorities, by which, of course, he meant the demands of feminists, civil rights activists, and other Metzenbaum supporters. This, as accusations go, was weak.

But a careful reading shows that there is something odd about this document. Rehnquist's argument against the ERA reads like the argument of a political consultant or pollster. There is nothing distinctively legal about his reasoning. He explains that three will be substantial opposition to the ratification of this measure by the several states (an accurate prognostication!) and suggests that it would be wise for the administration to align itself with those forces of opposition. He evades or barely mentions strictly constitutional concerns, such as whether the second section of the ERA constitutes a sweeping grant of indeterminate power to Congress. He evades, in other words, the concerns that would have been uniquely the concern of the Justice Department under the old dispensation of formalist jurisprudence. That is not an observation that would have fit well as a link in Metzenbaum's chain, but it is important for this study of the continuing decline and fall of the Supreme Court.

On September 17, the Senate voted consent sixty-five to thirty-three on the Rehnquist nomination, ninety-eight to none on Scalia's. The Rehnquist Court came into existence. Has the Court improved upon the performance of its predecessors as to church-state relations?

MORE ON CHURCH AND STATE

My answer is no. The following example is evidence in favor of that answer. A number of parents of public school students brought suit against Governor Edwin Edwards of Louisiana, seeking an injunction against enforcement of a statute that required that any teaching of evolution be balanced by the presentation of creationist views and arguments in the biology course of the public schools. Plaintiff prevailed in the courts below, and the defendant governor appealed to the Supreme Court, which heard the case in 1987. Seven justices of that Court voted to affirm the circuit court, striking the statute. As in <u>Stone</u>, the argument was not over the applicability of the three-part test itself but over the application of the first part of that test (the requirement of a secular purpose) to the facts at hand. The state argued that its purpose was not to "establish" the Genesis account of human origins but to provide "a more comprehensive science curriculum."

Justice Brennan, writing for the majority, found that the preeminent purpose of the law is religious. Comprehensiveness is not the goal of this statute, even on its face, because a school or teacher can obey the state's command by teaching neither the creationist nor the evolutionary material at issue and so balance with impeccable impartiality one silence against another. Furthermore, the law does not authorize teachers to include any material they could not include without it.[34]

If purpose is to be determined, not through the implications of the text but through the legislative history, the same conclusion is inevitable. The legislators who advocated this bill were, as Brennan inferred, trying to "provide persuasive advantage to a particular religious doctrine that rejects the factual basis of evolution in its entirety."[35]

Justice Powell's concurrence makes two points. Powell suggests that the Court should be wary of becoming a super school board. It may be a bit late to make such a point. After decades in which Court-ordered desegregation has shaded into Court-directed integration and in which just such supervision of public school secularity as the <u>Edwards</u> decision exemplifies has become commonplace, one cannot pretend that the Court's status as a national school board is still just a distant threat.

Somewhat more plausibly, Powell explained that the Court does not mean to exclude religion as an object of study from the public school curriculum.[36] It may provide some slight solace to people who loathe the godlessness of their children's education to read a judicial opinion stating, as does Powell's: "As a matter of history, schoolchildren can and should properly be informed of all aspects of this Nation's religious heritage . . . . Courses in comparative religion of course are customary and constitutionally appropriate."[37] What Powell ignores, and perhaps it is for the best that he does, is that in the secondary schools with which this litigation is concerned, courses on "comparative religion" or "aspects of this Nation's religious heritage" are almost invariably jejune intellectually and worthless pedagogically.

The new justice, Scalia, wrote a dissent for himself and Chief Justice Rehnquist. Scalia argued that any secular strand within a ball of intertwined legislative purposes can save the statute: "When the <u>Lemon</u> Court referred to 'a secular . . . purpose,' it meant '*a* secular purpose,' . . . Thus, the majority's invalidation of the Balanced Treatment Act is defensible only if the record indicates that the Louisiana legislature had *no* secular purpose."[38] Since Scalia did not find indication of that negative proposition in the trial record, he found that the Balanced Treatment Act is not impaled by the first prong of the traditional test. He gave a similar restraintist twist to his reading of each of the other two prongs and concluded that the act should stand.

Suppose Scalia's establishment clause restraintism should command a majority. What would follow? Restraintism does not lead very far from realism. Were the Court to hold that every state can regulate the curriculum of its public schools in the manner it deems best, perhaps with the caveat that rationality will be required, the next class of cases to reach the Court would demand enforcement particulars. Suppose an individual teacher gives the forbidden lesson or teaches the two sides of a mandated balance in a manner that higher authorities believe tips the scales. Is such a delinquency sufficient cause for firing that teacher? Is he or she entitled to a fair hearing? Will there be any due process safeguards at that hearing? Is the state entitled to affix criminal penalties for the miscreant? Without a formalist foundation, any restraintist solution to the problems posed by such cases as Edwards is but half a dam. It will not stop the water, nor will the rushing water let it stand.

Bowen v. Kendrick (1988) is my second example of the indefensible and chaotic character of today's church and state separation law[39] and of the Rehnquist Court's inability to bring order out of that chaos. The chief justice delivered the opinion of the Court upholding the Adolescent Family Life Act (AFLA), by which Congress offered financial assistance to private family-planning institutions, regardless of their religious affiliations. The plaintiffs drew upon arguments often made in the decisions that strike down or limit public aid to parochial schools. First, they said, this law is unconstitutional because it has the purpose of advancing certain theological positions over others; second, it will have the effect of subsidizing those churches that operate such institutions; third, any attempt on the part of the government to track or require an accounting for AFLA money will generate excessive entanglements between church and state.

On all three points the Court disagreed. It held that AFLA has the legitimate purpose of reducing the many problems associated with teenage pregnancies. The effects of AFLA need not include the advancement of religion, because the statute creates mechanisms for policing the use of the funds in question.[40] These very mechanisms do not constitute excessive entanglement of church and state because they do not require "extensive and permanent on-site monitoring" or benefit such "pervasively sectarian" institutions as the "Court has held parochial schools to be."[41]

Every time the Court tries to clarify any one of the three parts of this test, it increases the confusion. Here the Court was required to employ that question-begging formula, "excessive entanglement," and did so by splitting it into two formulas, two twigs from one of the three main branches of the tree. It is now the law of the land that an entanglement of church and state will be deemed excessive if it involves the subsidy of some institution deemed pervasively sectarian, or if it involves the extensive and permanent on-site monitoring of the activity of a religious institution. These subtests ought to inspire litigation over the following questions. When does sectarianism become pervasive? What of sporadic and temporary on-site monitoring? For example, would a bill fail if it provided for rare and randomly selected audit dates? Or if it provided for continuous on-site monitoring that was to end after a specific number of years (as with a sunset clause)? A packet of new conclusory labels does nothing to define the old conclusory labels.

Bowen makes it evident that, though we now have a Rehnquist Court, we do not have a postrealist Court. That negative conclusion is deserving of some regret.

NOTES

1. Lee & Lee, "The Gender Gap," The Freeman (March 1992) at 100.
2. L. Cannon, Reagan (New York, 1982), 313.
3. Id.
4. Udall, "A Master Stroke," Washington Post, July 13, 1981, op ed.
5. S. Carter, Reflections of an Affirmative Action Baby (New York, 1991). See also an intelligent review, Hayward, "Reversing Discrimination," Reason (December 1991), 48.
6. E. J. Dionne, Jr., Why Americans Hate Politics (New York, 1991), 207.
7. Id. 208.
8. "Congress shall make no law respecting an establishment of religion, or prohibiting the free exercise thereof."
9. Wallace v. Jaffree, 472 U.S. 38 (1985); Abington School District v. Schempp, 374 U.S. 203 (1963); Engel v. Vitale, 370 U.S. 421 (1962).
10.   Westside Comm. Schools v. Mergens, 496 U.S. 226 (1990).
11.   Meek v. Pittinger, 421 U.S. 349 (1975).
12.   463 U.S. 783 (1983).
13.   Id. 793 n. 14.
14.   Lemon v. Kurtzman, 403 U.S. 602 at 642 (J. Brennan, concurring) (1971). Also, see Mendelson, "Brennan's Revolution," 91 Commentary (February 1991), 31.
15.   Stone v. Graham, 449 U.S. 39 (1980).
16.   Id. 41.
17.   Id. 43.
18.   "Letter Accepting the Resignation of Warren E. Burger as Chief Justice of the United States Supreme Court," June 17, 1986, Public Papers of the Presidents: Ronald Reagan—1986, at 780.
19.   "Remarks on the Resignation of Chief Justice Warren E. Burger and the Nominations of William H. Rehnquist to be Chief Justice and Antonin Scalia to be Associate Justice," June 17, 1986, Public Papers, 781–788.
20.   "Radio Address to the Nation on the United States Supreme Court Nominations," August 9, 1986, Public Papers, 1067–1069.
21.   Reston, "Reagen and the Judges," New York Times, June 25, 1986, A27.
22.   19 How. 393 (1857).

23. D. E. Fehrenbacher, Slavery, Law, & Politics (Oxford, 1981), 241–243.

24. Ownby, "Deans enter the judicial nomination fray," Los Angeles Daily Journal, June 30, 1986, B14.

25. J. A. Broyles, The John Birch Society (Boston, 1964), 49–50.

26. "Reagan's Law" (cover story), Newsweek, June 30, 1986 at 14.

27. "Interview with Bruce Drake of the New York Daily News," July 8, 1986, Public Papers, 931–937, esp. 936–937.

28. O'Connor & Wright, "Bad Rx for Rehnquist?" Newsweek, August 25, 1986, 32.

29. Meyer & Wright, "Questions About Rehnquist," Newsweek, August 11, 1986, 21. Also, P. M. McGuigan, The Judges' War (Lanham, MD, 1987).

30. "Rehnquist and Scalia: Full Speed Ahead," Newsweek, August 18, 1986 at 17.

31. "Radio Address to the Nation on the United States Supreme Court Nominations," August 9, 1986, Public Papers, 1067–1069.

32. 132 Cong. Rec., Sept. 15, 1986, S. 12,556.

33. Id.

34. Edwards v. Aguillard, 482 U.S. 578 (1987).

35. Id. 592.

36. Id. 597.

37. Id., 606–07.

38. Id. 610.

39. Bowen v. Kendrick, 487 U.S. 589 (1988).

40. 42 U.S.C. §300z et seq.

41. 487 US. 589 at 616.

9

The Robert Bork Revue

On the day that President Reagan nominated Judge Robert Bork for the Supreme Court, Edward Kennedy spoke on the floor of the Senate in opposition. His speech was emphatic, attributing a variety of evils to what he called "Robert Bork's America." His charges set the agenda for the confirmation hearings that followed. The Senate voted on October 23, 1987, fifty-eight to forty-two against consent to this appointment. Judge Douglas Ginsberg was the president's second appointee for this post. Judge Anthony Kennedy was his third, and successful, nominee.

On June 9, 1987, Senator Joseph Biden, then the ranking majority member and accordingly the chairman of the Judiciary Committee, announced his campaign for the Democratic Party's nomination for president. In his speech at Wilmington, Delaware, Biden denounced what he saw as the climate of selfishness prevalent in the land and asked supporters to help him "rekindle the fire of idealism."[1]

One of Senator Biden's great virtues is that he sometimes makes explicit ideas and connections that are only implicit in the usual political mutterings of the day. His dichotomy between selfishness (which is bad) and the fire of idealism (good) is an example. Many of the best minds of the past three centuries have argued that such improvements in the lot of mankind as are within our grasp are to be expected from civilized, or channeled, selfishness.[2] But if one is to judge by contemporary discourse, it is as if these distinguished men and women have never spoken or written a word.

On June 26, Justice Lewis Powell announced his retirement. He was concerned that his "serious health problems" would "handicap the Court" should he continue in office. One of the recurrent themes of journalistic punditry in the following days was the opportunity this created for Chairman Biden. It was forecast that he would preside over hearings on the qualifications of Powell's successor and would do either great harm or much good to his presidential aspirations by virtue of the publicity this garnered. After all, as lobbyists for factions with a stake in these hearings alleged (assuming, as they did, the balance model), the Supreme Court was just "one Justice away from injustice."[3]

On July 1, the president announced the nomination of Judge Robert Bork of the U.S. Court of Appeals for the District of Columbia. Since that court hears cases brought by, and against, federal agencies, it is often regarded as an ideal training ground for the Supreme Court.

On the same day, Senator Kennedy of Massachusetts took to the Senate floor to deliver his views on the nomination. He declared:[4]

> Robert Bork's America is a land in which women would be forced into back-alley abortions, blacks would sit at segregated lunch counters, rogue police could break down citizens' doors in midnight raids, schoolchildren could not be taught about evolution, writer and artists would be censured at the whim of the government, and the doors of the federal courts would be shut on the fingers of millions of citizens for whom the judiciary is often the only protector of the individual rights that are the heart of our democracy.

This was a level of vituperation seldom heard before in such a context. No senator spoke in words so shrill about Haynsworth or Carswell, about Sessions or Manion, about Rehnquist or even, polarized though the politics of 1968 were, about Fortas. How had the Senate reached this point by 1987?

In part, the answer is to be found in the fluctuating fortunes of President Reagan. He had lost his majority in the Senate in 1986. He had also lost, through the Iran-contra scandal of the following spring, the ability a minority president often possesses, of building majorities ad hoc on the questions of greatest concern to him. At the moment when Bork's name went out to the world, there was as yet no administrative counteroffensive against the critics of its arms sales and its aid to the contra rebels in Nicaragua. A week later, Oliver North's testimony before a joint congressional committee created such a counteroffensive, but resentment outlasted North's television ratings. Reagan was weak, and the Democrats were strong and needed an issue on which to reassert themselves; Bork's nomination quickly became that issue. Other matters, such as the impending presidential campaign, Biden's role in both that campaign[5] and the confirmation hearings, and memories of Watergate and of Bork's part in the "Saturday night massacre," increased the chancy character of this particular nomination. The issues to which Senator Kennedy alludes in the strident oration just quoted remained in the forefront of the Bork debate, and his order of presentation will give order to the present discussion.

ABORTIONS AND LUNCH COUNTERS

Robert Bork's America, the senator had said, is a place where women "would be forced into back-alley abortions, blacks would sit at segregated lunch counters." Distortion begins with the word *would*. Bork, as a restraintist, believes that abortion law should be left to state legislators. In his view such matters as the use of Medicaid money for abortion or their availability on military bases may be left to Congress. The worst the advocates of legal abortion may say is that a world in which Bork's views prevail as to constitutional doctrine is one in which very restrictive abortion laws "could"—not that they "would"—be enacted and enforced. That distinction may be too subtle for the communicative powers of our mass media, but Senator Kennedy is certainly capable of it.

Blurring that distinction was not his only misrepresentation. Partisans of legal abortion forget that Bork was a valuable ally of theirs in one crucial fight. In 1981 Congress considered the Human Life Act, which would have declared that the legislature had determined that human life begins at conception. Sponsors hoped that the federal courts would infer that any state that distinguishes between abortion and homicide, subsequent to such a determination, encourages the former and so deprives a person of life without due process of law.

Senator Kennedy and his pro-abortion allies have short memories. In 1987 they first consigned to silence and, later, in their polemical excitement often outright denied the readily documented fact that Robert Bork testified against the Human Life Act.[6]

Eleanor Smeal, author of a weekly feminist newspaper, was another exploiter of this amnesia. In a late June issue she wrote:

> Women's groups and civil rights groups have pledged to fight a Right Wing ideological take-over of the Supreme Court with the nomination of U.S. Appeals Court Judge Robert Bork—or for that matter any nominee who will shift the majority of the Court to oppose legalized abortion, to destroy affirmative action, to abolish the right to privacy, or to roll back thirty years of civil rights and women's right progress. Group leaders who attended an emergency meeting of the Leadership Conference on Civil Rights made it clear they would fight one-two-or-more nominees who would give reactionaries the coveted fifth vote on the Court. Women's, civil rights, labor, senior citizen, and disabled groups see a possible Bork appointment as enabling the Right Wing to amend the Constitution with just one vote.[7]

The balance model of the Supreme Court and coverage of the just issued Webster decision conspired to put Roe v. Wade and the asserted right to privacy on the lips of everyone connected with the Bork confirmation debate.

But Smeal overestimated the staying power of the coalition of which she was a part. It held together for the fight against Bork, but there was no testing of its strength during the Ginsberg nomination that followed and that destroyed itself. There *was* a test of its staying power during the third, Anthony Kennedy, nomination, and the forces that had promised that they would oppose "two or more" nominees were nowhere to be found. Does this mean that Anthony Kennedy was not the "reactionary" that Bork was?[8] Or that stamina gave out? The most likely explanatory hypothesis for the gap between promise and performance is that Kennedy had the great tactical advantage of never having fired Archibald Cox.

The Cox firing was the great Unmentioned in the Bork debate. Confirmation opponents convened "focus groups" to help them decide what issues would be of most use in the effort to bring anti-Bork pressures to bear on key senators.[9] One important finding of this research was that the Cox firing did not move people; it was not a grassroots issue. After July, almost nothing was said about it. Yet memories of 1974 did stir the people who were trying to stir the grass roots. So the Cox issue should be understood as a kind of adhesive, keeping together the interest groups that worked against Bork, rather than as part of what they felt they had to do.

This self-assigned task was set forth in the September 1987 issue of Ms. in unusually ambitious terms. A contributor suggested that "if a Reagan nominee is rejected, there is a chance that a new President could appoint a judge even more progressive than Powell and we could begin to win back some things already lost, like gay rights and Medicaid abortion."[10]

Judge Bork, as a restraintist, would very likely have sustained any bill protecting "gay rights" that Congress could have passed. But what the words just quoted mean is that Bork would be unlikely to save the members of Congress the trouble of working out the details of such a bill, in that he would be unlikely to find a gay rights provision implicit in the Fourteenth Amendment. There are two possible places for such a finding. Sexual orientation might be considered a suspect category under the equal protection clause, or homosexual activity might be treated as a "liberty interest" under the substantive component of the due process clause, with or without the invocation of the word *privacy*. Even without Bork's presence, the Supreme Court has made no such finding under either clause. The editors of Ms. presumably hoped that a Democratic president would appoint a new justice who would tip the always precarious balance on the Court in the preferred direction, so that the Court would make one or the other of those findings. But the Senate did not keep the seat vacant long enough, and Ronald Reagan's successor was not a Democrat in any event.

Robert Bork would also have upheld against challenge a federal law funding abortions through the Medicaid system on the same principle that led him to oppose the Human Life Act. What Bork's opponents wanted was a Court that would save Congress the trouble of authorizing such expenditures, a Court that would take the terrible burden of a politically difficult choice off the shoulders of those elected officials whose job is to make politically difficult choices.

What is especially sad about the state of the debate on abortion is the loss of an opportunity for consensus. For one brief, shining moment, less than a decade before the Bork fight, it had seemed as if the body politic was coming to a decision that might be summarized in four words, "no prohibitions, no subsidies." Of course, neither Left nor Right could accept such a compromise, but between 1978 and 1981 it seemed as if the broad middle of opinion had reached that point and as if this center could hold.[11] Subsequent events—the Bork and Thomas confirmations prominent among them—show that it did not.

If the charge that Bork would force women into back-alley abortions was a symptom of the continuing polarization over the issue, the charge that Bork would send blacks back to segregated lunch counters was a symptom of our national fear that a tenuous consensus on civil rights embodied in the legislation of 1964–66 might fall apart. When Senator Kennedy, interviewed by the Boston Globe, defended his violent language, he said that he "had to be stark and direct, so as to sound the alarm and hold people in their places until we could get material together."[12] This is an admission that he had not "got together" the material to support his assertions when he made them; and that he was giving voice to prejudice in the hope that it would later acquire the status of informed judgment. That seems especially true of the "lunch counter" clause.

Elements of the "block Bork" coalition tried to make senators whose judgments were less hasty than Kennedy's pay a price for their hesitation. On July 6, Senator Daniel Patrick Moynihan (D-N.Y.), who is not on the Judiciary Committee, told the NAACP that he would take no position on Bork's confirmation until after that committee had completed its hearings. To this, one representative of that association replied: "I have the votes in New York to defeat him . . . I'll get what I want. It's strictly politics."[13] This final sentence sums up the thesis of this book, except for my addition of the word *alas*!

Racial politics also explains an ad with a Gregory Peck voice-over, produced by People for the American Way. This television spot ran for three weeks before and during Bork's hearings. Peck told America that Bork "defended poll taxes and literacy tests, which kept many Americans from voting." Simple fairness and an honest recognition of Judge Bork's judicial philosophy would have required a twofold explanation here. Bork never defended either the wisdom of such tests or their constitutionality if applied so as to discriminate. He had argued only that if race-neutral, they are constitutional.

The authors of The People Rising, a book that celebrates Bork's defeat as a triumph of grassroots organization, back away from the allegations in the Gregory Peck ads. The authors quote David Cohen, of the Advocacy Institute, who said that Peck's text was documented "to meet the zone of acceptability for feisty ads."[14] This is hardly an endorsement of accuracy. That the text was "feisty" is beyond doubt; clearly, the "zone of acceptability" expands and contracts according to the political weather.

Most of the well-known civil rights advocates and organizations did gather around the anti-Bork banner. But some usually reliable foot soldiers in that army went unmustered. Lloyd Cutler, former counsel to the president and a founder of the Lawyer's Committee for Civil Rights Under Law, broke with that committee when it lined up against Bork in July. Cutler explained, in the New York Times, that "in my view, Judge Bork is neither an ideologue nor an extreme right-winger, either in his judicial philosophy or in his personal position on current social issues."[15]

With regard to the interpretation of the equal protection clause of the Fourteenth Amendment, Bork, long before any question of appointment to the federal bench arose, had published an article supporting the result in Brown v. Board and the two-tier understanding of equal protection that arose from that decision.[16] Bork would limit the higher tier to classifications by race or ethnicity, and he has never accepted an "intermediate tier" for the adjudication of classifications by sex or alienage.[17]

This is, perhaps, the best place to note that Governor Bill Clinton of Arkansas played a small part in the Bork revue. Opponents of Reagan's nominee planned to include Clinton, as a representative of the new, and integrated, south, in their first group of witnesses before the Judiciary Committee. But Bork's own testimony took longer than expected, and on the date when Governor Clinton would have testified, he was out of the country.[18] Is it Clinton's fate, then, always to miss a chance to take a stand?

ROGUE POLICE AND SCHOOLCHILDREN

Robert Bork's America, continued Senator Kennedy, is a place where "rogue police could break down citizens' doors in midnight raids, schoolchildren could not be taught about evolution." Distortion here starts at *rogue*. It is sometimes appropriate for a police officer, even one who is not a rogue, to break down a door. Imagine a citizen sniping from the window of a high-rise apartment at people on the street below. Should the police not put a stop to this, even at the expense of breaking down the door? Even if the killer chooses midnight as the best time to begin firing? It is not only Robert Bork's but Senator Kennedy's America in which raiding that apartment would be considered reasonable and necessary. What, then, did the senator mean to make an issue here?

A Nader Organization, the Public Citizen Group, prepared a memorandum that may answer that question for us. "The Judicial Record of Judge Robert H. Bork" mentions no more than two cases in which Judge

Bork voted on an issue of criminal law or procedure in a split decision. The public citizens who put this material together found it ominous that Bork voted for the prosecution in both those cases. Statistically this gives no warrant for Kennedy's "midnight raid" language,[19] but one may look to the facts of those two decisions.

One concerns the admissibility and sufficiency of eyewitness testimony at trial.[20] These issues are important but involve no question of a raid on anyone. The other case may be what Kennedy had in mind. In United States v. Mount (1985),[21] the appeals court considered the appeal of a defendant convicted at trial of making a false statement on a passport application. This litigation arose out of an arrest made by British police officers after Charles M. Mount had failed to return his rental car on time. The officers searched Mount's room and found several passports bearing his photograph and a variety of names. They turned the information over to the American authorities. No official of the United States, then, ever searched any abode of Mount or initiated any action in anticipation of, or in cooperation with, the searches conducted by agents of the host country. Mount's appeal was an effort to make new law, to give the search and seizure provision of the Fourth Amendment extraterritorial effect. The Court refused that suggestion. The vote was unanimous, and the Public Citizen Group's representation of this case as a "split decision" is due to Bork's use of somewhat different reasoning in reaching his conclusion from that employed by his colleagues.

The gist of Bork's opinion was that the limits that he saw upon the "supervisory power of the federal courts over the administration of criminal justice." would be exceeded by an application of the exclusionary rule on these facts: "[W]e clearly lack supervisory power to create any exclusionary rule that expands the rule the Supreme Court has created under the Fourth Amendment. That forecloses any exclusion of evidence seized abroad by foreign police."[22] The Public Interest Group's book tried to make something ominous out of this and other declarations in Bork's opinion, arguing that they indicate a willingness on Judge Bork's part to abandon the exclusionary rule altogether. But all they indicate is that he accepts the truism that the lower courts must follow the authority of the Supreme Court.

Perhaps Robert Bork's England is a place where the police are allowed to engage in practices that Senator Kennedy associates with rogues. But that does not warrant the attribution of such practices to Robert Bork's America.

What can we say, though, to the senator's claim that the judge would not permit the teaching of evolution to schoolchildren? Neither as an academic nor as a judge has Bork played any large part in our nation's debates over the complex and difficult questions of the relation between church and state. Although it is hard to find any support for Kennedy's professed concerns in this area, it is true that an ardent polemicist (which Bork certainly is) will sooner or later express an opinion on almost every imaginable subject. On July 28, 1987, the Washington Post ran a front-page article on a meeting under the auspices of the Brookings Institute that Judge Bork attended, in September 1985, with several members of the clergy. At that meeting Bork spoke on church-state separation and argued in favor of greater restraint in judicial review of alleged entanglements. On August 6, the Post ran a letter from Joshua O. Haberman, who described himself as "a rabbi with a strong commitment to the separation of church and state" and as a participant at the Brookings Institute gathering. This eyewitness account indicates that Bork said little or nothing that would allow predictions about his decisions in particular cases:

> The judge showed great sensitivity to the ambiguities and dilemmas of the First Amendment. During an extraordinarily long exchange with the assembled clergy, Judge Bork was cautious, yet candid and open-minded . . . I do not recall the judge's ever stating how he would vote on matters such as prayer in public schools. Rather, I gained the impression that Judge Bork favors a pragmatic approach to the most controversial church-and-state issues, with all sides developing more flexibility. He sees a need to pull back from the growing polarization on these issues, which is highly damaging to the country and to religious bodies.

On September 24, Kenneth Dean, a Baptist minister from Rochester, New York, testified before the Senate Judiciary Committee to his memories of Bork's address at that conference. Dean quoted Bork as saying: "[T]here may be in man an ineradicable longing for the transcendent. If religion is officially removed from public celebration, other transcendent principles, some of them very ugly indeed, may replace them . . . . The public square will not remain naked. If religion departs, some other principle—perhaps political or racial—will arrive."[23] Dean inferred from these comments that Bork, if made a justice, would assist what Dean called "the right-wing evangelicals . . . in their attempt to gain control of the public square."[24]

Assuming that Bork said what Dean reports, the judge was obviously elaborating ideas inspired by Richard John Neuhaus, to whom the phrase "the naked public square" is due.[25] Whatever exactly is meant by the phrase *right-wing evangelical*, Father Neuhaus does not fit that bill. Nor does Dean seem to have grappled with the weighty argument that he quotes Bork as making. Indeed, if Dean is right it follows that Rabbi Haberman is right about the "candid and open-minded" frame of mind that Judge Bork displayed at that meeting.

By the time he retired from the appellate court and wrote his half-memoir, half-treatise, The Tempting of America, Bork seems to have forgotten Neuhaus and to have returned, when referring to Church and state relations, to the stale formulas of restraintism.[26]

One conclusion is inevitable. Neither in 1985 nor in 1987 did Bork oppose the teaching of evolution to schoolchildren.

WRITERS, ARTISTS, AND JUDGES

Is it the case that, in Robert Bork's America, "writers and artists would be censured at the whim of the government"? Let us make generous allowance for the usual Kennedy hyperbole, by substituting"could" for "would." The allegation remains very disturbing.

One of the prevalent journalistic clichés of 1987 was that of Bork's "paper trail." He had expressed opinions, publicly, about an enormous array of matters over so long a period and with such industry that nearly everyone could find reasons for offense. The item on this trail to which I take offense is an article he wrote in 1971 for publication by the Indiana Law Journal. It covered much ground (including the endorsement of Brown v. Board), but its chief concern was to resolve "First Amendment problems." These problems did notinvolve the religion clause, only free speech and the press.

Despite all I have said, in lamenting the extravagance of Bork's critics, I would, if magically transformed into the Senate, have great difficulty voting to confirm a justice who had argued for this conclusion: "Explicitly and predominantly political speech . . . seems to me the only form of speech that a principled judge can prefer to other claimed freedoms . . . . If the dialectical progression is not to become an analogical stampede, the protection of the first amendment must be cut off when it reaches the outer limits of political speech."[27] Bork's argument in favor of this position may be put briefly. In order to discern the purpose of the First Amendment, a jurist must decide what is unique about "speech" and "the press," what distinguishes these activities from such unprotected human pursuits as skeet-shooting or stamp collecting. Bork suggests that of all the functions speech can perform, only one is unique: the revelation and dissemination of political truths. On the theory that a rule should extend only so far as the reason for its existence, the protection of the First Amendment extends only so far as he indicated in the passage cited.

Bork's interpretation of the First Amendment would not protect works of fiction, even those far from any extant definition of "obscenity," from the force of law and the heat of a bonfire. Nor would it protect from suppression a scientifically disputed hypothesis, such as the Copernican theory of the solar system was once, and Immanuel Velikovsky's theory of colliding planets is now. The framers of the Bill of Rights considered Galileo a martyr to the cause of science.[28] It is even plausible to suppose that they had his silencing specifically in mind when they wrote the words that set Bork's "problems." It is not plausible that they meant to grant legitimacy to such a silencing. Any interpretation of "free speech" that would defend neither Galileo's Dialogue on the Great World Systems nor Vladimir

Nabokov's <u>Lolita</u> is to be presumed incorrect without further discussion. Additional examination of Bork's theory ought to be in the nature of an autopsy, not a medical checkup.

Where did Bork do wrong? I think the nub of his error is his assumption that a constitutionally grounded rule extends only so far as its purpose. This makes the plain language of the text subject to the extraneous check of philosophical speculation. Let me lay it down, rather, as an exegetical principle, that no constitutional rule is to be checked by any consideration extrinsic to itself, other than another constitutional rule. This principle allows the possibility that free speech can be checked by, for example, the demand of a fair trial. But free speech is not to be checked by a community's determination that a novel about a sexually precocious child must be "dirty" nor by some authority's devotion to the solar system as described by Ptolemy.

The old axiom <u>restringenda</u> <u>lex</u> <u>est</u>, <u>ut</u>, <u>cessante</u> <u>ratione</u>, <u>ipsa</u> <u>cessat</u> (the law is to be so restricted that when its reason ceases, so does its operation), which proved of great value in the development of the common law and is still of value in the construction of statutes, ought to be set aside or self-referentially applied when one sets out to interpret a document expressly designed to provide a fundamental law.

As Bork applies it, there seems to be a confusion between two meanings of the word *purpose*, or <u>ratione</u>. On one hand, a single clause has a purpose within the broader sentence or text of which it is a part. On the other hand, that whole sentence or text can have an extratextual purpose to which the single clause may be expected to contribute. Asking what the purpose is of the protection of speech is hazardous, because it seems to hold the one clause responsible for an extratextual purpose better attributed to the whole of the Bill of Rights. One cannot decide that a particular gear within a clock has the purpose of telling time. It has the purpose, rather, of transferring motion from the spring to a larger gear to which it is adjacent. Only the whole clock has the purpose of telling time. If it is to achieve this goal (or if the Bill of Rights is to achieve its goal of limiting the power of the sovereign and warding off abuses of that power), those of us who are not watchmakers had better not try tampering with the gears one by one.

To his credit, Judge Bork repudiated the thesis of his article in a letter in the <u>ABA</u> <u>Journal</u>[29] three years ahead of his nomination to the Supreme Court. Bork and the advocates of his confirmation laid great stress upon this repudiation and argued that the opposition was not fair in invoking a provocative, expressly tentative, and theoretical piece by a professor of law, that had been published sixteen years before the nomination, as if it were evidence of present intention.

But Bork's opponents were right to invoke that article, for it illustrates a direction of thought never since reversed. The ground upon which the judge rested his repudiation in 1984 of his thesis of 1971 is narrow and not at all reassuring. Apparently in later years Bork felt the force of the consideration that drawing the line between a political and nonpolitical speech would be a very difficult task. A pornographer could always end his novel with a page of policy proposals, more or less closely connected with what has gone before ("Legalize polygamy, and the graphically described adultery of this novel will be unnecessary!") The proposed principle would not, as Bork regretfully concluded, prevent the dialectical progression of free speech arguments from becoming an analogical stampede.

Bork's retraction, therefore, suggests only that his restraintism would still encourage him to let a legislature censor Galileo or Nabokov, if he could think of some more airtight way of reconciling that censorship with freedom for Henry George to argue for a single tax on land. Bork's old formula for reconciliation no longer satisfies him, but that dissatisfaction has apparently not led him to abandon the attempt. Since my objection to restraintism in First Amendment law is that the Supreme Court should _not_ be restrained in performing its proper functions and that protecting speech from legislators is one such function, I would not want on that Court a justice who continues to favor this restraint.

Now to the last of Kennedy's charges. The concluding feature of "Bork's America" is that "the doors of the federal courts would be shut on the fingers of millions of citizens for whom the judiciary is often the only protector of the individual rights that are the heart of our democracy." What is all that rhetoric about?

SHUTTING THE DOORS

The clause of the Constitution that established the courts, doors and all, authorizes their jurisdiction over "cases" and "controversies."[30] To be considered a case or controversy, a lawsuit must be initiated by a complaint wherein plaintiffs allege a _direct_ and _actual_ injury. A plaintiff who makes such an allegation against a defendant is said to have "standing." A plaintiff who alleges only a hypothetical injury ("The defendant's factory pollutes a lake where I may some day want to go fishing") or who alleges a real but indirect injury ("Acid rain caused by defendant's polluting practices results in expensive public reclamation projects, and I pay taxes that pay for those projects") will receive no hearing from the federal courts. A plaintiff might allege that industrial emissions have increased the acidity of the rain that falls into the lake on which he does fish and that the acidic fish have ruined his health, resulting in the medical costs documented in exhibit A. The plaintiff who sought to hold an industrial defendant liable for such actual damage, on such a theory, would state a claim that the courts could hear. He would have _standing_.

The preceding paragraph is noncontroversial. Any conceivable Supreme Court appointee would concur that there must be rules of standing, and the effect of those rules is, of course, to exclude many claims that sincere and aggrieved citizens want to present. If this constitutes "shutting the doors," then doors must be shut.

It is also true that Robert Bork has a somewhat more restrictive view of standing than many other jurists. Whether he is right or wrong in taking that position is a complicated question, which involves the proper balance between the demands of justice in many an individual dispute and the need for systemic judicial efficiency. Had Senator Kennedy said only that he doubted the rightness of the balance Bork struck, he might have made a valuable point, worthy of a discussion more tranquil than anything in his speech.

For an example of Bork's views on standing, I turn to one of the first decisions he wrote as a judge of the court of appeals, Vander Jagt v. O'Neill (1983).[31]   In this case, fourteen Republican members of the House of Representatives claimed that the defendants, Democratic leaders, systematically discriminated against them in the assignment of committee and subcommittee posts in a way that diluted their voting power and thereby the voting rights of their constituents. This claim was an invitation to the courts to change the rules of one of the houses of our nation's legislature, perhaps inspired, in part, by the precedent set by the litigation concerning Congressman Adam Clayton Powell. In that earlier case, the Supreme Court had announced that considerations of the separation of powers will not automatically prohibit judicial review of House rules.[32]

Powell obviously had standing to complain of his own exclusion from a legislative body to which he had won election. He asserted actual and direct injury. The defendants in Vander Jagt v. O'Neill claimed that this was not now the fact.

Judge James Gordon wrote the majority opinion for the appeals court.[33] Gordon reasoned (1) that the plaintiffs do have standing but (2) that the issue is nonetheless nonjusticiable: "Courts and commentators have long recognized that it is critical to distinguish questions about whether judicial power exists, from questions about whether judicial power should be exercised."[34]   The Court refrained from the exercise of power that it believed itself to possess, in order to keep its hands off the tar-baby of disputation about parliamentary rules.

Judge Bork, concurring in the judgment for the defendants, wrote separately in Vander Jagt to argue that the question of "remedial discretion" need never have arisen, because the plaintiffs had no standing. In this one instance, then, Bork argued for a stricter reading of the "case or controversy" requirement than the majority of the panel could accept. Neither this decision (of very limited importance as precedent for those "millions of Americans" not in Congress) nor any other Bork voted or wrote on during his judicial service closed the courthouse doors for those millions in Kennedy's mind.

Lloyd Cutler's testimony to the Judiciary Committee on September 22 included the observation that in <u>Allen</u> <u>v.</u> <u>Wright</u> (1984)[35] the U.S. Supreme Court cited with approval Bork's concurrence in <u>Vander</u> <u>Jagt</u>.[36] This undercut any intention Senator Kennedy may have harbored to argue that Bork's views on standing are "out of the mainstream" of contemporary American legal thought.

Aside from the doctrinal content of the Gordon and Bork opinions, the <u>Vander</u> <u>Jagt</u> litigation had repercussions at the Judiciary Committee hearings. On August 23, Judge Gordon wrote to the committee to express his opposition to the Bork appointment. He recalled his impression, at the judges' first meeting to discuss this case after oral argument, that he, Judge Roger Robb, and Judge Bork were all in agreement that Guy Vander Jagt's appeal must be dismissed on grounds of remedial discretion. He assigned Bork to write the unanimous opinion on that theory. Bork wrote his "lack of standing" opinion instead and circulated it to the offices of Gordon and Robb. Gordon came to the conclusion that Bork was maneuvering to have his view go forward as "the majority opinion of the Court when in fact, it was the minority opinion," his alone.[37] The trick, if that is what it was, failed. The summary I have given of the two published opinions implies as much. But Gordon thought it a disqualification that a prospective associate justice of the Supreme Court would try such a ruse: "I do not believe one who would resort to the actions toward his own colleagues and the majesty of the law as did Judge Bork in this instance possesses those qualities of character, forthrightness, and truthfulness necessary for those who would grace our highest court."[38]

This charge became public in the second week of September. Bork and his allies on the committee argued, in response, that it is quite common for a judge to begin writing an opinion with the intention of following one theory yet to change his views on a case in the middle of the task, that Bork circulated his first or "majority" draft on the standing issue in hopes of winning one of the other two judges over to his point of view, and that this was no such underhanded a scheme as Judge Gordon imagined but, at worst, a misunderstanding.

The Gordon accusation quickly faded from public attention. Yet the fact that a judge who had worked closely with the nominee came forward with so strong a view and one expressed not as a matter of judicial philosophy or political theory but as a matter of "character" and "forthrightness" no doubt contributed to the atmosphere of distrust in which memories of Watergate were also an element. Atmosphere did more to defeat Bork's nomination than did all the fireworks first ignited by Senator Kennedy.

On September 22 the <u>Washington</u> <u>Post</u> carried the report of the first Republican defection, that of Robert Packwood of Oregon, who made the grounds for his opposition to Bork very clear: "I am convinced that Judge Bork feels so strongly opposed to the right of privacy that he will do everything possible to cut and trim the liberties that the right of privacy protects."[39]

This issue of privacy, and so of reproductive freedom, arose in an industrial context inside the hearing room, when Bork's opponents discovered an emotion-provoking decision in the nominee's record as an appellate judge. Twenty years before President Reagan sent Bork's name to the Senate, the managers of a manufacturing plant had found that its processes released more lead into the air than the Occupational Safety and Health Administration (OSHA) allows if pregnant women are exposed. Management faced the choice of discharging women employees of childbearing age in the department affected or of subjecting itself to unlimited liability for exposing unborn children to grave danger. According to the findings of the administrative law Judge, there was <u>no existing technology</u> that would have allowed this production process to go forward without the release of the levels of lead that created the violation. The company, rather tactlessly, but under the circumstances understandably, informed female employees of childbearing age that they could keep their jobs if they were properly sterilized.

The Oil, Chemical & Atomic Workers' International Union took the position that offering this choice was itself a "hazardous condition of employment" and brought the matter before the OSHA administrative law judge. The judge reasoned that since "Congress conceived of occupational hazards in terms of processes and materials" rather than in terms of management personnel policies, the grievance did not state a claim on which he could grant relief. The Occupational Safety and Health Review Commission affirmed the judge's decision. The union appealed and lost again before the court of appeals for the District of Columbia, in a decision of 1984, written by Bork. The union did not petition the Supreme Court for review.

In 1987, People for the American Way, the same group that paid for the Gregory Peck television spot described earlier, ran a full-page ad in the <u>New York Times</u> under the caption "Robert Bork v. the People." One subhead was, "Sterilizing Workers."[40] The ad gave the following description of the facts:

> A major chemical company was pumping so much lead into the workplace that female employees who became pregnant were risking having babies with birth defects. Instead of cleaning up the air, the company ordered all women workers to be sterilized or lose their jobs. When the union took the company to court, Judge Bork ruled in favor of the company. Five women underwent

surgical sterilization. Within months, the company closed the dangerous part of the plant. And the sterilized women lost their jobs.

There are four lies in this account of <u>American Cyanamid</u>.[41] First, the verb *pumping* implies willfulness, as distinct from the unavoidable side effects of a lawful manufacturing process. Second, Judge Bork by himself could not "rule in favor" of anyone. He was one of three judges on a panel that arrived unanimously at that decision; he wrote for the Court. Third, it is a deception to skip over the two levels of administrative review that created the factual record available to Judge Bork and his colleagues when they received the case. If the ad had given these details, its authors might have been forced to state that the appellate judges are required to accept the findings of fact of the lower court and that these findings made it clear that "cleaning up the air" was <u>not</u> an available alternative. Finally, the ad deliberately confuses the sequence of events in order to imply that five women underwent sterilization as a result of Judge Bork's decision. Those who made that choice did so in 1978, four years before Bork even became a judge.

If organized feminism is, in fact, interested in opening up choices for women in the workplace, it will direct its collective attention toward the repeal of much of OSHA. The whole act could be replaced with a simply worded statute requiring full disclosure of all the conditions and risks of employment at the time of hiring and at any time thereafter when a change in those conditions occurs. Such a statute would leave everything else up to the negotiations of the parties in the marketplace. But much (not quite all) of what calls itself feminism today has been captured by an anticapitalist animus that makes such a proposal unthinkable.[42]

COUNTING THE VOTES

On October 6 the Judiciary Committee took its vote, nine to five to recommend against consent. All eight Democrats joined one Republican defector, Arlen Specter (Pa.) to produce this result. On the seventh, President Reagan met with his nominee, and they decided to push the matter to a full Senate vote. In the words of Bork's statement to the press on the eighth:

> The process of confirming Justices for our nation's highest Court has been transformed in a way that should not, indeed must not, be permitted to occur ever again.
>   The tactics and techniques of national political campaigns have been unleashed on the process of confirming judges. That is not simply disturbing. It is dangerous . . . .
>   If I withdraw now, that campaign would be seen as a success and it would be mounted against future nominees.[43]

This was Bork's finest hour. When he turned the debate on the Senate floor into an argument about the use of high-pressure partisan campaigns in confirmation hearings, he raised a banner deserving of salute.

The debate ended on October 23, when, at 2 P.M. the Senate voted fifty-eight to forty-two to deny consent. The fifty-eight votes included six Republicans. The forty-two votes included two Democrats. The near-perfect party discipline on both sides is indicative of the increasing polarization of the politics of judicial appointment.

On October 29, Reagan announced the nomination of Douglas Ginsberg (also on the court of appeals, D.C.) to the still-vacant Powell seat. On November 5, Judge Ginsberg admitted that a National Public Radio report on his marijuana use was correct, and two days later he withdraw his name from consideration. In subsequent weeks, several presidential candidates admitted to having "experimented" with marijuana in their respective college days, and since then such a charge has had little sting.

On November 11, the president announced the nomination of Anthony Kennedy of the Ninth Circuit Court of Appeals. One senator told the Washington Post that there would be no fight over the Kennedy nomination: "Nobody wants to go through that again. There's just too much blood on the floor."[44]

On January 14, 1988, Reagan accepted Bork's resignation from the federal bench.[45]

On February 3, the Senate confirmed Judge Kennedy ninety-seven to none. He was sworn in on the eighteenth. On the record that Justice Kennedy has created in his first six years in office, there is some reason to believe that he differs from Robert Bork in exactly the area where one would most want to find a difference—in his understanding of the First Amendment. He has held, for example, that the First Amendment protects the speech of a criminal describing his activities as a "wiseguy"—hardly the "explicitly political" speech of Robert Bork's article.[46] The director of the Reporters' Committee for Freedom of the Press has said that Kennedy is "solid on our issues."[47] If one believes that reporters are often on the better side of "their issues," this comment may be cheering. Perhaps a little of the "blood on the floor" was shed to a good end.

NOTES

1. Dionne, Jr., "Biden Joins Campaign for the Presidency," New York Times, June 10, 1987, p. A18.

2. Raimi, "Ambition and Compassion," The Freeman (January 1992), 13.

3. M. Pertschuk & W. Schaetzel, The People Rising (New York, 1989), 149.

4. 133 Cong. Rec. July 1, 1987, S. 9,188–9,189.

5. Dowd, "Biden's Debate Finale: An Echo from Abroad," New York Times, September 12, 1987, p. 1.

6. Sullivan, "The Bork Screw," The New Republic (October 19, 1987), 14.

7. Smeal, Eleanor Smeal Report, 5:1, p. 1 (June 28, 1987).

8. On the evidence available at the time of Kennedy's confirmation, he was "an agreeable Judge who votes like Judge Robert Bork and writes like Lewis Powell, Jr."—in the words of Alan Dershowitz, quoted in P. McGuigan & D. Weyrich, Ninth Justice (Lanham, MD, 1990) at xv.

9. Pertschuk & Schaetzel at 134.

10. Laurino, "Justice: The Battle of Bork," Ms (September 1987), p. 111.

11. Harris v. MacCrae, 448 U.S. 297 (1980).

12. R. Bork, Tempting at 282.

13. Noble, "Biden Vows to Lead Forces Against Bork's Confirmation," New York Times, July 9, 1987, A1.

14. Pertschuk & Schaetzel at 267.

15. Cutler, " Saving Bork From Both Friends and Enemies," New York Times, July 16, 1987, A27.

16. Bork, "Neutral Principles and Some First Amendment Problems," 47 Ind. L. J. 1 (1971) at 14.

17. U.S. Congress, Senate, Committee on the Judiciary, Nomination of Robert Bork, Hearings, 100th Cong., 1st Sess., September 15 to September 30, 1987, pp. 510–511.

18. E. Bronner, Battle For Justice. (New York, 1989), 285.

19. Bork Hearings, 1,725 et seq.

20. U.S. v. Singleton, 759 F.2d 176 (1985).

21. 757 F.2d 1315.

22. Id. 1324.

23. Bork Hearings, 3187 et seq.

24. Id. 3188.

25. R. Neuhaus, The Naked Public Square (Grand Rapids, MI, 1984).

26. "The Court has established a rigidly secularist view of the establishment clause, which would not have disturbed too many people if the clause had not been incorporated to prohibit religious practices that the states had employed for many years. The sense of outrage was particularly intense when the Court prohibited prayer in the public schools and years later even disapproved of some moments of silence. The application of the Bill of Rights to the states in this and other matters has done much to alter the moral tone of communities across the country." R. Bork, Tempting at 95.

27. Bork, "Neutral Principles" at 26–27.

28. T. Jefferson, Notes on the State of Virginia, ed. William Peden (Chapel Hill, 1955), 159–160.

29. Letter, "Judge Bork Replies," ABA Journal (February 1984), 132.

30. Art. III, §2.

31. 699 F.2d 1166 (1983).

32. Powell v. McCormick. 395 U.S. 486 (1969).

33. The appeals court seldom sits en banc, with all judges in attendance. Most cases are decided by a three-judge panel determined by rotation. Gordon was the senior judge on this panel (A. Kamen, "Federal Judge Assails Bork's Conduct in Controversial 1983 Case," Washington Post, September 9, 1987, A3).

34. 699 F.2d at 1170.

35. Bork Hearings at 2,349.

36. 468 U.S. 737.

37. Bork Hearings 318.

38. Id.

39. McGuigan & Weyrich at 142.

40. Id., 142–143.

41. Oil, Chemical, & Atomic Workers v. American Cyanamid Co., 741 F.2d 444 (D.C. Cir. 1984).

42. Postrel, "Why Women Can't Commit," Reason (June 1991), 4.

43. Quoted in Tempting, 313–315.

44. Bork, Tempting, 345–347. See also Cannon, "Reagan Resumes Attack on Bork's Senate Foes," Washington Post, October 14, 1987, p. A1.

45. "Letter Accepting the Resignation of Robert H. Bork as United State Circuit Judge," January 14, 1988, Public Papers of the Presidents: Ronald Reagan—1988, at 39.

46. Simon & Schuster v. New York State Crime Victims Bd., 112 S.Ct. 501 (1991) at 507 (J. Kennedy, concurring).

47. Barrett, "Kennedy's High Court Tenure Fails to Console Bork-Smitten Conservatives," Wall Street Journal, February 5, 1992, B5.

10

Staring into the Abyss . . .

The first section of the Fourteenth Amendment prohibits any state from denying any person the equal protection of the laws. The fifth section allows Congress to enact "appropriate legislation" to enforce the first. In the face of these two clauses, are there any limits left on congressional power? In 1976 New Hampshire, through David Souter, its attorney general, tried to answer that question yes. In 1990, when Souter came before the Senate as a Supreme Court nominee, Senator Kennedy thundered back no.

In 1973 New Hampshire filed with the Equal Employment Opportunity Commission the required reports known as EEO-4s. Contrary to regulation, the state refused to indicate the race or national origin of its employees and inserted the word *American* in place of the ethnic designations contained in the form prepared by the EEOC. In 1974 the state refused to file any EEO-4s at all. In July 1975 the United States of America brought suit against New Hampshire, alleging the violation of regulations that had been properly issued under the authority of the civil rights statutes.[1]

New Hampshire's actions were not negligent. They were the implementation of a policy announced by the duly elected governor, a policy of noncooperation with what Meldrim Thomson saw as the unconstitutional and discriminatory policies of the EEOC in its enforcement of Title VII of the Civil Rights Act of 1964.[2]

In December the district court granted the motion of the United States for summary judgment[3] and ordered state compliance with the regulations at issue.[4] The state appealed, and Attorney General David Souter, with the help of one of his assistants, prepared its brief for submission to the court of appeals, First Circuit.

It would have been an easier memorandum to prepare had the Supreme Court already published an opinion in <u>National League of Cities v. Usery</u>. A few months later, when that opinion appeared, it became the law of the land that the United States may not set a minimum wage for the employees of the constituent states. Souter's chief argument, that state sovereignty limits the regulatory power both of Congress and of agencies acting on Congress's behalf, was analogous to the argument of the Usery majority.[5]

Souter made other arguments. The enforced gathering of statistics on race and ethnicity is unconstitutional, he reasoned, by virtue of its potential for discriminatory abuse. A state policy of noncooperation with such a procedure ought to be commended for protecting the rights of that state's citizens, not condemned for allegedly infringing those rights. Furthermore, Souter argued, the constitutional "right to privacy" has meaning in the workplace as well as in the marital home. For the EEOC to demand information about the racial composition of the state's workforce violates the right of the people therein "to be left alone." In light of the confirmation debate of 1990, after Souter's nomination to the Supreme Court, it must be remembered that each of these arguments is to be understood as the contention of a professional advocate, on behalf of his client. Neither singly nor in combination do they allow any inference about David Souter's convictions on the issues.

The arguments did not prevail. The district court's judgment for the United States was affirmed by the appeals court in an opinion by Judge Edward McEntee. He reasoned that possible abuse of information is no argument for banning its collection; that Souter's privacy contention is not even "deserving of attention";[6] and that Congress does have authority over the states for the purpose of remedying racial discrimination. The U.S. Supreme Court refused to hear the case, thus letting Judge McEntee's opinion stand.[7]

It is important to understand that McEntee could reasonably have defended the same ruling even after the Supreme Court decision in Usery, for the civil rights laws have a unique constitutional status. When Congress acts to regulate wages, whether of public or of private employees, its authority proceeds from the original text of the Constitution, as a regulation of interstate commerce.[8] The short-lived Usery doctrine arose out of a chain of precedents interpreting this commerce clause and, accordingly, served as a limit upon the cognate power alone. On the other hand, when Congress acts to prohibit job discrimination, its authority proceeds, as McEntee's opinion observed, from section five of the Fourteenth Amendment: "The Congress shall have power to enforce, by appropriate legislation, the provisions of this article."

The first section of the Fourteenth Amendment guarantees to every person the equal protection of the laws. The fifth section allows Congress to enforce the first. Conjoined, these clauses may authorize Congress, or agencies created by Congress, to gather information germane to whether the states are denying their actual or potential employees that equal protection.

As for state sovereignty, the post–Civil War amendments were specifically designed to encroach upon matters that before the war had been left to the several states.

I submit that the argument of the last two paragraphs leaps too quickly to its conclusions. Perhaps the Supreme Court should have granted New Hampshire's petition for certiorari, not so that it might reverse the opinion of the courts below but so that it could explain what limits, if any, are left to congressional authority under §5 so understood. Is "appropriate legislation to enforce" the provisions of the Fourteenth Amendment whatever the Congress says that it is? One must hope not, for in such a case we live under legislative supremacy, and no check to the factions of that one branch remains. A close reading of §5 gives substance to one's hopes for the opposite. What this section authorizes is only legislation that is <u>appropriate</u>; the use of that modifier implies that there is some legislation that would not be appropriate to the specified ends and that Congress, by an additional inference, is not empowered to enact.

Governor Thomson's policy, by virtue of which his agents identified the employees of New Hampshire simply as Americans on the 1973 EEO-4, seems at least on its face perfectly consistent with the equal protection clause. Indeed, it seems conceived in the spirit of that clause and of Justice Harlan's dictum in his <u>Plessy</u> dissent that "the constitution is color-blind." One must hope that the federal courts, at every level, will become more particular than is now their custom about just how Congress derives its authority from the Fourteenth Amendment to override a state policy, so long as that policy is itself consistent with color-blind employment.

The reasoning that defends a broad regulatory power for the EEOC as an exercise by Congress of its §5 authority may also slide too quickly over the difficulties of "delegation." Congress did not order New Hampshire to collect information about the racial and ethnic backgrounds of its employees. Nor did Congress order the EEOC to require such a thing. How much may an agent presume upon the silence of its principal?[9]

NEW HAMPSHIRE AND VIRGINIA

In February 1988 George Bush's campaign for the Republican nomination for president was in trouble. Robert Dole had just won an impressive victory in the Iowa caucuses. Pat Robertson had come in second there, relegating the vice president to third place, with just 19 percent of the vote. A loss in New Hampshire in the February 16 primary would have left the Bush campaign, if indeed it was still alive, dangerously crippled. But with the enthusiastic support of Warren Rudman, a popular New Hampshire senator, Bush was able to win that primary, and his campaign rebounded with new vigor. Warren Rudman thereby became creditor to the president. Rudman was also, had long been, a friend and sometime mentor of David Souter, who was now an associate justice of the supreme court of New Hampshire and who was destined, with the assistance of Rudman and Bush, to join a still higher court.

On August 3, midway through that election year, the House of Representatives voted to impeach U.S. district court Judge Alcee Hastings (Southern District, Florida) for "high crimes and misdemeanors," although Hastings had been acquitted in a criminal trial of the charge of accepting a bribe from the racketeering defendants before his court, and that same accusation was at the heart of the articles of impeachment. Neither the principles of fairness that underlie the double jeopardy clause nor the tradition of comity for the judgments of trial courts on matters of fact could stand in the way of the rite of political purification that "impeachment" has become.

The Monday following George Bush's inauguration, in January 1989, the Supreme Court issued a much anticipated decision on civil rights and affirmative action, Richmond v. J.A. Croson Co.[10] The facts are these: the City of Richmond demanded that Croson, a construction contractor, give at least 30 percent of the dollar value of its subcontracted work to firms owned by U.S. citizens of specified racial and linguistic groups: "Blacks, Spanish-speaking, Orientals, Indians, Eskimos, or Aleuts." Since a municipality is a creature of the state by which it is chartered, there is no distinction between an act of Virginia and an act of Richmond for purposes of the application of the Fourteenth Amendment. Accordingly, Croson asked the federal district court in Virginia to strike the burdensome racial set-asides, which would be called "quotas" in a world where plain and accurate words are valued. The requirement was represented as depriving of the equal protection of the laws those subcontractors whose owners did not qualify as belonging to the enumerated groups. The district court granted judgment for plaintiff.

Richmond appealed to the Supreme Court, relying upon a 1980 decision, Fullilove v. Klutznick, as precedent.[11] In Fullilove, the Supreme Court upheld a federal law that specified a minority set-aside similar to the municipal program now at issue. But Fullilove, despite its name, does not "conquer all." In Croson, Justice Sandra Day O'Connor delivered a lengthy opinion, parts of which commanded the majority of the Court. In those parts, the judgment proper, O'Connor applied the standard "strict scrutiny" to Richmond's racial classifications and found: "The city has failed to demonstrate a compelling interest in apportioning public contracting opportunities on the basis of race . . . .[Its quota system is] contrary to both the letter and the spirit of a constitutional provision whose central command is equality."[12] In Part II of the O'Connor opinion, which did not command a majority and so must be treated as a concurrence, the justice argued that the judgment in Croson does not overturn Fullilove. O'Connor and the two justices who joined this part cited §5 of the Fourteenth Amendment and reminded the litigants that "Congress . . . has a specific constitutional mandate to . . . define situations which *Congress* determines threaten principles of equality and to adopt prophylactic rules to deal with those situations." Neither Virginia nor Richmond is the recipient of an analogous "specific constitutional mandate."

This attempted distinction raises anew the troubling issue of the scope of §5. Can Congress, by its own authority or through such agencies as the EEOC, take actions that would violate the equal protection clause if taken by the states? Could Congress authorize the states to take actions that they could not constitutionally take on their own initiative? Could Congress authorize Richmond, for example, to impose such racial quotas upon construction as its elected officials think best?

Language very similar to that of the Fourteenth Amendment clause at issue appears in six other constitutional amendments, and a provision of the same kind was attached to the Equal Rights Amendment passed by Congress in 1972 but denied ratification by the states. Indeed, fear of the extent of the powers that Congress would acquire through yet another such clause was one of the dominant issues of the long ERA ratification controversy.

For reasons that transcend even the monumental issue of racial fairness, interpreting the language of §5 is of enormous importance in the development of our constitutional system. Why did Congress, especially the post–Civil War Congress that passed the Thirteenth, Fourteenth, and Fifteenth Amendments and so set the pattern, first limit state authority and then give itself a vaguely worded power to "enforce" those limits? Traditional rules of construction demand that we give each clause a meaning that may be called nonsuperfluous. Legislation in the ordinary sense of the term is distinct from "enforcement," and legislation to enforce a provision that in and by itself simply limits the legislative powers of another body is a slippery idea.

Perhaps in its most recent uses, as in the case of the ERA, the enforcement language was included without careful thought as to its meaning; it routinely imitated the earlier phrasing. If that is so, then the opponents of the ERA are entitled to congratulate themselves on having kept one more loose cannon off the deck of constitutional law. But to speculate about it does nothing to tell us what the "enforcement" language meant when it was first written.

At least one reasonable hypothesis comes to mind. A Congress with a sharp memory of the Dred Scott decision might well have been concerned that judicial review would not always suffice to nullify state statutes that violate the requirement of equal protection. Congress may have meant to award itself a power concurrent with the courts' to find state actions unconstitutional and to declare them void. Raoul Berger has defended a

view of §5 similar to this.[13] But other views of the meaning of that section
are certainly possible. My concern is only to indicate that I agree with
Justice Kennedy, who wrote separately in <u>Croson</u>. He maintained that the
Court should not have asserted the continuing validity of <u>Fullilove</u>, a question
that was not properly before it. The Court ought to walk with small steps
through a field strewn with broken glass.[14]

In the closing weeks of the October 1988 term, the Court decided two
other conspicuous race relations cases. The first was a judgment on appeal
by Wards Cove packing, an Alaska salmon cannery, and the private
defendant in an equal employment opportunity lawsuit.[15] Plaintiff had
shown at trial that skilled jobs within defendant's workforce were held,
predominantly, by whites and that unskilled jobs were held, predominantly,
by nonwhites. Plaintiff contended that such statistics create a presumption
of race discrimination, which properly shifts the burden of proof to the
defendant. The Supreme Court held that this was a misreading of the civil
rights law. Justice Byron White's opinion explained that the plaintiff must
identify and prove the specific employment practices that are alleged to be
responsible for the statistical disparity. Only after a showing of a suspect
employment practice is the defendant employer required to show a bona fide
business justification for the challenged practice.

A few days later, the Court decided a case brought under an 1866 civil
rights act that provided that all persons "shall have the same right . . . to
make and enforce contracts . . . as is enjoyed by white citizens."[16] Brenda
Patterson, a black woman, complained that the defendant credit agency has
passed her over for promotions, favoring white employees with inferior
credentials, and that the 1866 act gave her a right to recover damages for
"racial harassment."[17] The Court characterized this suit as an effort to
circumvent the detailed remedial scheme of the 1964 Civil Rights Act and
upheld the holding of the courts below that Patterson had stated no claim on
which relief could be granted.

JUSTICE BRENNAN RETIRES

On March 6, 1990, the Senate approved Clarence Thomas, former EEOC
Chairman, for one of the vacancies on the court of appeals for the D.C.
Circuit. Several senators made it clear that they were suspicious of Thomas
and that they were willing to vote in his favor only because this was not a
Supreme Court appointment.[18] Thomas had to assuage two distinct
concerns: first, that he would prove to be an activist judge; and second, that
the ends of his activism would be other than those preferred by the members
of the majority party. To assuage such fears he declared: "[M]y obligation
in all circumstances would be to follow Supreme Court precedent, not to
establish law on my own. I do not think that district court judges or court
of appeals judges have the option of roaming unfettered on judicial terrain."[19]

His image here was probably stronger than his meaning. A "fetter" is a shackle attached to the legs of a prisoner just about the ankles. A Circuit Court Judge does have significant discretion and is guided, rather than "fettered," by Supreme Court precedent. I mention this only because there is a tendency toward hyperbole in Clarence Thomas's public utterances, a tendency that we shall meet again.

The Thomas appointment coincided with the bitter partisan reaction to Croson and the other civil rights decisions previously cited. To politicians the reasoning of an opinion is not important. What is important is who wins. What was important in Croson was that a municipality had taken an action hallowed under the label "civil rights" and that the Court had overturned that meritorious initiative. O'Connor's Part II, with its indefinitely expansive view of congressional powers under §5 of the Fourteenth Amendment, along with the unsuccessful argument of the plaintiff in Wards Cove that statistical evidence alone should be enough to create a prima facie case of discrimination, helped to generate much real and some feigned indignation and so encouraged the introduction of new civil rights acts into Congress. The sponsors of these acts strenuously argued that they would not require or encourage racial quotas. The reader can make her own judgment: any legislation that embraces the argument of the Wards Cove plaintiff encourages a statistically correct ethnic distribution of employees, a "race profile" that will relieve an employer from the burden of proof. If the reader believes that such legislation does not amount to a quota bill, then she sees a discrimination too fine for my eyes.

These bills, the double-talk of their advocates, President Bush's successful veto of such legislation in 1990, and the president's decision to sign a compromise bill in 1991—all provided the substance for the angriest politics of those two years, an anger that fueled the short-lived career and prominence of the Louisiana demagogue, David Duke.

In the midst of this tumultuous period, on July 20, 1990, Justice William Brennan announced his retirement from the Supreme Court. Brennan was the consummate ad hoc realist, the chief advocate of infinitely flexible three-part standards for obscenity laws and Church-State relations, and the architect of a constitutionalized law of defamation.[20] His departure presented President Bush with a first opportunity to change the direction of the court on each of these subjects.

On July 23, the president announced that he was nominating Judge David Souter to this vacancy. The president and his nominee held a joint news conference that day. Bush began by informing the assembled reporters that Souter is a magna cum laude graduate of Harvard, a Rhodes scholar at Oxford, and a graduate of Harvard Law School. With his nominee's credentials established, the president opened the floor to questions.

The first question was a familiar one, this time from Helen Thomas, of United Press International: "Did you ask Judge Souter for his views on abortion?" The president answered, "No."

Ann Compton of ABC News followed, asking with some incredulity, "You're not certain in your own mind how Judge Souter will vote if Roe v. Wade comes before the Court next year?" The president repeated, less succinctly than before, that he was not.

After a few more such questions, Bush said: "Look, you all can keep trying all day to get me to comment on abortion in relation to this nomination . . . please stop trying . . . . It would be unfair to Judge Souter."[21]

Democrats began at once to complain that Souter had no paper trail, that he was a "stealth candidate," leaving no discernible mark on the published record. He had had, of course, no opportunity to build a reputation on the court of appeals, where he had sat only since the preceding April, but on the record as a whole, the "stealth candidate" complaint is unfair. Souter had spent his professional life in practice, lacking Bork's academic niche but leaving behind him the papers one would expect: memoranda and advisory opinions as attorney general, published and unpublished opinions as a state judge. Potential opponents did manage to discover all this in time for the hearings and did come upon, for example, Souter's appellate brief in U.S. v. New Hampshire, which I cited for its "color-blind" position. It would have been appropriate for a senator opposing the Souter appointment to argue that the legal reasoning in that brief was below the level of cogency one ought to expect of a Supreme Court justice or that it was sloppily documented. Such charges, if demonstrated, would have been relevant to the issue of fitness, as were the charges advanced against the Manion nomination discussed earlier. But no one made an argument against Souter on grounds of fitness.

On the contrary, when the Judiciary Committee began its hearings on September 4, it heard first from the ABA which rated the nominee "well qualified" for the Supreme Court. On the thirteenth, the senators heard from Souter. He testified in such a way as to defuse opposition from defenders of Brennanesque doctrines. Souter told the committee, for example, that he had no interest in overturning Times v. Sullivan. This one proposition assured Chairman Biden, in particular, that Souter would not take an inordinately narrow, or Borkian, view of the First Amendment.[22]

One other assurance Souter gave to the senators received much more press attention than his position on the law of libel. Souter said, "I believe that the due process clause of the fourteenth amendment does recognize and does protect an unenumerated right to privacy."[23]

Is that unenumerated right simply another name for liberty? Or is it a derivation from the specifics of the Bill of Rights by way of penumbra or emanation? Or, again, does it derive from the reservation of rights in the Ninth Amendment? Is the right to privacy protected more securely, and does it warrant a level of scrutiny more strict, than does commercial liberty or (what is often the same thing) the right to property? All of these questions are raised by Souter's confessio fidei. Yet they are all a good deal less important, in political and factional reality, than the simple fact that the nominee spoke the magic words, "protect . . . privacy."

On September 27 the Judiciary Committee voted in Souter's favor thirteen to one. Senator Kennedy delivered the sole "nay." Some senators not on the committee would have eagerly seconded Kennedy's vote. On October 1, Senator Daniel Akaka (D-Hawaii) spoke and explained why he would have to oppose any nominee who did not pledge to uphold both Roe and Griswold. Silence on these points "places a cloud of uncertainty over well-settled legal precedents governing the right of individuals to make fundamental choices."[24] October 1 was a Monday, so, while Akaka was speaking, the Court began its new term, one member short.

One wonders what Akaka and others who would impose such a pledge would say to a retrospective application of their method. In February 1954 the Senate considered the nomination of Earl Warren to be chief justice. Warren was already serving in that capacity under a recess appointment and was not called to appear and pledge any course of action.[25] No member of the Senate had an opportunity to ask Warren whether he would vote to uphold Plessy v. Ferguson or what he thought in particular of its application to primary and secondary public schools.[26] Given the unquestioned standards of that time, it is certain that, if someone had asked, Warren would have refused to answer.

But suppose that he had answered and had told the truth. Would he have been confirmed? Would we ever have had Brown v. Board under such circumstances? Does the traditional refusal of nominees to answer questions on litigation that they expect will come before them serve any valuable purpose? I do not like to think that some precursor of Akaka's might have demanded an answer on Plessy and then denounced Warren's refusal to oblige on the ground that silence "places a cloud of uncertainty over well-settled legal precedents governing the ability of states and municipalities to make fundamental educational decisions."

Akaka was not on the Judiciary Committee and was therefore Johnny-come-lately in the argument over Souter. But Kennedy, being on the committee, simply renewed the arguments he had originated there when he spoke in the Senate debate:

> Judge Souter defended Governor Meldrim Thomson's decision to refuse to provide data on the racial composition of the state government work force . . . . His petition to the Supreme Court even took the extraordinary

position that the EEOC was violating a worker's right to privacy by requiring employers to report the overall racial composition of their workforce.

Judge Souter repeatedly defended the appropriateness of his actions as Attorney General in challenging the EEOC regulation. It was only after repeated questioning that Judge Souter finally admitted that the courts had been correct in rejecting his arguments.

His unenthusiastic after-the-fact endorsement of the Court's decision does not dispel the doubts raised by Judge Souter's reactionary arguments in this case.[27]

This passage makes three points worth remarking on. First, Kennedy executes a flip-flop on the very issue of privacy rights about which Souter had made his well-publicized concession. Souter told the committee that the Fourteenth amendment does protect privacy; Kennedy (as one might expect of a "liberal") now objects not that Souter's conception of privacy is too narrow but that it is too broad. It is too broad, moreover, on the old and bad assumption that privacy—and perhaps liberty itself—is of value only within the home. On this assumption, liberty deserves no constitutional protection in the workplace, and a former state attorney general who has argued that it does deserve such protection, who has even used the privileged word *privacy* in the service of that heresy, is a "reactionary." This is the rejection of Bernard Siegan all over again—except that at least Siegan was rejected for the expression of his own theories. What Senator Kennedy ignores—and this is the second peculiar feature of the quoted passage—is that when Souter was attorney general, it was precisely Souter's <u>duty</u> to defend the position taken by his governor. Of course, he could have resigned in protest had he received an order to defend a position that violated his conscience, for example, the contention (let us imagine) that New Hampshire has the authority to impose capital punishment on a first-offender pickpocket. But Souter was not obliged to resign at a mere difference of opinion, else few attorneys general would stay in their jobs for more than a month.

In the third place, what is most peculiar about Kennedy's argument is the importance it assigns to Souter's concession that "the courts had been correct in rejecting his arguments." Does this concession imply that Souter's action in setting forth the arguments he advanced was improper? It does not. An attorney general is not a judge; he is perfectly entitled to offer arguments that, he will later concede, the courts are correct to reject.

The upshot of this sequence of event is that the Senate walked to the very edge of a purely result-oriented, pledge-enforcing system of the confirmation of Supreme Court appointments. No other conclusion can be drawn from the statements made by Akaka and Kennedy on the floor of the chamber. But the Senate, in voting ninety to nine in favor of confirmation on October 3, decided not to walk over the edge this time. Neither did they walk away from the brink: the Judiciary Committee <u>had</u> extorted a pledge on the issue of <u>Times</u> <u>v.</u> <u>Sullivan</u> as well as an acknowledgment of a right of privacy, unspecified in character. If the optimist insists on seeing the glass as half-full, instead of half-empty, in the Souter debate only the outcome supplies grounds for optimism.

That outcome is a tribute to the foresight of the framers of the Constitution, whose concern was so great about the dangers of faction, dangers exemplified in the Kennedy and Akaka speeches. Publius wrote that the Senate would not deny confirmation for weak or spurious reasons, because the senators who voted that way would know that they faced further nominations by the same president. This consideration weighed heavily with Biden, who remarked on the Souter nomination: "His vision of the Constitiution is not mine, but it is clearly not that of the hardliners who believe that the Constitution is to be read very narrowly . . . . While he would not be my choice to exercise [judicial] power, I believe that he is the best we can hope for from this administration."[28] Such reasoning is at its strongest soon after an election. It weakens when, as happened with Fortas and Bork, the confirmation dispute comes during or close to an election year. Be this as it may, Judge Souter is now Justice Souter.

Has his presence made a difference to the work of the Court? The balance model persists, in common opinion, and pundits predicted that Justice Souter would, in the words of James J. Kirkpatrick, "provide the decisive swing vote for the conservative bloc in really close cases."[29] It did not turn out so. The October 1990 term saw the Court issue sixty-five split decisions. Only nineteen of those split five to four. Souter was on the winning side in only nine cases of those nineteen. Since the Court handed down 107 signed opinions in that term, a little arithmetic shows that the percentage of cases in which Souter could be said to have provided a swing vote is less than 8.5.

There was no landmark decision in constitutional law in the October 1990 term, nothing that will rival <u>Webster</u> or <u>Croson</u> in future textbooks. Yet measured not by space in books but by effect upon the lives of citizens with no special fondness for litigation, statutory interpretation is a more important part of the Court's work than is the exercise of judicial review; there were notable instances of statutory interpretation during Justice Souter's first year. To one of those instances I turn next.

THE MEANING OF A STATUTE

On March 20, 1991, the Supreme Court held, six to three, that Title VII of the Civil Rights Act, which provides for equal employment opportunities regardless of sex, prohibits "fetal protection policies." That is, a private employer may not ban women from positions in which it employs men on the ground that such employment will expose women to materials harmful to a developing fetus.[30] The defendant, Johnson Controls, Inc., claimed that the nonfertility of its male employees constitutes what, in the language of the statute, is called a bona fide occupational qualification, or "bfoq." The majority, Souter inclusive, in an opinion written by Justice Blackmun, rejected that claim. Men, too, Blackmun reasoned, suffer a risk of reproductive injury through exposure to the materials at issue, and birth defects may be carried through such damaged sperm. Since the claim of a bfoq fails, the fetal protection policy fails. Women must be permitted to take the jobs in question.

As medical science, this reasoning is specious. Some fetal injuries are genetically caused by malformed egg or sperm. Either malformation may result from lead poisoning of the parent, and in that respect, men and women are subjected to equivalent risks. But the injuries that the defendant company sought to avoid were those arising from a far more serious danger—a fetus's direct exposure to maternal blood lead. A man's presence in lead-bearing air does nothing to create or enhance this risk.[31]

As Justice White observed in his dissent, the reasoning of the majority avoids questions that it will force upon the attention of the courts below.[32] What of the enormous liabilities to which Johnson Controls will be exposed if work with dangerous materials leads to a miscarriage, a stillbirth, a live but short-lived infant, or a severely handicapped child? If the employees are made aware of the dangers when they take the job, there is perhaps a basis for the common law defense known as assumption of risk.[33] But, at best, only one of the two potential plaintiffs can be said to have assumed the risk. Or does the mother assume risks not only for herself but for an unborn or even an unconceived child when she accepts employment? Will the defendants in this hypothetical future litigation claim immunity on the ground that the proximate cause of infant plaintiff's injury was defendant's discharge of its duty under the law? When that case arises, will the Supreme Court acknowledge that immunity? Until such questions are resolved, it seems that the Supreme Court has placed itself in the anamolous position of ordering companies to injure the unborn and incur the associated costs.

On April 11, 1991, the Senate Judiciary Committee voted on President Bush's nomination of district court Judge Kenneth L. Ryskamp for a vacancy on the Eleventh Circuit Court of Appeals. Ryskamp's membership in a racially exclusive club incited opposition to his nomination. The Riviera Club had no rule prohibiting minority membership, but it did have a homogeneous screening committee and de facto racial and religious exclusivity.[34] Ryskamp's defenders argued that the nominee was not an officer of the club and had no responsibility for screening. Ryskamp himself testified that he had been misinformed that there were Jewish members. Senator Howard Metzenbaum replied, "That's just not good enough." The committee voted eight to six against confirmation.

Republican members of the committee moved that the nomination be sent to the full Senate without recommendation. They picked up one vote on this motion. But a tie vote is a loss for the affirmative, so the motion failed. This was the first loss suffered by the Bush administration on a judicial nomination. It may have contributed to the sense that future administration nominees are presumptively vulnerable. In that sense, the Ryskamp debate led to the Thomas imbroglio.

NOTES

1. <u>United States v. New Hampshire</u>, 539 F. 2d 277 at 279 (1st Cir. 1976).

2. 42 USCA §2000e-8(c).

3. Summary judgment is appropriate when a trial court finds that the matter before it can be decided without trial, either because no facts are in dispute or because the view of the facts most favorable to one side nonetheless requires a finding for the other. See <u>Fed. Rules of Civil Procedure</u>, 56.

4. 29 C.F.R. Part 1602.

5. See Chapter 7, infra.

6. 539 F.2d at 282, n. 6. (<u>Brief for Appellant</u>, February 20, 1976, at 45–50).

7. 429 U.S. 1023 (December 13, 1976), <u>cert. denied</u>.

8. U.S. Constitution, Art. I, §8, par. 3.

9. The limits of Congress's delegation of legislative authority to administrative agencies, limits for decades virtually ignored, have reappeared in Supreme Court decisions of recent years, as with the "Gramm-Rudman" case, <u>Bowshar v. Synar</u>, 478 U.S. 714 (1986).

10. 488 U.S. 469 (1989).

11. 448 U.S. 448 (1980).

12. 488 U.S. 469 at 505–506.

13. R. Berger, <u>Government by Judiciary</u> (Cambridge, MA, 1977) 221–229. Berger's own theory is that the framers of the Fourteenth Amendment preferred Congressional review of state actions over, and <u>to the exclusion of</u>, judicial review, with regard to the criteria set forth in §1 of that amendment.

14. 488 U.S. 469 at 518.

15. <u>Wards Cove Packing v. Atonio</u>, 490 U.S. 642 (1989).

16. 42 USCA §1981.

17. <u>Patterson v. McLean Credit Union</u>, 495 U.S. 617 (1988).

18. Berke, "Panel Plans to Press Court Nominee," <u>New York Times</u>, July 3, 1991 at D18, col. 2: "Some Senators who voted to confirm Judge Thomas last year for his seat on the United States Court of Appeals for the District of Columbia emphasized that this did not mean they would support him for the Supreme Court. 'The standards are entirely different and should be,' asserted Senator Patrick J. Leahy, a Vermont Democrat."

19. 1990 <u>Cong. Quarterly Almanac</u> 519.

20. Mendelson, "Brennan's Revolution," <u>Commentary</u> (February 1991), 31.

21. "Remarks Announcing the Nomination of David H. Souter to be an Associate Justice of the Supreme Court to the United States and a Question-and-Answer Session with Reporters," July 23, 1990, <u>Public Papers of the Presidents: George Bush—1990</u>, at 1046.

22.   136 Cong. Rec. S. 14,340 (October 2, 1990).

23.   1990 Cong. Quarterly Almanac 513.

24.   136 Cong. Rec. S. 14,291 (October 1, 1990).

25.   U.S. Congress, Senate, Committee on the Judiciary, Nomination of Earl Warren, Hearings, 83d Cong., 2d Sess., February 2, 1954.

26.   163 U.S. 537 (1896).

27.   136 Cong. Rec. S. 14,345.

28.   Id.

29.   Kirkpatrick, "Post-Mortem on a Ho-Hum Supreme Court Term," Springfield Union-News (Mass.) July 13, 1991, A13.

30.   United Auto Workers v. Johnson Controls, 111 S. Ct. 1196 (March 20, 1991). In light of the discussion of American Cyanamid in Chapter 9, supra, it is important to observe that the 1991 Supreme Court decision arose out of a procedural and statutory context very different from that of the 1984 circuit court ruling. The former did not overturn the latter.

31.   Id. (Brief for Respondent, July 19, 1990, at 10–13).

32.   111 S. Ct. 1196 at 1210.

33.   W. Prosser, Torts (4th ed. 1971) ch. 11, §68.

34.   Lewis, "Committee Rejects Bush Nominee to Key Appellate Court in South," New York Times, April 12, 1991, 1.

11

. . . And Stepping over the Edge

In 1991 the coalition of interest groups that had blocked the nomination of Robert Bork to the Supreme Court four years earlier declared its determination to "bork" Clarence Thomas. This time, the coalition failed. But the means that it employed, especially in its last-minute effort to avoid evident failure, were inconsistent with any respect for the Senate as a deliberative body. A vicious attack upon a decent person in public life is seen, in the 1990s, as an act without moral significance, as a simple matter of factional tactics.

In 1988 the police raided the apartment of Sonia Mayfield, who was allowing her boyfriend, Keith Long, to use it for the conduct of his business, the sale of cocaine. They found evidence of Long's trade as well as a handgun between the cushions of a sofa. They also found and arrested their suspect. While the police were still engaged in their search, the telephone rang. An officer picked up the receiver and told the caller that Keith was "busy." The caller asked whether Keith "still has any stuff" and whether "Mike" could come by to pick up his "fifty," a bag of cocaine sold for fifty dollars. The officer testified as to this conversation at Long's trial, when it was offered as proof of an intent to distribute the narcotics in defendant's possession. Long was convicted of possession of cocaine with intent to distribute and of the use of a firearm in connection with a drug trafficking crime. He appealed both convictions to the circuit court, Judge Clarence Thomas sitting on the panel that decided the appeal.[1]

One of the issues at stake was the scope of the rule of evidence that excludes hearsay testimony. Should the comments of the unnamed caller have been admitted into evidence? A second important issue was the prosecution's construction of the word *use* in the charge of "the use of a firearm in drug trafficking." The government argued from Long's use of the apartment and the presence there of a gun (unregistered and yielding no fingerprints), to a "constructive use" of the gun for the facilitation of the illegal business.

The court of appeals upheld the district court as to the conviction for intent to distribute but reversed for use of a firearm. Judge Thomas wrote the opinion. Its merits as an instance of the judicial protection of procedural due process are considerable, and it deserved—but did not receive—the attention of the committee during the debate on Thomas's nomination to the Supreme Court.

Thomas's opinion explains that the hearsay rule excludes the repetition by an in-court witness of an out-of-court statement, if that repetition is offered as proof of the truth of the matter asserted. Consider a noncontroversial example: Company X is in the business of selling a synthetic, apple-flavored concoction. The prosecution contends that X has defrauded the public into believing that this is genuine apple juice. A consumer's out-of-court statement, "Yum, this is fresh apple juice, all right!" may be repeated in court. It may be offered, that is, not as evidence of the matter asserted but as evidence of the success of the alleged pretense. Hearsay, then, must be defined both by where something was said first and by the reason for repeating it. Questions, however, are not <u>statements</u>; they do not assert anything, and so the evidentiary value of "Does Keith still have the stuff?" falls outside the exclusion of the hearsay rule. This may seem to constitute the splitting of a hair. But, if so, that appearance is deceptive. Thomas's distinction rests securely upon the justification for the evidentiary rule under discussion—that the falsehoods of an out-of-court witness are not subject to the checks of an oath or of cross-examination. As Thomas wrote, "When a declarant does not intend to communicate anything . . . his sincerity is not in question and the need for cross-examination is sharply diminished."[2]

As to the use of a firearm, Thomas understood that the government must not be allowed to put citizens in prison for alleged violations of statutes that use words that have no preexisting or well-defined meaning, or even despite compliance with the meanings that the words <u>do</u> have:

> Upholding the conviction of a defendant in the absence of any indicia of a possession would stretch the meaning of "use" beyond the breaking point. We readily acknowledge that the word "use" is expansive, but the difficulty of pinpointing the outer limits of its meaning does not imply that no such limits exist. To affirm Long's conviction for "using" the revolver in the sofa would be to concede that the word "use" has no discernable boundaries.[3]

Both where the appellant won and where he lost, it is clear that Thomas' concern as a jurist was where it ought to be—on the plain meaning of the ordinary English words involved, words no more recondite than *use* or *statement*, and on the application of those meanings to the facts at hand.

What is more, his opinion is a model of clarity; it ought on that ground alone to be mandatory reading for Justice Thomas's eight colleagues.

A FORMALIST AND HIS OPPONENTS

On June 27, 1991, Justice Thurgood Marshall announced his retirement from the Supreme Court. On July 1, President George Bush nominated Judge Clarence Thomas to fill that vacancy. Because the president opposed racial quotas in the debates over <u>Croson</u>, <u>Wards Cove</u>, and proposed civil rights legislation, it was natural for his critics to observe that the president was replacing the first black man ever to sit on the Court with a second and for them to ask whether this nomination was due to an implicit racial quota. At the first opportunity, Bush denied that he was moved by any such concern: "The fact that he is black, a minority, has nothing to do with this. He is the best qualified."[4]

I believe that, at least in one very important respect, the president was telling the truth. He was right to nominate Thomas on the merits, and those merits have "nothing to do" with Thomas's race. The widespread assumption that the nomination <u>must</u> have been motivated by racial politics, that it could not possibly have been a merited appointment, is itself an excellent example of the harm that what I have called the demographic theory of representation does to those whom it affects to help; it denigrates genuine achievement and stigmatizes honorable ambition.[5]

My belief that Thomas is an excellent appointment follows from my contention that the cause of the decay of contemporary jurisprudence is neither judicial activism nor partisan balance: the former is half of a false dichotomy; the latter is a mirage. The cause of the decay is so-called realism. The period chronicled in this book has seen a slow shift of the Supreme Court away from the <u>activist</u> realism associated with the Warren Court and toward the <u>restraintist</u> realism associated with the Rehnquist Court. But that shift is of little moment to the <u>dignitas</u> of the law, the one thing needful for the stability of a republic. Of a formalist restoration that would make an end of realism there is little sign. The only justice appointed between 1940 and 1990 to whom the label "formalist" can be applied was John Paul Stevens. The case in favor of Thomas, then, is that he was and is the Court's second sitting formalist.

His individual variety within this style of jurisprudence has a purist, rather than a moderate, tendency, and, as I remarked earlier, pure formalism is subject to both logical and psychological objections. Thomas displayed one of the weaknesses of his philosophy when he told the Judiciary Committee: "I think . . . it is important for us . . . to eliminate agendas, to eliminate ideologies. And when one becomes a judge . . . that's precisely what you start doing. You start putting the speeches away. You begin to decline forming opinions in important areas that could come before your court because you want to be stripped down like a runner."[6] I confess that I would hold Thomas's judgment in even higher esteem than I now do, had he said that he makes an effort, as a judge, to acknowledge and offset his extrajudicial "agendas" and "ideologies." But for him to suggest that he has "eliminated" such potential biases from his mind seems an instance of a habit of hyperbole. Nonetheless, in the 1990s and for the foreseeable future, Justice Thomas's formalist view of the law and the Constitution can only improve the work, and consequently the public prestige, of the Court to which he has been appointed.

Although race is not among Thomas's qualifications and may have had nothing to do with his selection, his race and the story of his first years of life had much to do with shielding him from attacks. Clarence Thomas was born in June 1948 to poor parents living in the countryside outside Savannah, Georgia. His father left home while he was very young. When he was seven, his mother sent him to live with her parents. These grandparents enrolled Clarence in an all-black Catholic school, where he was educated by nuns. When Thomas spoke to the press in 1991 about his nomination, he praised his mother, grandparents, and teachers, "all of whom were adamant that I grow up to make something of myself."[7]

Thomas did that. He graduated from Yale Law School in 1974 and went to work for the attorney general of Missouri, John C. Danforth. By 1991 Danforth was Missouri's senior senator, and he was responsible for the compromise civil rights bill of that year—a bill the president signed—that brought an end (for the moment) to the legislative controversy that <u>Croson</u> had aroused. This accomplishment seems to have brought Danforth credibility with his colleagues, credibility that he employed with extraordinary energy in pushing for Thomas' confirmation.

Opposition groups took up arms long before the Judiciary Committee began its hearings. Patricia Ireland, speaking as the leader of the National Organization for Women (NOW), gave a succinct summary of the goals of the coalition of which that organization was but a part. "We're going to bork him," she said,[8] and the use of Judge Bork's name as a verb (a confession in itself) soon caught on. "Borking" was incompatible with scruples. This was evident as soon as Douglas Wilder, the governor of Virginia who was then contemplating a campaign for President, suggested that it would be unwise to put a Catholic on the Supreme Court. Aside from the implication that he would impose an unconstitutional religious test for public office,[9] Wilder's suggestion suffers from irrelevance and inaccuracy. Despite his early education by nuns, Clarence Thomas was not at the time of his nomination a Catholic.

The Thomas debates mark the final appearance into my narrative of the Harvard Law Professor, Laurence Tribe. In 1987 Tribe's testimony bolstered the intellectual prestige of the opposition to Robert Bork. Tribe told the

Senate that Bork was out of the mainstream of American jurisprudence because he refused to acknowledge the existence of unenumerated but protected constitutional rights that people possess simply by virtue of their personhood.[10] Tribe reminded the committee that the United States was founded by men who believed in "the laws of nature and of nature's God," and he believed that the Constitution must be read in the context of that conviction. It was, or should have been, a great surprise when the same Laurence Tribe emerged in the early stages of the Thomas controversy to argue that this nominee was a dangerous figure precisely because of his announced interest in the jurisprudence of natural law.[11]

According to one report, natural law theory was the chief subject of a courtesy call that Thomas paid on Senator Metzenbaum on July eleventh. When the senator asked the judge to explain his views, Thomas answered with a question of his own: "Do you think it's proper for a human being to own another human being?" Metzenbaum said that it was not. Thomas explained that "the reason you think that's wrong is because we all have natural rights." Of course, the enactment of this principle into positive law took place with the ratification of the Thirteenth Amendment in 1865. But before that enactment and before the war that made it possible, the only rational premise for an argument against slavery was the argument drawn from human nature. Such was, and is, Thomas's view.[12]

THE FIRST ROUND OF HEARINGS

As the inquiry opened, Senator Biden told the nominee of Biden's concern that a justice who reasons from natural law will vote in favor of "radical constitutional departures." Finding out what such theories meant to the nominee, therefore, was "the most important task of these hearings." The nominee repled that his earlier statements on natural law were made "in the context of political theory" and were not meant to describe a basis for adjudication.[13] He assured the committee that as justice he would make decisions just as he had been making them as a judge, using "the traditional tools of constitutional interpretation . . . and statutory construction," that is, abiding by the positive law.

Some observers considered this a retreat. Indeed, a phrase that Professor Tribe had introduced into the Bork hearings, "confirmation conversion," became a catch phrase on this point. Senator Kennedy referred with open skepticism to his "vanishing views."[14] But such a reading of Judge Thomas's remarks shows the impoverishment of political theory in the age of the sound bite. The incredulity, the accusations even of bad faith, that greeted many of Thomas's assertions before the committee arose from the anachronistic sound of formalism. Such accusations soon acquired in stylishness what they would continue to lack in cogency.

When abstract disquisitions on human nature tired committee chairman Biden, he turned the attention of the nominee to the two conclusions from constitutional premises that concerned him most: the right to procure an abortion, which he was afraid Thomas would not protect, and the right to own and use one's own property, which he was afraid Thomas would protect.

Biden held aloft a copy of a book by Richard Epstein, professor of law at the University of Chicago. The book was Takings (1985), and while the cameras got their pictures, Biden asked Thomas whether natural law theory would lead him to the results Epstein advocates—vigorous judicial enforcement of a hitherto neglected clause of the Bill of Rights that prohibits the "taking" of private property "for public use without just compensation."[15] Biden explained that "there is a whole new school of thought that up until about five years ago spoke only to one another [and] that is now receiving wider credence and credibility." Thomas reminded the senator that the school of thought involved is a bit more than five years old: "There is a Takings Clause in the Constitution and there's also a reference to property in our Constitution."[16] Thomas also made the cogent point that property rights and racial fairness are not severable issues. The Jim Crow laws, he said, "did not allow my grandfather to enjoy the fruits of his labor."[17]

Among those who wanted Thomas "borked," the issue of abortion fired the passions a good deal more than did Epstein's book. Senator Pat Leahy (D-Vt.), one of those Democrats whose vote Thomas's Republican strategists hoped to win, questioned the judge on this point and received an answer many thought evasive:

Leahy: Have you ever had discussion of Roe v. Wade other than in this room, in the 17 or 18 years it has been there?

Thomas: Only, I guess, Senator, in the fact, in the most general sense, that other individuals express concerns one way or the other and you listen and you try to be thoughtful. If you are asking me whether I have ever debated the contents of it, the answer to that is no, Senator.[18]

In the weeks that followed, one heard repeatedly the canard that Thomas had denied ever discussing abortion with anyone or ever being in a room when the subject was discussed. When the Senate had to pit Thomas's credibility against that of Professor Hill, the simplified version of the preceding quoted exchange was polished off and offered as evidence of the untrustworthiness of the former's sworn statements. Thomas' actual answer deserved some scrutiny.

The first sentence seems to say that he had never initiated discussions of Roe, only listened when others expressed concern. The final clause, in which Thomas asserts that he tried to be thoughtful, is somewhat obscure. Does it mean that he made thoughtful replies? If so, a yes answer to Leahy's question would have been better. Or does it refer to an effort at being thoughtful limited to a somber facial expression and a sage nod of the head?

The second sentence answers a somewhat different question from the one Leahy asked. If the senator wanted to know whether Thomas had ever "debated the contents" of Roe, then the right answer is no. But Leahy had used the word *discussion*. Even on abortion, there are surely discussions that fall short of "debates." Whether or not he intended to evade, Thomas certainly did avoid Leahy's question.

Other senators tried to learn Thomas's views on Roe by asking him about an article written by Lewis Lehrman entitled "The Declaration of Independence and the Right to Life," in which Lehrman invoked his understanding of natural law to argue against a right to abort. In 1987, when speaking at the Heritage Foundation of Washington, in a room named after one of the patrons, the Lehrman Auditorium, Thomas praised Lehrman's article. He invoked its use of a higher law and treated it as a analog to his own view. The Judiciary Committee wanted to know whether he meant to endorse Lehrman's opinion on abortion in particular. Thomas said that he had not. Lehrman's reasoning was simply an instance of a type of reasoning that he would like to promote, and his mention of that article was a "throw-away line" meant to gain the attention of his audience.[19] He also explained that if he was successful in persuading conservatives, who are often skeptical of natural law, to endorse such a philosophy, the effect would be to broaden the constituency for an aggressive enforcement of civil rights.

At these hearings, civil rights did not become the great issue some had expected, and on July 31, 1991, when the governing board of the NAACP voted to oppose Thomas's nomination, the chairman held a press conference in which he refused three times to say whether there had been any contrary votes.[20] The executive director, Benjamin Hooks, stated publicly on another occasion that Judge Thomas had "good points" and that were he rejected the next nominee would be white and as far right as Genghis Khan.[21]

Was Genghis Khan on the "Right" of intra-Mongol politics in his day? Was there another party (the "Left") that opposed the power of the military-equine complex? Or is this an allusion to the broader Eurasian scene, on the assumption that the subjugated always belong to the Left, their conquerors always to the Right? Hooks is not alone in this use of Khan's name. But it remains a puzzling allusion, however often it is employed.

In tactical partisan calculations, the two varieties of senator of special interest during a confirmation fight are southern Democrats and northeastern Republicans. Arlen Specter was the Judiciary Committee's sample of the latter. He was also a rare Republican defector from the cause of Robert Bork in 1987. Indeed, Bork in his memoir singles Specter out for special censure as an opponent who "could not comprehend what I was saying about the first amendment, the equal protection clause . . . or the dangers of letting judges decide cases with no more authority or guidance than a phrase not in the Constitution, such as 'fairness,' or 'the needs of the nation.'"[22] As one might expect, Bork's opponents had a higher opinion of Specter's performance on that occasion, and Thomas's opponents hoped to bring him around to their side this time, too.

During the first round, Specter sought to gain Thomas's assent to a typology of judicial conservatism. Was he more akin to Scalia or to O'Connor? Specter sought to persuade Thomas to take sides. Thomas refused to answer directly, but he did admit to some "skepticism" about Scalia's jurisprudence, insofar as it results in a narrowing of the scope of individual rights.[23] Such answers seem to have offended no one and (most important) to have satisfied Specter, who became one of Thomas's most ardent defenders when the fate of his nomination came to turn on issues more suited to the front page of a tabloid than to the inside of a law review. Indeed, it was Specter whose aggressive questioning of Anita Hill called down upon his head the cry of "Shame! Shame!" from that most dependable opponent of the judicial nominees of Republican presidents, Senator Kennedy of Massachusetts.

Southern Democrats had been crucial to the Bork defeat, and strategists for both sides of the Thomas bout considered their votes crucial once again. Until the day before the vote, Thomas's supporters awaited Howard Heflin's decision with some hope. But Heflin, of Alabama, announced on September 26 that he would vote nay. Interested parties either desired or feared that Heflin would prove to be a bellwether.

On September 27 the Committee voted seven to seven on a motion to endorse the nomination, that is, failed to endorse it. The only Democratic vote Thomas received was that of DeConcini (Ariz.). The nomination was referred to the full Senate without recommendation.[24]

On October 1, five southern Democrats announced that they would vote for Thomas: Richard Selby (Ala.), Sam Nunn (Ga.), Ernest Hollings (S.C.), Bennett Johnston, and John Breaux (La.). Despite the firestorm that followed, each of these senators kept his commitment when the final vote came. It appears that southern Democrats are not a voting bloc but a set of independent minds and wills.

By October 1, it seemed to those who could follow only the public side of this conflict that the anti-Thomas forces were proving only their own ineffectuality, their inability to "bork" anyone who does not have the bad luck of having fired Archibald Cox in 1973. It also seemed that Thomas's opponents had misunderstood their earlier success. The anti-Bork coalition had said and written much about the reasons for their victory. They apparently believed that they had won by taking their case, as the cliché goes, "to the people" and that the broad demographic categories whom the groups professed to represent (racial minorities, women, labor) rose up in anger against this judicial but injudicious threat to their nonnegotiable interests.

What happened in the Bork case, though, was something more pedestrian. The intra-Washington lobbying efforts were successful because of the weakness of the Reagan administration in 1987, the need felt by he new Democratic majority in the Senate to assert itself, and the atmosphere of personal mistrust toward Bork, initiated by the Cox firing and intensified by Judge Gordon's letter of objection. Bork's defeat was not a case of the people's rising. It was a case of the politicians' burrowing. Because Thomas's opponents misunderstood themselves, they tried this time to do what they thought they had done before. They tried to win this fight out in the countryside, in places like Compton, California, and Hartford, Connecticut. They got nowhere. Only in the later rounds did they begin to use an intra-Washington strategy—too late, though barely so.

THE SECOND ROUND OF HEARINGS

Such would have been the conclusion of an observer of the public side of this dispute, on October 1, 1991. A month before, cloaked in privacy, the would-be "borkers" had begun to prepare what one might call their "Plan B." In the first week of September an aide to Senator Kennedy named Ricki Seidman got in touch with Anita Hill, a professor at the Law School of the University of Oklahoma at Norman. In this conversation, Hill said nothing accusatory about Clarence Thomas's behavior during the years 1981 to 1983, when she worked for him at the Department of Education first and then at the EEOC. Only on September 9, during a second conversation with Seidman, did Hill first make her accusation. She later talked to James Brudney, a Metzenbaum aide whom Hill knew from their days as students at Yale Law School. On September 10, Brudney gave the allegations to Harriet Grant, chief nomination counsel for the committee. On the nineteenth, Hill agreed that her name could be released, but only to the FBI and members of the committee. This was a formula for half-secrecy, for a smear campaign too obscure to be countered by its target but too widely spread to prevent leaks and adverse publicity. This was the worst possible arrangement for any protection of the rights of the accused.

The events of the next two weeks require only chronological order to tell their own story. On September 25, Senator Biden briefed each member of his Committee. He gave Hill's name. On the twenth-seventh, the committee took the vote mentioned before, and the Senate leadership scheduled the floor debate for October 8. By October 1 the professional vote-counters were saying that confirmation was within Thomas's grasp. On October 4, Senator Orrin Hatch predicted that an attempt would be made over the weekend to stop the nomination. Certain it was that if a campaign of selective leaking was to work at all, now was the moment for the bombshell disclosure. On Sunday, October 6, the Hill allegation appeared in <u>Newsday</u>, a Long Island, New York, newspaper. It was also aired by Nina Totenberg on National Public Radio's "Weekend Edition."

By Tuesday evening, the eighth, it appeared that the tactical leak had worked. Senator Dole, the minority leader and a Thomas supporter, said, "We just don't have the votes." Senator Danforth, speaking as <u>the</u> supporter of Thomas, asked that the scheduled vote be delayed. The Republicans had decided to force the accusations of sexual harassment contained in Hill's affidavit into the full glare of publicity.[25] With such a forum, Thomas would have the senatorial equivalent of what every accused person deserves, "his day in court."

On October 11 Anita Hill came, however reluctantly, before the Senate Judiciary Committee and the world. She repeated the story now familiar to the general public: Thomas had asked her for dates while she was working on his staff. She had refused. He had retaliated by repeatedly embarrassing her with lewd discussions of sex.

Hill told of her hospitalization in 1983 for stomach pains that she attributed to stress brought on by Thomas's harassment. That was an assertion of cause for which she had no medical authority, but it was well adapted to playing on the sympathies of what was now a national and transfixed television audience.

In the morning session of her testimony, Arlen Specter questioned Hill repeatedly as to whether she had expected Thomas to withdraw quietly after he heard of the existence of her affidavit:

Specter: Did anyone tell you that by providing the statement that there would be a move to press Judge Thomas to withdraw his nomination?

Hill: I don't recall any story about pressing—using this to press anyone . . .

Specter: But was there any suggestion, however slight, that the statement with these serious charges would result in a withdrawal so that it wouldn't have to be necessary for your identity to be known . . .

Hill: There was no—not that I recall. I don't recall anything being said about him being pressed to resign.[26]

It seemed odd to Specter that a woman who claimed detailed memory of events a decade old would deny any "recall" on so crucial a matter four to five weeks earlier. It may have seemed odd to Professor Hill, too, for during the lunch break her memory improved. In the afternoon, without another question to prompt her, she returned to the point of whether she had been assured that Thomas would withdraw quietly. She said that her early conversations with senatorial staff members "even included something to the effect that the information might be presented to the candidate and to the White House. There was some indication that the candidate or, excuse me, the nominee, might not wish to continue the process." This was precisely the information for which Specter had pressed.[27]

Specter attached the name of Metzenbaum's staffer to this admission:

Specter: So Mr. Brudney did tell you that Judge Thomas might not wish to go forward with this nomination if you came forward?

Hill: Yes.[28]

Specter later commented that, had Hill not retracted her morning testimony in the afternoon, she might have been subject to prosecution for perjury.[29] That is not plausible. Hill never denied that she had received such a suggestion from Brudney. She had said, "I do not recall." Since jurors in a perjury prosecution would be unable to get inside her skull to divine the real state of her recall at that moment, and since they would be unwilling to discount the known vagaries of human memory, it seems to me that Specter, in raising the threat of such a prosecution, was stretching a valid point, which is that the episode sheds an unflattering light on Anita Hill's credibility as a witness.

That light did not become any more flattering through the infamous lie detector test, administered on Sunday by an expert chosen by Hill's attorneys. Indeed, the chairman of the Judiciary Committee, Joseph Biden, committed though he was to opposing Thomas's confirmation on jurisprudential grounds, ruled that the results of a polygraph would be inadmissible at this hearing.

In two respects the Hill charges recall the 1986 attacks on Justice Rehnquist. First, there is the slippery term *harassment* itself, a catchall word vague enough to serve as a smear. In 1986, Rehnquist was said to have harassed minority voters by challenging their credentials. In 1991, Thomas was said to have harassed an employee by making crude remarks. In neither case was it clear what counts as evidence, for or against such a charge. Second, there was in each case an unabashedly personal character to such attacks—charges of drug abuse in 1986 and of a taste for pornography in 1991.* A society in which such attacks are routine will drive decent people out of public life and will leave that sphere of government to the more shameless of its rodents.[30]

---

* Robert and Mary Ellen Bork regularly rent movie videotapes. They have a taste for the classics, notably for Cary Grant. In 1987 an enterprising reporter, undoubtedly hoping for something more headline-worthy, obtained the records of the rental outlet that they patronize.

On the evening of October 11, Judge Thomas came before the committee to answer the charge against him. He testified that he had not watched Professor Hill's testimony but that he was familiar with the gist of it. He denied it categorically ("unequivocally"). For a moment, though, he sounded like a man who had been beaten, who would withdraw, because "no job is worth what I've been though—no job. No horror in my life has been so debilitating." But he had not been beaten and would not, he soon declared, "provide the rope" for his own lynching; "I'd rather die than withdraw." He thus put an end to the lure with which Brudney and others had lured Hill. What Thomas did not say is what many expected him to say—that some events akin to those described by Hill had taken place but that she had misunderstood or misremembered details that would prove that it was all a joke or minor lapse of taste. Instead, Thomas said, simply, no, nothing of the sort had ever happened.[31]

The following morning, Saturday, Thomas returned to complete his testimony. He complained that Hill had played upon stereotypes about the sexual prowess of black men, that the lynching of black men had long been associated with just such language, and that these accusations are of the sort that an innocent person "cannot shake off." Biden asked who it was, exactly, who had decided to raise those poisonous stereotypes? Thomas insisted on answering only in the passive voice: "I believe that in combination this story was developed, or concocted, to destroy me." The who did not matter to the accused in contrast to the to whom and the what.

One of the few sensible essays about the whole Anita Hill affair that appeared in its wake was an editorial by Virginia Postrel in Reason.[32] It deals with the what, the nature of these concoctions. Postrel writes: "Feminists like to claim that 'sexual harassment is not about sex—it's about power.' The truth is a bit more complicated. First, sexual harassment is very clearly about sex. Lots of bosses harass their employees in non-sexual ways. They make them run personal errands. They berate them in front of other employees. They play favorites. But these actions are not illegal, nor should they be." One ought to add that if Clarence Thomas's harassment or alleged harassment of Anita Hill had been of the nonsexual variety Postrel describes, a televised Senate hearing featuring his demands for errands or his office favoritism is hardly imaginable. Nor would such a complaint have given Thomas reason to mention long-standing and poisonous racial stereotypes.

If one believes, as I do, that Hill's accusation was without merit, one must face the much-discussed question of motive. Furthermore, even if one believes that Anita Hill was telling the truth and that the charge has weight as a disqualification, the motive question remains. Hill had not come forward with this story when Thomas was nominated for the circuit court. Was it irrelevant to Thomas's judicial qualifications in March 1990? Hill did not even mention her charge during her first conversation with Ricki

Seidman, in the first week of September 1991. Again, supposing Hill was telling the truth, what was her motive in coming forward just when she did? If she was not telling the truth, what was her motive for beginning to lie, or expanding on long-since-forgotten lies, at that time?

The most plausible answer to either variant of the motive question, the answer suggested by all the earlier material of this chapter, is that: the interest groups that had promised to "bork" this nominee, that had gambled all their prestige, in a city that honors nothing so much as demonstrated power, on their success in stopping this nomination, saw their chances of doing so by any means other than personal attack fading away; and they enlisted Hill to reinvigorate their campaign. No need to speculate here about the mix of threats, promises, or appeals that might have produced Hill's enlistment. The point is simply that the controversy, if not the accusation itself, was certainly "about power." It was about the power of an accuser over an accused.

It was also about the pass to which legal realism has come. The law and the courts and the Senate hearing rooms, where their sanctity as institutions ought to be protected by themselves and respected by others, have come to be just so many back alleys for knife fights between well-tailored equivalents of the Jets and the Sharks.

The Judiciary Committee capped this memorable weekend with a rare Sunday session, during which the senators heard from character witnesses on behalf of each antagonist, Hill and Thomas. Some of the pro-Hill witnesses testified that she had told them of an incident of sexual harassment years before. On questioning, it became evident that what she had told them was very different from, and very much less than, what she was saying now. There was no testimony of any earlier mention of the memorable particulars, of Long Dong Silver, of the Coca-Cola can, or of any discussion of organ size. These elaborations had no provable existence prior to Hill's enlistment with the anti-Thomas coalition, the "borking" brigade, in September 1991. Particulars are all-important. The phrase *sexual harassment* is otherwise just a conclusory label, not a fact. So the evidentiary value of third-party reports about unparticularized conversations with Anita Hill must be rated low, not to say trifling.

Some have argued that it is unfair to characterize Anita Hill as a participant in a partisan political scheme, that she was a conservative Republican herself, and that her Reaganite politics should induce an objective observer to give credence to her testimony against a nominee of the same persuasion. This argument, like so much else in the attendant controversy, is specious. First, whatever exactly a "conservative" is, there is no reason to believe that Anita Hill is one.[33] She was never a political appointee of the Reagan administration. She was in the civil service as a schedule A employee, so that her jobs there say nothing whatsoever about her opinions.[34] Second, her party affiliation is not Republican. Voting records in Tulsa County show that she was registered there as a Democrat during the very weeks of her secret contacts with members of the staffs of senators on the Judiciary Committee. She reregistered in Cleveland County, which includes Norman, on October 4, two days before the Totenberg story aired.   Here, too, she registered as a Democrat.   Some of the best-remembered facts about this affair just are not so.

On October 15 the Senate finally voted on the Thomas nomination. Since vice president Dan Quayle, presiding, was empowered to break a tie, Thomas's opponents needed fifty-one nays.   Shortly before the vote, reporters outside the Senate chamber witnessed a symbolic tableau—Betty Friedan, feminist author, exchanging strong words with Alan Simpson, Republican whip.

The vote-counters believed that Thomas could rely upon forty-one of the Senate's forty-three Republicans; the two crossovers, as expected, were James Jeffors of Vermont and Robert Packwood of Oregon. The same oracles postulated the presence of fourteen persuadable Democrats. Arithmetic did the rest. Thomas would need at least nine of the fourteen swing votes to secure a tie or better. When the votes were cast, the nominee received all of his forty-one root affirmatives, plus ten of the fourteen hinge votes, and a bonus: Chuck Robb of Virginia, a Democrat who had not been on anyone's persuadable list, voted to confirm. That added up to fifty-two votes for consent to this appointment and forty-eight opposed.

There were two women in the Senate, and they split. Nancy Kassenbaum voted aye, and Barbara Mikulski nay.

Thomas took his oath of office and became the 106th justice of the Supreme Court on November 1.

NOTES

1. United States v. Long, 905 F.2d 1572 (D.C. Cir. 1990).

2. Id. 1580.

3. Id. 1577.

4. "The President's News Conference in Kennebunkport, Maine," July 1, 1991, Public Papers of the Presidents: George Bush—1991, at 801.

5. Dworkin, "Justice for Clarence Thomas," New York Review of Books (Nov. 7, 1991), 41 is especially egregious in flaunting its author's refusal to believe that a Republican President could possibly have chosen a black judge on grounds of merit.

6. Blumenthal, "The Drifter," The New Republic (November 4, 1991), 23.

7. Margolick, "Influence of Savannah Nuns Lives on in Judge Thomas," New York Times (July 2, 1991), A1.

8. Nieves, "With Rising Voice, Acting Head of Feminist Group Assumes Mantle," New York Times (July 7, 1991), 10. Perhaps, though, the Times is in error, and it was Florence Kennedy who, at the NOW press conference, used this

phrase. See Lukacs, "Why I Can't 'Bork' Clarence Thomas," Wall Street Journal (September 5, 1991), A15.

9. Article VI, par. 3, "No religious test shall ever be required as a qualification to any office or public trust under the United States."

10. Weisberg, "Supreme Courtier," The New Republic (September 30, 1991), 16.

11. Soper, "Some Natural Confusions about Natural Law," 90 Mich. L. Rev. 2393 (1992).

12. Barnes, "Weirdo Alert," The New Republic (August 5, 1991), 7. For a scholarly discussion of the issues involved in this stage of the Thomas hearings, one which has acquired timelessness with its age, see E. S. Corwin, The "Higher Law" Background of American Constitutional Law (Ithaca, N.Y., 1928).

13. "Excerpts From Senate's Hearings on the Thomas Nomination," New York Times (September 11, 1991), A22.

14. Lewis, "Thomas Ends Testimony But Senators Grumble Over Elusive Views," New York Times (September 17, 1991), A14.

15. Fifth Amendment, "nor shall private property be taken for public use without just compensation." R. Epstein, Takings (Cambridge, MA, 1985) is the book Biden found so threatening.

16. Editorial, "Biden Meets Epstein," Wall Street Journal (December 2, 1991), A12.

17. Id.

18. Editorial, "Thomas Said That? Never Mind," Wall Street Journal (December 2, 1991), A12. See also J. C. Danforth, Resurrection (New York, 1994), 23–25.

19. Barrett, "Thomas Softens His Remarks On Natural Law," Wall Street Journal (September 11, 1991), A3.

20. Editorial, "Racial Correctness," Wall Street Journal (August 1, 1991), A12. See also J. C. Danforth, Resurrection (New York, 1994), 17.

21. Id. See T. Phelps & H. Winternitz, Capitol Games (New York, 1992), 72–80.

22. Tempting 306.

23. Barrett, "Thomas Criticized by Bar Association for Inexperience," Wall Street Journal (September 17, 1991), A18.

24. Phelps & Winternitz, 224.

25. Barrett & Calmes, "Senate Delays Thomas Vote By a Week to Study Charges," Wall Street Journal (October 9, 1991), A3.

26. Garment, "Why Anita Hill Lost," Commentary (January 1992), 27.

27. Id. at 30.

28. Id.

29. Id.

30. E. Bronner, Battle for Justice (New York, 1989), 274.

31. Hertzberg, "Washington Diarist: What a Whopper," The New Republic (November 4, 1991), 42. Hertzberg says that he was disappointed by Thomas's line of defense. He had hoped Thomas would portray the "whole thing" as "a 33-year-old divorced man's clumsy attempt at courtship and ribald humor." But if "the whole thing" in fact never happened, shouldn't Thomas have said so? Which, of course, is what he did say. Hertzberg's article is typical of the non sequiturs that filled the frosty air of the final months of 1991.

32. Postrel, "Poetic Injustice," Reason (December 1991), 4.

33.   D. Brock, The Real Anita Hill (New York, 1993), 318–20.
34.   Weymouth, "Some Clues to Anita Hill's Motive," Wall Street Journal (November 20, 1991), A16.

12

The Meaning of the Rehnquist Court

The Supreme Court's term begins on the first Monday of October and ends in late June or early July of the following year. Since newsworthy litigation often generates protracted debate among the justices, the headline-making decisions cluster together in an annual end-term rush. The decisions of June 1992 might have contributed weighty issues to the election campaign of that autumn—they bore on federalism, public school prayer, abortion, and private property rights. But the campaign and the campaigners passed by such matters (crying, "It's the economy, stupid!").

On June 19, 1992, the Supreme Court announced its decision in New York v. United States.[1] Justice O'Connor wrote for the Court in an opinion that struck a federal law that had required every state to "take title" to the low-level nuclear waste commercially generated within its borders.[2] The law was designed to force each state to find sites for waste dumps. New York brought suit in 1990, requesting a declaration that it need not take title. The district court dismissed the lawsuit, reasoning that the solution Congress had adopted for this nationwide problem was a constitutional exercise of Congress's power under the commerce clause, as that clause has been understood since the Garcia decision. The Second Circuit affirmed that dismissal.[3] The Supreme Court reversed both courts below, granting the requested declaratory relief.

O'Connor's opinion does not overturn Garcia; there was no reason why it should. At broadest, Garcia stands for the proposition that the United States can regulate commerce by means of uniform national standards that apply not merely within every state but to the states themselves insofar as they act as commercial entities. Garcia does not authorize the legislation at issue in New York v. United States, legislation through which Congress sought not to apply, but to avoid, uniform national standards. Congress bucked responsibility, ordering every state to legislate site-selection procedures in its own domain. As the Court rightly observed, this act hijacked the state legislatures, turning them into adjuncts of Congress, administrative entities within the central government's scheme. The "take title" provision fell; Garcia stands.

Yet it appears that the conflict between the commercial regulatory powers of the federal government and the sovereignty of the states is as yet unresolved, and perhaps the advocates of the earlier Usery rule—that is, of the theory that state autonomy imposes a substantial limit on the commerce clause power—will have their innings once again.[4]

On June 24, the Court returned to the eerie terrain of church-state relations. One way to think about the decision that made this voyage[5] is to ask oneself whether high school graduates are more akin to state representatives or to pupils in a classroom. State legislators may be subjected to state-sponsored prayer because they are adults, with minds presumably formed against sectarian indoctrination, and peer pressure will not keep them in seats they would prefer to leave. Pupils in a classroom in a public school may not be subjected to state-sponsored prayer or to lessons in creationism, because they are not adults, their minds are unformed, and their susceptibility to peer pressure is profound. A high school graduation is the traditional rite of passage from the one status to the other in American society, from childhood to adulthood, and so it may be said that exposure to state-sponsored prayer becomes constitutional subsequent to that event. But is such exposure constitutional during that event? This is a neat "borderline" issue.

Unfortunately, the case in which the Supreme Court dealt with this issue was an inappropriate vehicle. As Justice Kennedy's opinion explains,[6] this case arose from the exercises of a middle school, and "we are unfamiliar with any fixed custom or practice at middle school graduations."[7] The rest of the opinion proceeds as if a high school graduation were at issue, because such exercises "are such an integral part of American cultural life that we can with confidence describe their customary features."[8] This is an odd transposition. I suppose one might defend it thus: what is unconstitutional for the older graduates is also unconstitutional for the younger. Since the Court found prayer unconstitutional in the borderline case, it disposed of the case before it a fortiori.

Kennedy's opinion also explains that the district court applied the three-part test of Lemon v. Kurtzman[9] and held that the primary effect of these prayers is the advancement of religion. Thus, the practice under challenge fails under the second part of the traditional standard. The court of appeals for the First Circuit affirmed the district court.

The Supreme Court also affirmed. Much has been made of the psychological character of Kennedy's reasoning. Scalia, in dissent,[10] went so far as to claim that the majority had "replaced Lemon with its psycho-coercion test . . . as infinitely expandable as the reasons for psychotherapy itself."[11]   But that seems to be a misrepresentation of Kennedy's approach. His journey into the psyches of graduates was a plausible effort to clarify just what is meant by the second part of the Lemon test and so what was meant by the judgment of the lower courts. Not only does Kennedy's opinion not overturn existing jurisprudence, but it is probably the best opinion that could have been written within that framework. In so saying, of course, I do not mean to retract my strictures on the whole line of precedents that led the Court to this point.

On to abortion, inevitably. As noted in Chapter 7, the Webster decision of 1989 authorized the states to regulate abortion in many respects, but it did not authorize a prohibition or a recriminalization of that operation. On June 29, 1992, the Supreme Court handed down its decision in Planned Parenthood v. Casey.[12] The state regulations at issue in this suit against the Governor of Pennsylvania were informed consent, parental consent, a twenty-four-hour waiting period, record-keeping requirements, and spousal notification. The last of these was found to be an "undue burden" on the exercise of the right to choose to have an abortion and so was struck. The other regulations at issue survived review.

The effect was to restate and strengthen the distinction that Webster had announced. What was new was that, while in 1989 the plurality deferred consideration of whether a state law prohibiting abortion would be unconstitutional, in 1992 the plurality did consider that question and answered it no.

Also new to 1992 was a set of partisan reactions to this restatement of what had, after all, been the law for three years. On one hand, the advocates of a broad right to privacy, who made some pro forma protests, had every reason to be—and not far below the surface they were—delighted. Justice Blackmun, always their voice on the Court, wrote that just when many vote-counters or balance theorists had "expected the darkness to fall, the flame has grown bright."[13]

On the other hand, the opponents of legalized abortion were shocked and felt betrayed. They had thought of Webster not as a resting place for the law but as a transition. With the departure of Brennan and Marshall in the intervening years, these partisans were confident that 1992 would see that transition complete and Roe straightforwardly abolished. When the Casey opinion let them know that Webster's distinction between regulation and prohibition is a rule of law, to be taken seriously as such, and that their contrary confidence was misplaced, they howled. The founder of Operation Rescue said that the Court has "stabbed justice in the back." A spokesman for the National Right to Life Committee said that his side has lost "95% of the battle."[14]

Each side had believed, in accord with the bad old model, that the Court was in balance in 1989 and that the two appointments since then had tipped that balance in the direction the one feared, the other desired. Casey confirms one of the themes of this book, that the balance model has no predictive value, that its only use is in squeezing money out of a movement's direct mailing list and otherwise rallying the troops.

Scalia and Rehnquist each wrote a dissent. Scalia's is the most quoted of the two, and there is good reason for that: his prose is pungent and quotable:

> The Court's reliance upon stare decisis can best be described as contrived . . . I confess never to have heard of this new, keep-what-you-want-and-throw-away-the-rest version . . . . Roe fanned into life an issue that has inflamed our national politics in general, and has obscured with its smoke the selection of Justices to this Court in particular, ever since. And by keeping us in the abortion-umpiring business, it is the perpetuation of that disruption, rather than of any pax Roeana, that the Court's new majority decrees.[15]

Scalia was also the author of what is, from the standpoint of those who believe that the Court ought to return to its role as guardian of property rights and commercial liberty, that term's most heartening opinion, Lucas v. South Carolina Coastal Council.[16]

In 1986, David Lucas bought two plots of land on the Isle of Palms, along the Carolina coast. His property was exempt from the beachfront construction restrictions in effect at the time of purchase, as it was more than three hundred feet from shore. He planned to build a house on each plot, one for his own use, and the other for sale. Before he could build, South Carolina changed its definition of "beachfront."[17] Lucas now owned land on which no "improvements" were allowed and had lost the value of his property, insofar as market value cannot be presumed to include a discount for the probability that the next session of the legislature will enact an expropriation.

Lucas sued, demanding a declaration that his land had been taken for public use and that he was entitled to just compensation. The Supreme Court, Scalia writing for six, ruled that Lucas may be so entitled. It ordered that a trial be held on certain factual issues that this majority considered dispositive: specifically, whether Lucas has lost "all economically viable use of his land" and whether either Lucas's legal title or the common-law rules in effect in South Carolina would have prohibited the construction he had planned even without the contested statute. If this case does not fall into either of those categories, then the owner will be entitled to compensation just as if he had been subjected to eminent domain and his land paved over for a stretch of a new interstate highway.

That is very good news. But what does it mean for other individuals with title to property, real or other, faced with somewhat less drastic or less complete regulatory takings? Such issues may not be settled except through litigation as yet uncontemplated, by decisions as yet unimaginable, on patterns of fact as yet unforeseen.

So ends my narrative. Some closing thoughts of a higher level of generality may now be in order. Just as the decline of the Supreme Court made possible the decline of the Senate as a constitutional partner in the appointment of justices, so only a renewal of the original role of the Supreme Court can bring about a restoration of senatorial *dignitas* in general and in that partnership in particular.

One final illustration from the struggles of our nation's Founders may make such a renewal seem more plausible than in bare statement it may seem. In 1760 the royal customs collectors at Boston applied to the superior court of the colony of Massachusetts for what was then known as a writ of assistance, that is, a general warrant that would allow an officer to enter *any* premises at *any* time in search of suspected smuggled goods.

A Boston lawyer named James Otis resigned his office as king's advocate in protest. In 1761 he argued to the court that it should not issue the requested writs because warrants of this degree of generality, of this unreasonableness, violated natural right, as well as the fundamental laws of the British Empire. What was more startling, he argued that the court ought to refuse to grant such writs just for that reason, despite their authorization by a recent act of Parliament. Otis declared that "an act against the Constitution is void; an act against natural equity is void."[18]

The court issued the writs nonetheless. But John Adams, another young lawyer, sat in the audience to hear Otis argue, and he was inspired. In later years Adams said that American independence was born at that moment. Otis's words threw on fertile ground "the seeds of patriots and heroes."[19]

Whether independence was born that day, certainly the institution of "judicial review," as Americans have since come to know it, received a great boost. Also, thirty years later the states would ratify an amendment to the new Constitution, the Fourth Amendment, providing what Otis had demanded, that "the right of the people to be secure in their persons, houses, papers, and effects, against unreasonable searches and seizures, shall not be violated."

One should not, then, underestimate the power that the right arguments, grounded in history, conforming to equity and nature, can possess. Such arguments as Otis's directed at our Supreme Court may yet recall it to the path of formalism, the path of Otis himself, of John Adams, of Publius, and of John Marshall. Let the Court once again walk that path, and much else of immeasurable value will follow.

NOTES

1. 112 S.Ct. 2408 (1992).

2. O'Connor's opinion quotes from the Federalist Papers (No. 82): "The erection of a new government, whatever care or wisdom may distinguish the work, cannot fail to originate questions of intricacy and nicety; and these may, in a particular manner, be expected to flow from the establishment of a constitution founded upon the total or partial incorporation of a number of distinct sovereignties." So although Publius could hardly have foreseen the Low-Level Radioactive Waste Policy Amendments Act of 1990, he did foresee the need for a continued grappling with federalism and understood that the relations of the distinct sovereignties would have to be sufficiently adaptable to meet the unforeseeable (Id. 2417).

3. New York v. United States, 942 F.2d 114 (2d Cir. 1991).

4. 112 S.Ct. 2435, 2441.

5. Lee v. Weisman, 112 S.Ct. 2649 (1992).

6. Id. 2653.

7. Id.

8. Id.

9. 403 U.S. 602 (1971).

10. 112 S.Ct. at 2678.

11. 112 S.Ct. at 2685.

12. 112 S.Ct. 2791.

13. 112 S.Ct. 2843, 2844.

14. Barrett, "Supreme Court Curbs, But Won't Overrule, Right to Abortion," Wall Street Journal, June 30, 1992, p. 1, col. 1.

15. 112 S.Ct. 2873, 2881–2882.

16. 112 S.Ct. 2886 (1992).

17. The Beachfront Management Act, So. Car. Code, §48–39–250 et. seq. (Supp. 1990).

18. E. S. Corwin, The "Higher Law" Background of American Constitutional Law (Ithaca, New York, 1928), 77.

19. K. Wroth & H. Zobel, eds., Legal Papers of John Adams 3 vols. (Cambridge, MA, 1965), 2: 107.

Epilogue: The Clinton Presidency and the Electoral Arithmetic

In the introduction to this book I stated certain conclusions. I deferred the supportive reasoning until this point. Specifically, I predicted that President Clinton would nominate to the bench people with a "hawkish" reputation on matters of great emotional heft within American politics and that in defense of such nominees there will be opportunities for an alignment of Republicans with the Clinton loyalists among the Democrats. The obverse proposition is also true: There will be a large bloc of "dovish" Democrats within the Senate and within the supportive interest group network who will oppose those appointments, who will continue their sport of "borking" judicial nominees under this administration the sport they perfected under the two preceding administrations.[1]

I believe this to be the case because I believe that President Clinton aims at his own reelection in 1996 and hopes to build a White House dynasty for the start of the new millennium. If such are his aims and hopes, he will naturally attend to the arithmetic that determines presidential elections. What is the prescription for the election of Democratic presidents? There is a clear formula, with just three ingredients.

First, the party must nominate a southerner. Once upon a time it was thought that giving the second spot on the ticket to a southerner would suffice. That did suffice in 1960, the year of the victory of a Boston-Austin ticket. But since that year the party of Jefferson and Jackson has won the White House only three times—1964, 1976, and 1992, in each case with a prominent southerner as the presidential candidate. In 1988, that party tried another Boston-Austin combination. Lloyd Bentsen did not enable the Dukakis ticket to make any inroads on the map of the South.

Second, the candidate and his tacticians must remember that regional identity will not suffice to win the election. If that were enough, then the president from Georgia would have won his reelection in 1980. The Democrats must consolidate their base, the states of the Northeast and of the Pacific coast. In the task of harvesting that party's advantage in these two regions, the economics of 1992 gave a great assist. Those were the regions in which the end of the cold war hurt, because military bases and defense-related industries had been an integral part of the local scene for decades. In these two areas the recession lingered longest and hardest; here the statistics of recovery seemed only empty and abstract.

Third, Democrats have to take the fight out of their base. They have to move forcefully into the old Northwest and the mountain West. In this, Clinton and Gore succeeded. They won Colorado, Montana, Nevada, and New Mexico in the mountain West. They also won every one of the states lying in the great "V" between the rivers Mississippi and Ohio, except for Vice President Quayle's home state of Indiana. Clinton and Gore did not do well in the Great Plains, and in their native South they did no better than middlin'. But arithmetic did not require that they do better there.

In 1992, accordingly, the Democratic candidate for president, William Jefferson Clinton, former governor of Arkansas, won that office with 370 electoral votes, the victor in thirty-two states and the District of Columbia. Those of us who plan no such campaign should concern ourselves with the particulars of this arithmetic, because they determine the kind of Democrat who can be elected. To satisfy this recipe, a candidate is well advised to appeal to his base on issues of the cerebrum and to go beyond that base to strike into the middle of the continent on issues of the gut. He can do both if and only if he follows a social-democratic line on the former sort of issue and portrays himself as a hawk as to the latter sort.

I do not mean to say that President Clinton is bound to establish a dynasty of these hawkish social democrats. If I could foretell such matters, I would not look forward each morning to the arrival of that day's newspaper with such curiosity. As it happens, I look forward to the successive papers I shall receive in the mornings of 1996 with a political junkie's relish. In the meantime, I think it is safe to say the following:

1. If Clinton is to found a dynasty, he must be a hawkish social democrat—or a "new Democrat," if the two terms are synonyms.
2. Clinton has pursued precisely the mix of policies and pronouncements best adapted to that result.
3. The federal courts have not been perceived by the public at large for some time as an economic policy-making body and probably are not seen predominately as such within the White House today. Appointments thereto are likely to be made not for the brain of the electorate but for its intestines.

This is good news and bad news. It is all to the good in that this public and presidential perception will free the courts and the Supreme Court in particular from the sorts of pressure to which the Federal Reserve shall continue to be subject. It is bad because it leaves the appointment process as Armageddon for the most divisive and emotion-laden issues of our time. There is a great likelihood that Clinton will use further appointments as pawns in a complicated chess game, his continuing effort to prove that "my center" is identical to the "political center."

There is nothing in the politics of the 1990s that seems likely to restore the Court to what it was before 1937 or even to what it was at the time of the first of the Brown v. Board decisions. It is a forum of legal realists. It seems likely to remain such for the foreseeable future, and the damage that fact has done to the advice and consent role of the Senate shall go unrepaired.[2]

NOTES

1. Editorial, "Breyer Conflicts," The Nation, July 18, 1994, p. 75.
2. S. Carter, The Confirmation Mess (New York, 1994).

Select Bibliography

PRIMARY SOURCES

The Constitution of the United States
Sections of the Constitution that are especially relevant include Art. I, §§ 1–2, 6, and 8; Art. II, §§ 1–2; Art. III, §§ 1–2; Art. IV, § 2; Art. VI; Amendments I, IV, V, VI, IX, XIII, XIV, XV, and XVII.

The United States Code (USC)
Sections of the USC that are especially relevant include the National Labor Relations Act, 29 USC §§ 141–187; Age Discrimination in Employment Act, 29 USC §§ 621–634; Occupational Safety and Health Act, 29 USC §§ 651–678; Civil Rights Act of 1964, as amended, 42 USC § 2000a ("Title II"), Public Accommodations; 42 USC § 2000e ("Title VII"), Equal Employment Opportunity; 42 USC § 2000e(k), Pregnancy Discrimination Act.

Official and Semiofficial Publications

Congressional Quarterly Almanac. Washington, DC: Congressional Quarterly.

Congressional Record. Washington, DC: U.S. Government Printing Office.

Earle, Edmund M., ed. The Federalist: A Commentary on the Constitution of the United States. New York: Random House, 1937.

Fleming, Peter, Jr. Report of Temporary Special Independent Counsel. Washington, DC: U.S. Government Printing Office, 1992.

Jaspan, Stanley S. Brief on behalf of Johnson Controls, Inc., UAW v. Johnson Controls, July 19, 1990.

Souter, Attorney General David. Brief on behalf of New Hampshire, United States v. New Hampshire, February 20, 1976.

Storing, Herbert J., ed. The Complete Anti-Federalist. Chicago: University of Chicago Press, 1981.

First-Person Accounts

Bork, Robert H. The Tempting of America: The Political Seduction of the Law. New York: Simon & Schuster, 1990.

Douglas, William O. The Autobiography of William O. Douglas: The Court Years. New York: Random House, 1980.

Freedman, Max, ed. Roosevelt and Frankfurter: Their Correspondence, 1928–1945. Boston: Little, Brown, 1969.

Salisbury, Harrison E. Without Fear or Favor: The New York Times and Its Times. New York: Times Publications, 1980.

Sirica, John. To Set the Record Straight. New York: New American Library, 1979.

SECONDARY SOURCES

Books

Ambrose, Stephen E. Nixon: The Triumph of a Politician, 1962–1972. New York: Simon & Schuster, 1989.

Baker, Livia. Felix Frankfurter. New York: Coward-McCann, 1969.

———. Miranda. New York: Atheneum, 1983.

Berger, Raoul. Government by Judiciary. Cambridge: Harvard University Press, 1977.

Bronner, Ethan. Battle for Justice. New York: W.W. Norton & Co., 1989.

Burnham, Walter Dean. Critical Elections and the Mainsprings of American Politics. New York: Norton, 1970.

Cannon, Lou. Reagan. New York: Putnam's, 1982.

Caro, Robert. The Years of Lyndon Johnson Vol. 1, The Path to Power. New York: Knopf, 1982.

———. The Years of Lyndon Johnson Vol. 2, Means of Ascent. New York: Knopf, 1989.

Carter, Stephen. Reflections of an Affirmative Action Baby. New York: Basic Books, 1991.

Collier, Peter & Horowitz, David. The Kennedys. New York: Simon & Schuster, 1984.

Cortner, Richard C. The Iron Horse and the Constitution: The Railroads and the Transformation of the Fourteenth Amendment. Westport, CT: Greenwood Press, 1993.

———. The Supreme Court and the Second Bill of Rights. Madison: University of Wisconsin Press, 1981.

Dionne, E. J. Jr. Why Americans Hate Politics. New York: Simon & Schuster, 1991.

Dunne, Gerald T. Hugo Black and the Judicial Revolution. New York: Simon & Schuster, 1977.

Ely, John Hart. Democracy and Distrust. Cambridge: Harvard University Press, 1980.

Epstein, Richard. Forbidden Grounds. Cambridge: Harvard University Press, 1992.

———. Takings. Cambridge: Harvard University Press, 1985.

Evans, Rowland & Novak, Robert. LBJ. New York: New American Library, 1966.

Goldenweiser, E. A. American Monetary Policy. New York: Committee for Economic Development, 1951.

Goldstein, Leslie Friedman. In Defense of the Text. Savage, MD: Rowman & Littlefield, 1991.

Goulden, Joseph C. The Superlawyers. New York: Weybright & Talley, 1971.

Grieder, William. Secrets of the Temple. New York: Simon & Schuster, 1987.

Harris, Robert J. The Quest for Equality: The Constitution, Congress, and the Supreme Court. Westport, CT: Greenwood Press, 1977.

Hecht, Marie B. Odd Destiny: The Life of Alexander Hamilton. New York: Mac Millan, 1982.

Jaffa, Harry V. Crisis of the House Divided. New York: Doubleday, 1959.

Kearns, Doris. Lyndon Johnson and the American Dream. New York: Harper & Row, 1976.

Kohlmeier, Louis M., Jr. God Save This Honorable Court. New York: Scribner's, 1972.

Levy, Leonard W. & Mahoney, Dennis J., eds. The Framing and Ratification of the Constitution. New York: Mac Millan, 1987.

McGuigan, Patrick & Weyrich, Dawn M. The Ninth Justice: The Fight for Bork. Lanham, MD: Free Congress Foundation, 1990.

McKeever, Porter. Adlai Stevenson: His Life and Legacy. New York: Morrow, 1989.

May, Dean L. From New Deal to New Economics. New York: Garland, 1987.

Murphy, Bruce A. Fortas. New York: Morrow, 1988.

Neuhaus, Richard John. The Naked Public Square. Grand Rapids, MI: Eerdsmans, 1984.

Pertschuk, Michael & Schaetzel, Wendy. The People Rising. New York: Thunder's Mouth Press, 1989.

Samuelson, Paul. Economics. 10th Ed. New York: McGraw-Hill, 1976.

Schlesinger, Arthur, Jr. A Thousand Days. Boston: Houghton Mifflin, 1965.

————. The Age of Roosevelt: The Politics of Upheaval. Boston: Houghton Mifflin, 1960.

Schwartz, Bernard. Super Chief. New York: New York University Press, 1983.

Sickels, Robert J. John Paul Stevens and the Constitution. University Park: Pennsylvania State University Press, 1988.

Siegan, Bernard. Economic Liberties and the Constitution. Chicago: University of Chicago Press, 1980.

Smith, Richard N. Patriarch: George Washington and the New American Nation. Boston: Houghton Mifflin, 1993.

Tugwell, Rexford G. The Emerging Constitution. New York: Harper's Magazine Press, 1974.

————. Off Course. New York: Praeger, 1971.

Wicker, Tom. One of Us. New York: Random House, 1991.

Wilkinson, J. Harvie. From Brown to Bakke. New York: Oxford University Press, 1979.

Williams, Charlotte. Hugo Black, A Study in the Judicial Process. Baltimore: Johns Hopkins University Press, 1950.

Articles

Anderson, David "The Origins of the Press Clause." 30 UCLA L. Rev. 455 (1981).

Barnes, Fred, "Weirdo Alert." The New Republic, August 5, 1991, at 7.

Black, Hugo, "The Bill of Rights," 35 N. Y. U. L. Rev. 865 (1960).

Bork, Robert "Neutral Principles and some First Amendment Problems," 47 Ind. L. J. 1 (1971).

Cox, Archibald, "Executive Privilege," 122 U. Pa. L. Rev. 1383 (1974).

Dworkin, Ronald, "Justice for Clarence Thomas." New York Review of Books, November 7, 1991, at 41.

Ervin, Sam, "The Exclusionary Rule: An Essential Ingredient of the Fourth Amendment," 1983 S. Ct. Rev. 283.

Garment, Suzanne, "Why Anita Hill Lost," Commentary (January 1992).

Ginsburg, Ruth B., "Some Thoughts on Autonomy and Equality in Relation to Roe v. Wade." 63 N. Car. L. Rev. 375 (1985).

Hayward, Steven, "Reversing Discrimination." Reason, December 1991 at 7.

Miller, Geoffrey, "The True Story of Carolene Products," 1987 S. Ct. Rev. 397.

Postrel, Virginia, "Why Women Can't Commit: Feminists Won't Let Them." Reason, June 1991, at 4.

Raimi, Ralph, "Ambition and Compassion," The Freeman, January 1992 at 13.

Sullivan, Andrew, "The Bork Screw." The New Republic, October 19, 1987, at 14.

Williams, Wendy, "Firing the Woman to Protect the Fetus: The Reconciliation of Fetal Protection with Employment Opportunity Goals under Title VII," 69 Geo. L. J. 641 (1981).

Case Table

Index

About the Author

CHRISTOPHER C. FAILLE is a graduate of Marist College and the Western New England School of Law. He is a contributor to the *Federal Bar News & Journal* and is author of *These Last Four Centuries* (1988).

ISBN 0-275-94826-9

HARDCOVER BAR CODE